Property and Liability Insurance Principles

Property and Liability Insurance Principles

Constance M. Luthardt, CPCU, AAI, AIM

Eric A. Wiening, CPCU, ARM, AU

Coordinating Author

Martin J. Frappolli, CPCU, AIS

Fourth Edition • Fifth Printing

American Institute for Chartered Property Casualty
Underwriters/Insurance Institute of America
720 Providence Road, Suite 100
Malvern, Pennsylvania 19355-3433

Fourth Edition · Fifth Printing · February 2008

Library of Congress Control Number: 2005929202

ISBN 978-0-89463-249-5

Printed in Canada

Foreword

The American Institute for Chartered Property Casualty Underwriters and the Insurance Institute of America (the Institutes) are independent, not-for-profit organizations committed to expanding the knowledge of professionals in risk management, insurance, financial services, and related fields through education and research.

In accordance with our belief that professionalism is grounded in education, experience, and ethical behavior, the Institutes provide a wide range of educational programs designed to meet the needs of individuals working in risk management and property-casualty insurance The American Institute offers the Chartered Property Casualty Underwriter (CPCU®) professional designation, designed to provide a broad understanding of the property-casualty insurance industry. CPCU students may select either a commercial or a personal risk management and insurance focus, depending on their professional needs.

The Insurance Institute of America (IIA) offers designations and certificate programs in a variety of disciplines, including the following:

- Claims
- Commercial underwriting
- Fidelity and surety bonding
- General insurance
- Insurance accounting and finance
- Insurance information technology
- Insurance production and agency management
- Insurance regulation and compliance
- Management
- Marine insurance
- Personal insurance
- Premium auditing
- Quality insurance services
- Reinsurance
- Risk management
- Surplus lines

You may choose to take a single course to fill a knowledge gap, complete a program leading to a designation, or take multiple courses and programs throughout your career. No matter which approach you choose, you will gain practical knowledge and skills that will contribute to your professional growth and enhance your education and qualifications in the expanding insurance market. In addition, many CPCU and IIA courses qualify for credits toward certain associate, bachelor's, and master's degrees at several prestigious colleges and universities, and all CPCU and IIA courses carry college credit recommendations from the American Council on Education.

The American Institute for CPCU was founded in 1942 through a collaborative effort between industry professionals and academics, led by faculty members at The Wharton School of the University of Pennsylvania. In 1953, the American Institute for CPCU merged with the Insurance Institute of America, which was founded in 1909 and which remains the oldest continuously functioning national organization offering educational programs for the property-casualty insurance business.

The Insurance Research Council (IRC), founded in 1977, helps the Institutes fulfill the research aspect of their mission. A division of the Institutes, the IRC is supported by industry members. This not-for-profit research organization examines public policy issues of interest to property-casualty insurers, insurance customers, and the general public. IRC research reports are distributed widely to insurance-related organizations, public policy authorities, and the media.

The Institutes strive to provide current, relevant educational programs in formats and delivery methods that meet the needs of insurance professionals and the organizations that employ them. Institute textbooks are an essential component of the education we provide. Each book is designed to clearly and concisely provide the practical knowledge and skills you need to enhance your job performance and career. The content is developed by the Institutes in collaboration with risk management and insurance professionals and members of the academic community. We welcome comments from our students and course leaders; your feedback helps us continue to improve the quality of our study materials.

Peter L. Miller, CPCU
President and CEO
American Institute for CPCU
Insurance Institute of America

Preface

Property and Liability Insurance Principles is the textbook for the first course (INS 21) in the three-part Program in General Insurance (INS) of the American Institute for CPCU/Insurance Institute of America (the Institutes). In conjunction with the INS 21 Course Guide and Practice Exam CD-ROM, this text will help students prepare for the INS 21 examination. The INS 21 course serves as a broad introduction to property-casualty insurance and as a foundation for studying the other two courses in the INS program.

This text is divided into three segments. Segment A—Fundamentals of Insurance—provides information on what insurance is, who provides it, how it is regulated, and how the financial performance of insurers is measured. Segment B—Insurance Operations—describes the functions of marketing, underwriting, and claims. Finally, Segment C—Insurance Contracts, Loss Exposures, and Risk Management—discusses insurance as a contract, introduces both property and liability loss exposures and policy provisions, and provides a basic discussion of risk management as a means of managing loss exposures.

I am grateful to many insurance professionals for their contribution to this textbook:

Thomas J. DeFalco, FCAS, MAAA

Gary Grasmann

Christopher J. Jones, CPCU, CIDM, AIS

Dean Ockerbloom, CPCU, ARM, AU

Charles A. Prall, CPA

Kevin M. Quinley, CPCU, ARM, AIC

Beth Gamble Riggins, CPCU, AIC, AAI

Christine A. Sullivan, CPCU, AIM

Marcia Tepp, CPCU, ARM, AIAF

David Ueeck, CPCU, CLU, ChFC

Andrew Zagrzejewski, CPCU, CLU, AIC

The policy provisions that are quoted throughout this text are from insurance policies developed by Insurance Services Office, Inc. The Institutes remain grateful for ISO's continuing cooperation.

Finally, I wish to thank all the students and course leaders who have provided their constructive comments regarding the INS text materials. With your help, we can continue to improve this text to give you the best educational tools for your insurance and risk management studies.

For more information about the Institutes' programs, please call our Customer Support Department at (800) 644-2101, e-mail us at customersupport@cpcuiia.org, or visit our Web site at www.aicpcu.org.

Martin J. Frappolli

Contents

Segment A

Fundamentals of Insurance

Direct Your Learning

Insurance: What Is It?

After learning the content of this chapter and completing the corresponding course guide assignment, you should be able to:

- ■ Describe the role of insurance in risk management.
- ■ Explain how insurance works as a transfer system.
- ■ Explain how the law of large numbers operates and applies to insurance.
- ■ Describe the major types of loss exposures.
- ■ Describe the characteristics of an ideally insurable loss exposure.
- ■ Explain why government insurance is needed, and give examples of federal insurance programs and state insurance programs.
- ■ Describe the major business operations of insurers.
- ■ Explain why and how state insurance departments regulate insurers.
- ■ Describe the benefits of insurance.
- ■ Describe the costs of insurance.
- ■ Distinguish among the major types of property and liability insurance.
- ■ Distinguish among the major types of life and health insurance.
- ■ Define or describe each of the Key Words and Phrases for this chapter.

Develop Your Perspective

What are the main topics covered in the chapter?

Insurance fills a wide range of roles as a financial institution that transfers the costs of losses. This chapter provides an overview of insurance operations, types of insurers, and regulation. The benefits as well as the costs of insurance are addressed.

Identify the many roles that insurance fills on a macro scale.

- How large and diverse is the insurance industry?
- What are the major types of insurance offered?

Why is it important to learn about these topics?

By creating a framework regarding the many aspects of insurance, you will be able to better comprehend information that you learn in the future about insurance.

Consider how private insurance and government insurance work to address the major types of loss exposures.

- How do insurers price insurance using the law of large numbers?
- Why are some loss exposures not ideally insurable?
- How does government insurance address those loss exposures that are not ideally insurable?

How can you use what you will learn?

Evaluate the benefits versus the costs of insurance.

- Do the benefits outweigh the costs?
- What actions would help to reduce the costs of insurance?

Chapter 1

Insurance: What Is It?

Almost every person, family, and organization needs insurance of some type to protect assets against unforeseen events that could cause financial hardship. Sometimes insurance is even required to satisfy a contractual obligation, such as when a homeowner buys insurance on a home to protect the mortgage company's investment in the event the home is damaged or destroyed. Almost everyone needs insurance, but not everyone fully understands it. What exactly *is* insurance?

Insurance is essentially the following four things:

1. A *risk management technique* that enables a person or an organization to deal with loss exposures and their financial consequences. A **loss exposure** is any condition or situation that presents the possibility of a loss.

2. A *transfer system*, in which one party—the insured—transfers the chance of financial loss to another party—the insurer.

3. A *business*, which includes various operations that must be conducted in a way that generates sufficient revenue to pay claims and provide a reasonable profit for its owners.

4. A *contract* between the insured and the insurer that states what potential costs of loss the insured is transferring to the insurer and expresses the insurer's promise to pay for those costs of loss in exchange for a stated payment by the insured.

This chapter discusses these four aspects of insurance.

Loss exposure
Any condition or situation that presents the possibility of a loss.

INSURANCE AS A RISK MANAGEMENT TECHNIQUE

Individuals, families, and organizations face loss exposures every day. Many of these loss exposures can have serious financial consequences. For example, a person operating an automobile may cause an accident leading to thousands of dollars of damage to the property of others and medical expenses for those involved. Businesses face a variety of loss exposures, such as damage to premises, injury to workers, and harm to customers from defective products or workmanship.

A person or an organization can retain some loss exposures. For instance, a flat tire is a nuisance and a minor expense, but it does not threaten a family's financial situation. Some loss exposures have the potential to create financial ruin; prudent persons and organizations must find other ways to deal with these exposures. The process of making and implementing decisions to handle loss exposures is known as risk management and is explored fully in a subsequent chapter. To mitigate the financial consequences of loss exposures, several risk management techniques are available.

A person or an organization may choose to avoid a particular type of loss exposure. For example, a city dweller may avoid the loss exposures arising from the ownership, maintenance, and use of an automobile by not owning one and choosing public transportation. Loss exposures may also be controlled by loss prevention measures (such as safety goggles and helmets for construction workers to reduce the frequency of injuries) and loss reduction measures (such as placement of fire extinguishers in the home or workplace to reduce the severity of fire losses).

Some loss exposures are not easy to retain, avoid, or control. Consider the following example: Ming lives sixteen miles from his workplace and no public transportation is available. He also needs a car for grocery shopping, running errands, and seeing friends. Owning and operating a motor vehicle makes sense for him. However, this creates loss exposures for Ming; the bodily injury or property damage that can result from his negligent operation of the automobile could reach hundreds of thousands of dollars. He cannot afford to retain such loss exposures, and it is not practical to avoid them. Though he may choose a sturdy car and drive safely to control these loss exposures, he cannot be certain of avoiding or minimizing the financial consequences of a serious accident. For Ming, the best risk management technique may be transfer, so that the financial consequences of loss will be borne by another party. Ming could use forms of noninsurance transfer, but insurance is probably the most economically viable choice for him.

INSURANCE AS A TRANSFER SYSTEM

Insurance is a system that enables a person, a family, or an organization to transfer the costs of losses (the potential financial consequences of certain loss exposures) to an insurer. The insurer, in turn, pays for covered losses and, in effect, distributes the costs of losses among all insureds (that is, all insureds share the cost of a loss). Thus, insurance is a system of both transferring and sharing the costs of losses.

Transferring the Costs of Losses

By transferring the costs of their losses to insurers, insureds exchange the possibility of a large loss for the certainty of a much smaller, periodic payment (the premium that the insured pays for insurance coverage). This transfer is accomplished through insurance policies. An insurance policy is a contract that states the rights and duties of both the insured and the insurer regarding the transfer of the costs of losses.

Transferring the costs of losses to an insurer would be unnecessary, however, if there were no exposures to loss—that is, no possibility that losses would occur. A loss need not occur for a loss exposure to exist; there simply must be the possibility of a loss. For example, every home has a fire loss exposure; in other words, the possibility exists that a fire could occur and cause a financial loss to the homeowner.

Sharing the Costs of Losses

Insurance also involves sharing the costs of losses. The insurer pools premiums paid by insureds, and insureds who incur covered losses are paid from the insurer's pooled funds. The total cost of losses is thereby spread (or shared) among all insureds. Insurers estimate future losses and expenses to determine how much they must collect from insureds in premiums. Predicting future losses is based on past loss experience.

The **law of large numbers** is a mathematical principle that enables insurers to make predictions about losses. According to the law of large numbers, as the number of similar but independent exposure units increases, the relative accuracy of predictions about future outcomes (losses) based on these exposure units also increases. An **exposure unit** is a measure of the loss exposure assumed by the insurer. Exposure units are independent to the extent that they are not generally subject to the same loss-causing event. Because insurers have large numbers of independent exposure units (the cars and houses of all their insureds, for example), they can predict the number of losses that all similar exposure units combined are likely to experience.

Law of large numbers
A mathematical principle stating that as the number of similar but independent exposure units increases, the relative accuracy of predictions about future outcomes (losses) based on these exposure units also increases.

Exposure unit
A measure of the loss exposure assumed by the insurer, used in pricing insurance.

For example, a homeowner is uncertain whether a fire will damage his or her home and transfers this uncertainty to an insurer. The insurer insures thousands of homes whose owners face the same uncertainty. Because of the large number of homes, the insurer can, with a great deal of accuracy, predict the number of homes that will be damaged by fire during a given period. Based on this prediction, the insurer can determine the amount of premiums that it needs to pay for the fire losses during that period.

Types of Loss Exposures

Before types of loss exposures are discussed, consider the following scenario. A fire sweeps through the ballroom and lower floors of a crowded hotel, killing or injuring 200 hotel guests and employees. An investigation later reveals that the number of people occupying the ballroom exceeded its legal capacity and that a disgruntled former employee intentionally started the fire. It also becomes apparent that the hotel owners had not taken proper steps to deal with a possible fire emergency. For example, the owners had not installed an automatic sprinkler system, firewalls were insufficient, exits were unlighted, and no plan was in place for safe evacuation of the hotel occupants.

The hotel fire illustrates the following three major types of loss exposures that are useful in identifying and categorizing potential losses:

- Property loss exposures
- Liability loss exposures
- Personal and personnel loss exposures

Property Loss Exposures

Property loss exposure
Any condition or situation that presents the possibility that a property loss will happen.

A **property loss exposure** is any condition or situation that presents the possibility that a property loss will occur. Property includes real property and personal property. **Real property** is land, buildings, and any other property attached to it. A house, a storage shed, a swimming pool, a factory building, a flagpole, and an underground sewer pipe are all items of real property, as is the land where each is situated. All tangible or intangible property that is not real property is **personal property**. Examples of personal property include the inventory of a retail merchant, furniture and tableware in a restaurant, equipment and machinery in a factory building, contents of a dwelling, computers, money, securities, automobiles, patents, and copyrights.

Real property
Land, buildings, and other structures attached to the land or embedded in it.

Personal property
All tangible or intangible property that is not real property.

In the case of the hotel fire, damage to the building and the personal property of the owners and others totaled several million dollars. The hotel building was badly damaged and had to be repaired. Much of the furniture and carpeting in the hotel was damaged or destroyed and had to be replaced.

Net income
Revenue minus expenses and taxes during a given time period.

Damage to property can also cause an indirect loss, such as a net income loss. **Net income** is revenue minus expenses and taxes during a given time period. Generally, individuals, families, and businesses must generate revenue that covers expenses in order to remain financially sound. A reduction in revenue, an increase in expenses, or both is commonly called a **net income loss** in the risk management and insurance communities. The net income losses of a business often greatly exceed the property loss that caused them, as in the case of the hotel fire.

Net income loss
An indirect loss caused by a reduction in revenue, an increase in expenses, or both during a given time period.

While the damaged rooms in the hotel were being repaired and cleaned, the hotel's revenue fell because guest rooms were empty. The hotel had to cancel social and business functions, and close its restaurants and shops. Because of negative publicity about the fire, the hotel permanently lost some of its revenue to competition. The hotel also incurred increased expenses for overtime pay for some employees while it was being restored.

Liability Loss Exposures

Liability loss exposure
Any condition or situation that presents the possibility of a claim alleging legal responsibility of a person or business for injury or damage suffered by another party.

A **liability loss exposure** is any condition or situation that presents the possibility of a claim alleging legal responsibility of a person or business for injury or damage suffered by another party. Some liability claims result in a lawsuit. Even if the lawsuit is groundless, the defendant may incur substantial expenses to defend against the suit. Liability claims may result from bodily injury, property damage, libel, slander, humiliation, or invasion of privacy.

A **liability loss** is a claim for monetary damages that results from one party negligently causing injury to another party or causing damage to another party's property. In the hotel fire example, the hotel owners were judged to be negligent for various reasons, including failure to take proper precautions to handle a fire emergency. As a result of the fire, the hotel incurred liability losses that included payments for medical expenses, rehabilitation costs, and pain and suffering experienced by the guests, employees, and others injured in the fire. Liability losses also included payments for damage to property belonging to guests and payments to survivors of people who were killed in the fire.

Liability loss
A claim for monetary damages because of injury to another party or damage to another party's property.

Personal and Personnel Loss Exposures

A **personal loss exposure** is any condition or situation that presents the possibility of a financial loss to an individual or a family because of death, disability, or unemployment. For example, a family would face a loss of income if a wage earner died or became disabled or unemployed.

Personal loss exposure
Any condition or situation that presents the possibility of a financial loss to an individual or a family by such causes as death, sickness, injury, or unemployment.

Personnel loss exposures, on the other hand, affect businesses. A **personnel loss exposure** is any condition or situation that presents the possibility of a financial loss to a business because of the death, disability, retirement, or resignation of key employees. For example, a business could face a financial loss if a key executive, sales representative, or product developer died, became disabled, or resigned and could not be quickly replaced.

Personnel loss exposure
Any condition or situation that presents the possibility of a financial loss to a business because of the death, disability, retirement, or resignation of key employees.

In the case of the hotel fire, if a key employee (such as the master chef) died in the fire, the hotel owners would experience a personnel loss. The chef's family and the families of others killed or injured by the fire would suffer personal losses.

Ideally Insurable Loss Exposures

Insurance covers events that may or may not happen. When covered events do occur, a financial loss usually results. By transferring the potential costs of the uncertain event to an insurer, the insured reduces or eliminates the possibility of suffering a large financial loss. By charging a premium in return, the insurer can make a profit if it handles a volume of similar transactions efficiently. Therefore, each party to the contract receives some benefit from the transaction. However, the transaction is not likely to be advantageous to the insurer unless the loss exposure has certain characteristics that make it ideally insurable from the insurer's standpoint. Insurers generally prefer to provide insurance for the potential financial consequences of loss exposures that have the following characteristics:

- Loss exposure involves pure, not speculative, risk.
- Loss exposure is subject to accidental loss from the insured's standpoint.
- Loss exposure is subject to losses that are definite in time and that are measurable.

- Loss exposure is one of a large number of similar, but independent, exposures.
- Loss exposure is not subject to a loss that would simultaneously affect many other similar loss exposures; loss would not be catastrophic.
- Loss exposure is economically feasible to insure.

Loss Exposure Involves Pure, Not Speculative, Risk

One purpose of insurance is to make the insured financially whole after a loss, that is, to restore the insured to the same financial position the insured had before the loss. A speculative risk offers the possibility of gain as well as loss. Therefore, if a loss exposure involved a speculative risk and the insured gained as a result of that risk, this purpose of insurance would be defeated.

Loss Exposure Is Subject to Accidental Loss From the Insured's Standpoint

An ideally insurable loss exposure also involves a potential loss that is accidental from the insured's standpoint. If the insured has some control over whether a loss will occur, the insurer is at a disadvantage because the insured may have an incentive to cause a loss. If losses are not accidental, the insurer cannot calculate an appropriate premium because the chance of a loss could increase as soon as a policy is issued. If the loss exposure involves only accidental losses, the insurer can better estimate future losses and calculate an adequate premium for the exposure.

A loss that is not accidental may be a case of insurance fraud—as when an insured intentionally deceives an agent or an insurer to collect money. Controlling insurance fraud is considered as one way to keep insurance rates reasonable. For such reasons, it is contrary to public policy for insurers to cover intentional losses.

Loss Exposure Is Subject to Losses That Are Definite in Time and That Are Measurable

To be insurable, a loss should have a definite time and place of occurrence, and the amount of the loss must be measurable in monetary terms. If the time and location of a loss cannot be precisely determined and the amount of the loss cannot be measured, writing (that is, issuing) an insurance policy that defines what claims to pay and how much to pay for them becomes difficult. Also, losses are impossible to predict if they cannot be measured. For example, the sudden bursting of a water pipe that causes water damage in the insured's bathroom is an occurrence that has a definite time and place. It can therefore be measured and insured. However, if a slow leak in the pipe causes decay and rotting of the insured's bathroom floor over several years, the resulting loss does not have a definite time of occurrence and is generally not insurable.

Loss Exposure Is One of a Large Number of Similar, But Independent, Exposures

An ideally insurable loss exposure must be common enough that the insurer can pool a large number of homogeneous, or similar, exposure units. This characteristic is important because it enables the insurer to predict losses accurately and to determine appropriate premiums.

Loss exposures that satisfy this requirement, such as the possibility of damage to homes, offices, trucks, or automobiles, allow the insurer to take advantage of the law of large numbers. The insurer can determine appropriate premiums based on the experience of thousands of similar exposure units and make reasonably accurate predictions about losses.

On the other hand, predicting the number of losses each year to space stations in outer space would be difficult, because there are very few exposure units. Moreover, each loss could drastically affect the profitability of an insurer and the insurance business as a whole. The inability of insurers to predict losses, and thus to determine adequate premiums, makes most insurers reluctant to insure unusual loss exposures such as those represented by space stations.

Loss Exposure Is Not Subject to a Loss That Would Simultaneously Affect Many Other Similar Loss Exposures; Loss Would Not Be Catastrophic

Effective pooling of exposure units assumes that the exposure units are independent. Independence means that a loss suffered by one insured does not affect any other insured or group of insureds. If exposure units are not independent, a single catastrophe could cause losses to a sizable proportion of insureds at the same time. For example, if all of the homes and businesses in a particular city were insured by the same insurer, the insurer would probably suffer a financial disaster if a hurricane leveled the city. The insurer would be unlikely to have the financial resources to pay all claims of all the insureds affected by the hurricane.

The tendency of insurers to avoid insuring catastrophic losses does not mean that hurricane damage to property is not insurable. Coverage for windstorm damage, including hurricane and tornado damage, is readily available throughout most of the United States. However, an insurer avoids possible financial disaster by managing its pool of insureds in such a way that it does not have a large proportion of its insureds exposed to loss in any single event. For windstorm coverage, the insurer must diversify the homes and businesses it insures so that it does not have a large concentration of insureds in any one geographic area. Consequently, the insurer maintains as much independence as possible among its insureds. If each of many insurers issued a relatively small number of policies in the city devastated by the hurricane, no one insurer would face financial ruin. Some insurers failed to maintain such independence among loss exposures in 1992 when Hurricane Andrew swept across Florida, resulting in several insurer insolvencies.

Loss Exposure Is Economically Feasible to Insure

Insurers seek to cover only loss exposures that are economically feasible to insure. Because of this constraint, loss exposures involving only small losses as well as those involving a high probability of loss are generally considered uninsurable. Writing insurance to cover small losses does not make sense when the expense of providing the insurance probably exceeds the amount of potential losses. Insurance to cover the disappearance of office supplies from a company, for example, could require the insurer to spend more to issue claim checks than it would to pay for the claims. It also does not make sense to write insurance to cover losses that are almost certain to occur. In such a situation, the premium would probably be as high as or higher than the potential amount of the loss. For example, insurers generally do not cover damage due to wear and tear of an automobile because autos are certain to incur such damage over time.

INSURANCE AS A BUSINESS

The insurance business (including property-casualty insurers, life and health insurers, agents, and brokers) provides about 2.3 million jobs in the U.S. In the most recent figures insurance premiums in the U.S. were nearly $1.1 trillion, and worldwide premiums totaled $2.9 trillion. More than 3,300 insurers sell property and liability insurance in the U.S. Property-casualty insurers employ about 606,000 people. In addition, another 628,000 people work in insurance-related agencies and brokerage firms, and about 209,000 in other insurance activities.[1]

Private (nongovernment) insurers vary enormously in size and structure, the products they sell, and the territories they serve; collectively they represent a substantial segment of business in the U.S. Despite their size and number, however, private insurers do not fill every insurance need. In some instances, federal and state governments provide insurance to meet the property and liability insurance needs of the public.

Through their insurance departments, state governments closely regulate the business of insurance. Private insurers must be licensed (for most types in insurance) in the states where they sell insurance. Because regulation of licensed insurers encompasses all insurer operations, state insurance regulators review insurance rates, policy forms, underwriting practices, claim practices, and financial performance. Regulators can revoke the licenses of insurers that do not fully comply with state regulations.

This section provides a brief overview of insurance as a business, regarding the following:

- Types of insurers
- Insurer operations
- Financial performance of insurers

- State insurance regulation
- Benefits of insurance
- Costs of insurance

These topics are all covered in greater detail in later chapters.

Types of Insurers

Many different types of private insurers offer various types of insurance. The federal government and state governments also provide insurance. In some cases, government insurance plans supply the same types of insurance as private insurers; in other cases, government insurance provides coverage that is not available from private insurers.

Private Insurers

There are three major types of private insurers as follows:

1. Stock insurers, which are corporations owned by stockholders
2. Mutual insurers, which are corporations owned by their policyholders
3. Reciprocal insurance exchanges (also known as an interinsurance exchanges), which are unincorporated associations that provide insurance services to their members, often called subscribers

Other private providers of insurance include Lloyd's, American Lloyds, captive insurers, and reinsurers. A later chapter will discuss these types of insurance providers in more detail.

Federal Government Insurance Programs

Some federal government insurance programs exist because of the huge amount of financial resources needed to provide certain types of coverage to citizens and because the government has the authority to require mandatory coverage. Social Security is the best example of such a program. Private insurers provide some benefits similar to those provided by the Social Security program, but the number of Social Security beneficiaries (in effect, claimants) and the range of coverages make providing this type of insurance beyond the resources of private insurers. Further, eligibility for payments—retirement—is a certainty, so this is not an ideally insurable exposure.

In addition to the Social Security program, the federal government provides insurance for certain kinds of catastrophic losses. The National Flood Insurance Program provides insurance for owners of property located in flood-prone areas and for others concerned about the exposure of flooding. The Federal Crop Insurance Program insures farmers against damage to their crops by drought, insects, hail, and other causes. The federal government also insures depositors against loss resulting from the failure or insolvency of banks (through the Federal Deposit Insurance Corporation) and credit unions (through the National Credit Union Administration).

State Government Insurance Programs

State governments also offer insurance programs to ensure that certain types of coverage considered necessary to protect the public are available. All states require that employers meet the financial obligations to injured workers, based on workers' compensation laws. In place of or in addition to private insurers, some states sell workers' compensation insurance to employers. Depending on the state, the state workers' compensation insurance program may be the employers' only option, or it may be one of several options available to employers to meet their obligations.

In addition, state governments operate unemployment insurance plans, which provide some measure of continuing income for eligible workers who become unemployed. Fair Access to Insurance Requirements (FAIR) plans have been implemented in many states to provide basic property insurance for property owners who cannot otherwise obtain needed coverage on the open market. Through automobile insurance plans and other programs, states make auto insurance available to drivers who have difficulty obtaining such insurance from private insurers.

Insurer Operations

An insurer must take great care in arranging the insurance it agrees to provide, not only to ensure that it can meet its commitments to insureds to pay for covered losses, but also to collect enough premiums to earn a reasonable profit after paying those losses. The insurer must market its products and services effectively to gain enough customers to operate economically. The insurer must also decide which potential customers to insure, what coverages to offer, and what premiums to charge so that customers are adequately insured and the insurer can operate profitably. On a daily basis, the insurer must determine which losses sustained by its customers are covered and, if covered, the amount to be paid.

To accomplish these objectives, insurers engage in the following operations, all of which are discussed briefly here and covered in greater detail in later chapters:

- Marketing
- Underwriting
- Claim handling
- Ratemaking

Marketing is the process of determining customers' needs and then promoting and selling products or services to meet those needs. Insurance marketing enables insurers to reach potential customers and retain current ones. Insurance producers (agents and brokers) are an integral part of insurance marketing because they represent insurers to the public. Other important aspects of marketing are advertising, producer supervision and motivation, and product management.

Underwriting is the process by which insurers decide which potential customers to insure and what coverage to offer them. Underwriters are responsible for selecting insureds, pricing coverage, and determining policy terms and conditions. For some types of insurance, such as personal automobile, policy terms and conditions are largely standardized, and pricing is performed by computer rating programs. Still, the underwriter affects the outcome by determining the insured's eligibility for any of the insurer's policy provisions, and by properly classifying the insured for the automatic rating system. Effective underwriting enables insurers to provide the coverage needed by insureds and to be reasonably certain that the premiums collected will be sufficient to pay for their losses.

Claim handling enables insurers to determine whether a covered loss has occurred and, if so, the amount to be paid for the loss. The role of a claim representative is to satisfy the insurer's obligations under an insurance policy by promptly responding to claims and gathering the information necessary to evaluate a claim properly and reach a fair settlement.

Ratemaking is the process by which insurers determine the rates for each category, or classification, of similar but independent insureds. Insurers need appropriate rates to have enough money to pay for losses, cover operating expenses, and earn a reasonable profit.

To support their operations, insurers process vast amounts of data, relying on computers to process most of that data and to generate information necessary for running their businesses. Insurers use computers to process applications, to issue and renew policies, to generate invoices, to keep records of claims and loss payments, and to maintain accounting records and statistical reports. In addition to insurance-related information, insurers use computers in the same way that other businesses do: to generate management information reports and to store and retrieve data relating to employees, investments, customers, suppliers, and other matters.

Financial Performance of Insurers

An insurer's revenue must, in the long run, match or exceed the amount it pays for claims and administrative expenses if the insurer is to remain financially viable. Therefore, an insurer's financial performance is very important, but not just to the insurer. State insurance regulators, insurance producers, stockholders, and insureds also need to be assured of an insurer's financial health.

The primary sources of revenue for insurers are premiums and investment income. Insurers have investments because they receive premiums before they pay for losses and expenses. Insurers invest the money in the meantime and receive investment income as a result. One of the goals of insurers is to generate enough revenue from premiums and income from investments to pay for losses, meet other expenses, and earn a reasonable profit.

In addition to loss payments, insurers incur several other types of expenses. Insurers have loss settlement expenses, which include the costs of investigating and settling claims. They also incur expenses to acquire new business (such as advertising costs and producers' commissions), and general expenses (such as salaries, employee benefits, utilities, telephones, and computer equipment). Insurers pay premium taxes, income taxes, and various licensing and other fees. Insurers have expenses associated with investment activities, such as the salaries of investment department staff members. The ability to pay these expenses and still make a reasonable profit is a measure of an insurer's solvency, that is, its long-term financial strength.

State Insurance Regulation

Insurers must be able to meet their obligations to insureds. A financially weak insurer may not have the resources necessary to meet its obligations. Therefore, insurance regulators closely monitor the financial condition of insurers and take actions necessary to prevent insurer insolvency.

Every state has an insurance department that regulates the insurers doing business in that state. The insurance department regulates almost all aspects of the insurance business to some degree, but most insurance regulation deals with rates, insurer solvency, and consumer protection.

State insurance departments regulate insurance rates to protect consumers from inadequate, excessive, or unfairly discriminatory rates. Adequate rates are necessary for insurers to earn enough premium revenue to pay for losses and other expenses while generating a reasonable profit. At the same time, regulators believe that excessive rates are unfair to insurance consumers. Though regulators in some states trust open competition to produce lower rates for customers, many place tight caps on rates and enforce restrictions on changes to existing rates.

Insurance rates should reflect the insured's loss exposures. Therefore, insureds with similar loss exposures are grouped together in a single rating class and charged the same rate. Although other insureds may be grouped in a different rating class and charged a different rate, that rate must reflect the group's loss exposures. It would be unfair, however, if the different rate reflected characteristics of the group that had no bearing on their loss exposures. Therefore, rates based on such characteristics would not be permitted because they would be unfairly discriminatory. What constitutes unfair discrimination varies by state, and some states no longer allow discrimination based on such characteristics as age and sex for certain types of insurance, such as personal auto.

Insurance regulation also deals with insurer solvency. Through solvency surveillance, insurance regulators monitor the financial condition of insurers. Such surveillance enables regulators to work with insurers that have financial difficulties to keep the insurers in business and maintain their ability to meet obligations to insureds.

Finally, insurance regulation deals with consumer protection. Insurance regulation protects consumers in several ways. Insurers must be licensed to write insurance policies (for most types of insurance) in a given state, and licensing requires an insurer to meet tests of financial strength. In addition to licensing insurers, states require that certain representatives of insurers also be licensed. Such licensing requirements apply to insurance producers and may also apply to claim representatives and others.

Most states require that insurers file their policy forms with the insurance department so that the department can approve policy language. States also monitor specific insurer practices concerning marketing, underwriting, and claims. In addition, state insurance departments investigate complaints against insurers and their representatives and enforce standards regarding their conduct. All of these activities help to protect consumers.

Benefits of Insurance

Insurance provides many benefits to individuals, families, businesses, and society as a whole. These benefits include the following:

- Indemnifying for the costs of covered losses
- Reducing the insured's financial uncertainty
- Promoting insurers' loss control activities
- Using resources efficiently
- Providing support for credit
- Satisfying legal requirements
- Satisfying business requirements
- Providing a source of investment funds
- Reducing social burdens

Indemnifying for Losses

The primary role of insurance is to indemnify individuals, families, and businesses for covered losses. To **indemnify** means to restore a party who has sustained a loss to the same financial position that party held before the loss. Consider the aftermath of a loss for those who have no insurance to recognize the value of payment for losses. If fire destroys the home of a family with no insurance, the family members may be left without the financial resources to repair their home or to replace their belongings; they may also have no place to live. A business can incur bankruptcy as the result of a liability judgment it cannot pay, and the employees and owners of the business are suddenly unemployed. By indemnifying insureds, insurance provides some degree of financial security and stability for individuals, families, and businesses.

Indemnify
To restore a party who has sustained a loss to the same financial position that party held before the loss occurred.

Reducing Uncertainty

Because insurance provides financial compensation when covered losses occur, it greatly reduces the uncertainty created by many loss exposures. A family's major financial concerns, for example, often center on the possibility of a wage earner's death or the destruction of a home. If the family transfers the uncertainty about the financial consequences of such losses to an insurer, the family practically eliminates these financial concerns. Insurers have greater certainty than individuals about losses, because the law of large numbers enables them to predict the number of losses that are likely to occur and the financial effects of those losses.

Promoting Loss Control

Insurers often promote loss control by recommending loss control techniques that people and businesses can implement. Loss control means taking measures to prevent some losses from occurring or to reduce the financial consequences of losses that do occur. For example, individuals, families, and businesses can use loss control measures such as burglar alarms, smoke alarms, and dead bolt locks to prevent or reduce property loss exposures. Loss control generally reduces the amount of money insurers must pay in claims. Consequently, loss control helps to improve the financial results of insurers and to reduce insurance costs to consumers. Thus, society benefits from activities that prevent and reduce losses.

Using Resources Efficiently

People and businesses that face an uncertain future often set aside funds to pay for future losses. Insurance makes it unnecessary to set aside a large amount of money to pay for the financial consequences of loss exposures that can be insured. Money that would otherwise be set aside to pay for possible losses can be used to improve a family's quality of life or to contribute to the growth of a business. In exchange for a relatively small premium, families and businesses can free up additional funds that they would otherwise need to reserve to pay for unforeseen future losses, such as the loss of a house because of fire.

Providing Support for Credit

Before making a loan, a lender wants assurance that the money will be repaid. When a lender loans money to a borrower to purchase property, the lender usually acquires a legal interest in that property. The lender often can repossess a car or foreclose a home mortgage if the loan is not repaid. However, the lender would be less likely to make loans if it did not have some assurance of getting back its money if the car or house were destroyed or if the borrower died or became disabled before the loan was paid in full.

Insurance facilitates loans to individuals and businesses by guaranteeing that the lender will be paid if the collateral for the loan (such as a house or a commercial building) is destroyed or damaged by an insured event, thereby reducing the lender's uncertainty.

Satisfying Legal Requirements

Insurance is often used or required to satisfy legal requirements. In many states, for example, automobile owners must prove they have auto liability insurance before they can register their autos. All states have laws that require employers to pay for job-related injuries or illnesses of their employees, and employers generally purchase workers' compensation insurance to meet this financial obligation.

Satisfying Business Requirements

Certain business relationships require proof of insurance. For example, building contractors are usually required to provide evidence of liability insurance before a construction contract is granted. In fact, almost anyone who provides a service to the public, from an architect to a tree trimmer, may need to prove that he or she has liability insurance before being awarded a contract for services.

Providing a Source of Investment Funds

One of the greatest benefits of insurance is that it provides funds for investment. When insurers collect premiums, they usually do not need funds immediately to pay losses and expenses. Insurers use some of these funds to purchase stocks and bonds. Such investments provide businesses with money for projects such as new construction, research, and technology. Investment funds promote economic growth and job creation. Investment brings additional funding to insurers in the form of interest; this additional income helps to keep insurance premiums at a reasonable level for individuals and businesses. Insurers also invest in social projects, such as cultural events, education, and economic development.

Reducing Social Burdens

Uncompensated accident victims can be a serious burden to society. Insurance helps to reduce this burden by providing compensation to such injured persons. For example, workers' compensation insurance provides payment to injured employees for medical expenses, lost wages, and rehabilitation, as well as death benefits to survivors of employees killed by workplace accidents or diseases. Compulsory auto insurance is another example, because it provides compensation to auto accident victims who may otherwise be unable to afford proper medical care or who may be unable to work. Without insurance, victims of job-related injuries or auto accidents may need state welfare or the assistance of another social program.

Costs of Insurance

The benefits of insurance are not cost-free. However, the benefits of insurance outweigh the costs, and insurance is generally considered to provide a meaningful economic and social purpose. Among the costs of insurance are both direct and indirect costs, including the following:

- Premiums paid by insureds
- Operating costs of insurers
- Opportunity costs
- Increased losses
- Increased lawsuits

Premiums Paid by Insureds

Insurers must charge premiums to have the funds necessary to make loss payments. In fact, an insurer's total revenue (premiums and investment income) must equal or exceed the amount needed to pay for losses and to cover its costs of doing business. For example, an insurer may use eighty cents of every premium dollar to pay for losses and twenty-five cents for other expenses. If the insurer can earn an amount equal to five percent of its premiums on its investments, it can break even. By law, insurance premiums must not be excessive; however, insureds may believe that their premiums are too high. Realistically, insurance premiums may also be considered as a cost of living and doing business in an industrialized society.

Operating Costs of Insurers

Like any business, an insurer has operating costs that must be paid to run the day-to-day operations of the company. Those costs include salaries, producers' commissions, advertising, building expenses, equipment, taxes, licensing fees, and many others. In addition, most insurers are in business to make a profit, just like any other business. Therefore, a reasonable amount of profit must be calculated in the cost of insurance that insureds pay.

Opportunity Costs

If capital and labor were not being used in the insurance business, they could be used elsewhere and could be making other productive contributions to society. Therefore, whatever resources the insurance industry uses in its operations represent lost opportunities in other areas—in other words, opportunity costs. These opportunity costs are one of the costs of insurance.

Increased Losses

The existence of insurance may encourage losses to some extent. Although insurers have an economic incentive to provide and encourage loss control measures, insurance may sometimes provide an economic incentive for insureds to have losses. For example, a person may intentionally cause a loss or exaggerate a loss that has occurred. It is estimated that 37,500 structural fires and 30,500 vehicle fires in 2003 were intentional. Property damage from these fires amounted to approximately $692 million in structural damage and $132 million in vehicle damage. These figures do not include indirect costs, such as business interruption, loss of use, and temporary shelter costs, nor do they take into consideration human suffering and human loss exposure costs, such as medical expenses and funeral costs.[2] Many cases of arson or suspected arson involve insurance—some property owners would rather have the insurance money than the property.

Arson is an intentionally staged accident and it represents one form of insurance fraud. The intentional exaggeration or loss in an otherwise legitimate claim is a more common form of insurance fraud. These exaggerations are also referred to as claim buildup. For example, an insured may claim that four items were lost rather than the actual three or that the items were worth more than their actual value. In liability claims, claimants may exaggerate the severity of their bodily injury or property damage. Physicians, lawyers, contractors, and auto body shop operators can also be participants in claim buildup.

Insurers are actively involved in the fight against insurance fraud and use various techniques to detect and investigate suspicious claims. Nevertheless, insurance fraud is a serious problem that results in billions of dollars in excess insurance payments each year. Fraudulent claims increase costs for both insurers (in terms of both payment for fraudulent claims and the cost of investigating and resisting fraud) and insureds (who pay increased premiums to help cover the cost of those who defraud insurers).

Some losses may not be deliberately caused, but they may result from carelessness on the part of an insured because insurance is available to pay for losses if they do occur. Routinely leaving the keys in an unlocked car is an example of such carelessness. If the car is stolen, the insured would suffer only minimal financial consequences because the insurer will pay for the loss. The additional losses that result from insureds' carelessness increase the cost of insurance for everyone because insurers often pay for injuries and damage that insureds could have prevented.

Increased Lawsuits

The number of liability lawsuits has increased steadily in recent years. One reason for this increase is that liability insurers often pay large sums of money to persons who have been injured. Liability insurance is intended to protect people who may be responsible for injury to someone else or damage to someone's property. However, some people may view liability insurance as a pool of money available to anyone who has suffered injury or damage, with little regard given to fault. The increase in frivolous lawsuits is an unfortunate cost of insurance in today's society.

INSURANCE AS A CONTRACT

An insurance policy is a contract between the insurer and the insured. Through insurance policies, insureds transfer the possible costs of losses to insurers. In return for the premiums paid by insureds, insurers promise to pay for the losses covered by the insurance policy. As noted, this promise reduces the uncertainty or insecurity that insureds have about paying for losses that may occur. The coverage provided by insurance policies enables individuals, families, businesses, and organizations to protect their assets and minimize the adverse financial effects of losses.

The four basic types of insurance—property, liability, life, and health—are generally divided into two broad categories, as follows:

1.   Property/liability insurance
2.   Life/health insurance

Property insurance provides coverage for property and net income loss exposures. It protects an insured's assets by paying to repair or replace property that is damaged, lost, or destroyed, or by replacing the net income lost and the extra expenses incurred as a result of a property loss. Liability insurance covers liability loss exposures. It provides for payment on behalf of the insured for injury to others or damage to others' property for which the insured is legally responsible.

Life insurance and health insurance cover the financial consequences of personal and personnel loss exposures. Life insurance replaces the income-earning potential lost through death and also helps to pay expenses related to an insured's death. Health insurance protects individuals and families from financial losses caused by sickness and accidents. Disability insurance is a form of health insurance that replaces an insured's income if the insured is unable to work because of illness or injury.

Property Insurance

Property insurance covers the costs of accidental losses to an insured's property. The insured could be a family insuring its house and personal property or a business insuring its building, inventory, and equipment. When the insured experiences a loss, such as fire damage to a house, the insured deals directly with the insurer to settle the loss and receive payment.

Many types of insurance are classified as property insurance, such as the following:

* Fire and allied lines insurance
* Business income insurance
* Crime insurance
* Ocean marine insurance
* Inland marine insurance
* Auto physical damage insurance

Fire and allied lines insurance generally covers direct damage to or loss of insured property, such as buildings and personal property, at a fixed location or locations described in the policy. The term "allied lines" refers to insurance against causes of loss usually written with (allied to) fire insurance, such as windstorm, hail, smoke, explosion, vandalism, and others. Examples of fire and allied lines insurance policies are a dwelling policy and a commercial property policy.

Business income insurance, traditionally called **business interruption insurance**, covers the loss of net income or additional expenses incurred by a business as the result of a covered loss to its property. For example, when a business has a serious fire, it may have to close until repairs to the building are made and personal property is replaced. A resulting loss of net income occurs over time. Business income insurance pays the insured for the loss of income or additional expenses that the insured incurs because of the loss during the time needed to restore the business to its pre-loss condition.

Crime insurance covers money, securities, merchandise, and other property from various causes of loss such as burglary, robbery, theft, and employee dishonesty. Coverage for crime losses that a business may incur is usually provided by separate policies that insure specific types of property against specific crime losses. Crime losses that a person or family may suffer are usually insured under a homeowners policy.

Ocean marine insurance, one of the oldest forms of insurance, covers ships and their cargo against such causes of loss as fire, lightning, and "perils of the seas," which include high winds, rough waters, running aground, and collision with other ships or objects.

Inland marine insurance covers miscellaneous types of property, such as movable property, goods in domestic transit, and property used in transportation and communication. It was originally developed to provide coverage for losses to cargo transported over land but now covers many different types of property in addition to goods in transit.

Auto physical damage insurance covers loss of or damage to specified vehicles from collision, fire, theft, or other causes. It is usually part of a policy that also provides auto liability coverage, such as a personal auto policy or a business auto policy.

Liability Insurance

Because an insurance policy is a contract between the insured and the insurer, these two are usually the only parties involved in a property loss. Liability insurance, however, is sometimes called third-party insurance because three parties are involved in a liability loss: the insured, the insurer, and the party who is injured or whose property is damaged by the insured. (The third party is usually called the claimant.) The insurer pays the claimant *on behalf of the insured* if the insured is legally liable for the injury or damage. An insured's

---

Fire and allied lines insurance
Insurance that covers direct damage to or loss of insured property.

Business income insurance, or **business interruption insurance**
Insurance that covers the loss of net income or additional expenses incurred by a business as the result of a covered loss to its property.

Crime insurance
Insurance that covers money, securities, merchandise, and other property from various causes of loss such as burglary, robbery, theft, and employee dishonesty.

Ocean marine insurance
Insurance that covers ships and their cargo against such causes of loss as fire, lightning, and "perils of the seas."

Inland marine insurance
Insurance that covers miscellaneous types of property, such as movable property, goods in domestic transit, and property used in transportation and communication.

Auto physical damage insurance
Insurance that covers loss of or damage to specified vehicles from collision, fire, theft, or other causes.

legal liability for injury or damage is often the result of a negligent act, but there are other sources of liability as well. Examples of liability insurance include the following:

- Auto liability insurance
- Commercial general liability insurance
- Personal liability insurance
- Professional liability insurance

Auto liability insurance
Insurance that covers an insured's legal liability arising out of the ownership, maintenance, or use of an automobile.

Auto liability insurance covers an insured's legal liability arising out of the ownership, maintenance, or use of an automobile. The legal costs of defending the insured against lawsuits are also covered when such defense is necessary. The personal auto policy and the business auto policy are the most widely used auto insurance policies. These policies can include coverage for both auto liability and auto physical damage losses.

Commercial general liability insurance
Insurance that covers liability loss exposures arising from a business organization's premises and operations, its products, or its completed work.

Commercial general liability insurance covers liability loss exposures arising from a business organization's premises and operations, its products, or its completed work. The following examples of liability claims against an appliance store illustrate the various ways that a business can be liable for the bodily injury or property damage suffered by others:

- *Premises.* A customer whose finger was caught in a revolving door incurred medical expenses for treatment in a hospital emergency room.
- *Business operations.* Employees broke a water pipe while installing a dishwasher in an apartment, causing substantial water damage to property in the apartment below.
- *Products.* A customer's face was cut when an electric mixer sold to the customer malfunctioned and shattered a glass mixing bowl.
- *Completed operations.* A short circuit developed in an electric stove incorrectly installed by employees and caused a fire that damaged the customer's kitchen.

Personal liability insurance
Insurance that provides liability coverage to individuals and families for bodily injury and property damage arising from the insured's personal premises or activities.

Personal liability insurance provides liability coverage to individuals and families for bodily injury and property damage arising from the insured's personal premises or activities. As mentioned previously, in most instances, the liability arises from the insured's negligence. For example, a visitor to the insured's home may slip and fall on the insured's icy driveway, or the insured may hit a golf ball that accidentally strikes a pedestrian in the head. This type of coverage is included in all homeowners policies.

Professional liability insurance
Insurance that provides liability coverage to professionals for errors and omissions arising out of their professional duties.

Professional liability insurance provides liability coverage to professionals for errors and omissions arising out of their professional duties. Medical malpractice insurance, which covers doctors and other healthcare providers, is probably the best known type of professional liability insurance, but similar coverage is available to other types of professionals, including insurance producers, attorneys, architects, and engineers.

Life Insurance

One of the most severe causes of financial loss to a family is the premature death of a family member, especially the primary wage earner. Life insurance can greatly reduce the adverse financial consequences of premature death by providing funds to replace lost income to pay uncovered medical expenses (when necessary) and cover the funeral costs.

Although there are many variations of life insurance, the following three basic types are commonly sold:

- Whole life insurance
- Term insurance
- Universal life insurance

Whole life insurance provides lifetime (for the insured's whole life) protection, accrues cash value, and has premiums that remain unchanged during the insured's lifetime. **Cash value** is the monetary amount, considered to be a form of savings, that accumulates in the policy. A policyholder can borrow the cash value after a policy has been in effect for a specified number of years. Whole life insurance is purchased when a consumer wants lifetime protection with a level (constant) premium and a savings element.

Term insurance provides coverage for a specified period, such as ten or twenty years, with no cash value. A term life insurance policy is used when the consumer wants the maximum amount of life insurance protection available at the lowest cost. Parents of young children may buy twenty-year term insurance to provide financial security until their children are grown.

Universal life insurance provides life insurance protection and a savings component. The policyholder has a cash value account that is credited with the premiums paid, less a deduction for the cost of the insurance protection and expenses charged. The balance in the account is then credited with interest at a specified rate. If the policyholder surrenders the policy, the cash value account may be reduced by a surrender charge to determine the surrender value paid to the policyholder.

Some life insurance policies are sold directly to individuals, while other life insurance policies cover a group of insureds. Such group policies are usually term insurance policies arranged through an employer or an association.

Whole life insurance
Life insurance that provides lifetime protection, accrues cash value, and has premiums that remain unchanged during the insured's lifetime.

Cash value
The monetary amount, considered to be a form of savings, that accumulates in a whole life insurance policy.

Term insurance
Life insurance that provides coverage for a specified period, such as ten or twenty years, with no cash value.

Universal life insurance
Insurance that provides life insurance protection and a savings component.

Health Insurance

Health insurance is designed to protect individuals and families from financial loss caused by accidents and sickness. Like life insurance, health insurance is issued on either an individual or a group basis. The various types of health insurance policies can be classified as either medical insurance or disability insurance. **Medical insurance** covers medical expenses that result from illness

Medical insurance
Insurance that covers medical expenses that result from illness or injury.

Disability income insurance
A type of health insurance that provides periodic income payments to an insured who is unable to work because of sickness or injury.

or injury. **Disability income insurance** provides periodic income payments to an insured who is unable to work because of sickness or injury. Disability insurance is primarily income replacement insurance that pays weekly or monthly benefits until the insured can return to work or until a maximum period has elapsed.

SUMMARY

Every individual, family, and business organization needs insurance. Insurance is actually four things: a risk management technique, a transfer system, a business, and a contract.

For loss exposures that an individual or organization cannot easily retain, avoid, or control, insurance is often the best available risk management technique.

The key elements of insurance as a transfer system are transfer and sharing. An insured transfers the potential financial consequences of loss exposures to an insurer, thereby exchanging the possibility of a large loss for the certainty of a much smaller periodic payment (the premium). The sharing aspect of insurance requires the insurer to pool the premiums paid by insureds into a loss fund from which covered losses are paid. Although the insurer does not expect all insureds to experience a loss, all insureds share in the cost of losses because their premiums make up the loss fund. Because of the law of large numbers, insurers can predict the number of losses that may occur and thus the amount of premium to be paid by each insured.

The need for insurance exists because everyone faces exposures to loss, that is, the possibility that a loss will occur. Loss exposures can give rise to three major types of loss: property loss (including net income loss), liability loss, and personal and personnel loss. The role of insurance is to protect insureds' assets from the financial consequences of loss. However, insurers prefer to provide insurance for loss exposures that are considered ideally insurable.

The insurance business provides jobs to millions of workers in the U.S. Private insurers provide most insurance, but federal and state government insurance programs also provide insurance for loss exposures that private insurers are unable or reluctant to insure.

Insurer operations include marketing, underwriting, claim handling, and ratemaking, as well as information processing. The states regulate many of the operations of insurers. Regulators, insureds, and others need to be assured of insurers' financial stability. To protect consumers, state insurance departments regulate insurance rates and monitor insurer solvency.

In addition to payment for losses, the insurance business offers many benefits to insureds and to society as a whole. However, there are both direct and indirect costs associated with insurance.

An insurance policy, which is a contract between the insured and the insurer, states the rights and duties of each party with regard to losses. The four basic types of insurance are property insurance, liability insurance, life insurance, and health insurance. Each of these types of insurance is provided through contracts between the insured and the insurer.

CHAPTER NOTES

1.　Insurance Information Institute, *The III Insurance Fact Book 2005* (New York: Insurance Information Institute, 2005), pp. 1–7, 13.

2.　Insurance Information Institute, *The III Insurance Fact Book 2005*, p. 102.

Chapter 2

Direct Your Learning

Who Provides Insurance and How Is It Regulated?

After learning the content of this chapter and completing the corresponding course guide assignment, you should be able to:

- Describe the various types of private insurers that provide property-casualty insurance:
  - Stock insurers
  - Mutual insurers
  - Reciprocal insurance exchanges
  - Lloyd's
  - American Lloyds
  - Captive insurers
  - Reinsurance companies
- Describe the federal government Social Security program.
- Identify other federal insurance programs.
- Describe common state government insurance programs:
  - Workers' compensation insurance funds
  - Unemployment insurance programs
  - Automobile insurance plans
  - Fair Access to Insurance Requirements (FAIR) plans
  - Beachfront and windstorm pools
  - Insurance guarantee funds
- Describe the purpose and activities of the National Association of Insurance Commissioners (NAIC).
- Explain how insurance rates are developed.
- Describe the objectives of rate regulation.
- Describe the different types of insurance rating laws.
- Explain how insurance regulators monitor insurers' financial condition and protect consumers.
- Explain how the excess and surplus lines market meets the needs of various classes of business that are often unable to find insurance in the standard market.
- Define or describe each of the Key Words and Phrases for this chapter.

Develop Your Perspective

What are the main topics covered in the chapter?

Although most property-casualty insurance in the United States is provided by private insurers, government insurance fills important voids for loss exposures that are difficult for private insurers to address. Insurance is regulated on a state basis. State regulators ensure the solvency and performance of private insurers to protect consumers.

Describe the providers of property-casualty insurance.

- What loss exposures are ideally insurable, and why are private insurers reluctant to insure those that are not?

- What loss exposures are assumed by the federal and state governments?

- Why is excess and surplus insurance necessary?

Why is it important to learn about these topics?

The providers of insurance fill an important role in addressing the loss exposures of most individuals and organizations.

Consider how the insurance market would change if any of the providers were missing.

- How would society in the U.S. change if the government did not provide the Social Security program?

- How would construction and land development change if the National Flood Insurance Program did not provide flood insurance and various states did not provide windstorm insurance pools?

How can you use what you will learn?

Evaluate the state regulation of private insurers.

- How does regulation benefit insurers that do business in a particular state and the residents of that state?

- How might federal regulation of private insurers enhance or diminish those benefits?

Chapter 2

Who Provides Insurance and How Is It Regulated?

Insurance is a risk management technique, a transfer system, a business, and a contract, and it is provided by several types of insurers. This chapter describes these different types of insurers and how state governments regulate them. Regulatory mechanisms are designed to maintain the integrity of insurers, govern rates, and address the needs of customers who cannot purchase insurance from "mainstream" insurance companies.

The insurance industry is not well understood or held in high regard by much of the purchasing public. The mechanism of insurance is relatively complex in comparison to purchases of other goods and services. A family that buys a car examines and compares vehicles to determine which provides the best value for the lowest price. In contrast, the purchase of insurance is an exchange of money now for a future promise (payment for covered claims) as stated in a contract. In choosing an automobile insurance policy for the new car, it may be difficult for a family to compare the promises made by various insurers and their track records in fulfilling those promises. In the past, some unscrupulous insurance companies may have taken advantage of policyholders by failing to fulfill the promises made in their contracts, heightening the public's suspicions regarding all insurers.

To maintain and strengthen the integrity of the insurance industry, regulations govern the actions and practices of insurers. This chapter describes some of those regulatory activities as well as the insurers who provide coverage.

TYPES OF INSURANCE ORGANIZATIONS

Private (nongovernment) insurers provide most of the property-casualty insurance in the United States. Private insurers also provide some insurance through government-sponsored insurance programs. The federal government and the various state governments also act as insurers for certain types of loss exposures. This section discusses the various types of private insurers and then examines common federal and state government insurance programs.

Private Insurers

Numerous kinds of private insurers provide property and liability coverage for individuals, families, and businesses. Private insurers differ from one another in several ways, primarily in terms of:

- The purpose for which they were formed
- Their legal form of organization
- Their ownership
- Their method of operation

Some of these differences developed through historical circumstances; others resulted from legislative action or the interests of the parties that formed the insurer.

All insurers provide a means to indemnify insureds if a covered loss occurs, and to spread the cost of losses among insureds. Although all insurers perform these basic functions, the underlying motives of the parties forming different types of insurers are not the same. Some types of insurers are formed in the expectation that the insurer's operations will make a profit or provide some other direct financial benefit for its owners. Other insurers are formed by or on behalf of groups of insureds with the motive of making insurance more readily available or making insurance available at a cost lower than if it were purchased through the general insurance market.

This section discusses the following types of private insurers:

- Stock insurers
- Mutual insurers
- Reciprocal insurance exchanges
- Lloyd's
- American Lloyds
- Captive insurers
- Reinsurance companies

Exhibit 2-1 outlines the major differences among these kinds of private insurers. Insurers may also differ according to their licensing status, the marketing systems they use, and the types of insurance coverage they provide. Each type of insurer is discussed in greater detail next.

Stock Insurers

Stock insurer
An insurer that is owned by its stockholders and formed as a corporation for the purpose of earning a profit for the stockholders.

Insurers formed for the purpose of making a profit for their owners are typically organized as stock corporations. As such, a **stock insurer** is owned by its stockholders and formed as a corporation for the purpose of earning a profit for the stockholders. By purchasing stock in a for-profit insurer, stockholders supply the capital the insurer needs when it is formed or the additional capital needed to expand the insurer's operations. These stockholders expect to

EXHIBIT 2-1

Differences Among Major Types of Private Insurers (and Lloyd's)

Type	Purpose for Which Formed	Legal Form	Ownership	Method of Operation
Stock insurer	To earn a profit for its stockholders	Corporation	Stockholders	The board of directors, elected by stockholders, appoints officers to manage the company.
Mutual insurer	To provide insurance for its owners (policyholders)	Corporation	Policyholders	The board of directors, elected by policyholders, appoints officers to manage the company.
Reciprocal insurance exchange (interinsurance exchange)	To provide reciprocity for subscribers (to cover each other's losses)	Unincorporated association	Subscribers (members)	Subscribers choose an attorney-in-fact to operate the reciprocal.
Lloyd's	To earn a profit for its individual investors ("Names") and its corporate investors	Unincorporated association	Investors	Lloyd's is regulated by the U.K. Financial Services Authority (FSA), which delegates much authority to the Council of Lloyd's.

receive a return on their investment in the form of stock dividends, increased stock value, or both. Therefore, one of the primary objectives of a stock insurer is returning a profit to its stockholders. Many of the largest property-casualty insurers in the U.S. are stock insurers. These companies have been able to attract and retain stockholders by the expectation of investment returns.

Stockholders have the right to elect the board of directors, which has the authority to control the insurer's activities. The board of directors creates and oversees corporate goals and objectives and appoints a chief executive officer (CEO) to carry out the insurer's operations. The CEO and a team of senior management personnel are given authority by the board of directors to implement the programs necessary to operate the company.

The stock form of ownership also provides financial flexibility for the insurer. For example, the management of a stock insurer may decide to expand its operations by purchasing another insurance company, by expanding into new territories, developing new product lines, or by purchasing a noninsurance company to diversify its operations. One way that a stock insurer can finance such expansion is by selling additional shares of common stock. The ability to raise additional funds by selling common stock is an important aspect of the stock form of organization.

Mutual Insurers

A **mutual insurer** is owned by its policyholders and formed as a corporation for the purpose of providing insurance to them. The corporation of a traditional mutual insurer issues no common stock, so it has no stockholders. The policyholders of a mutual company have voting rights similar to those of the stockholders of a stock company. They elect a board of directors that performs the same functions as the board of directors of a stock company. Mutual companies include some very large national insurers and many more regional ones.

Although initially formed to provide insurance for their owners, mutual insurers today generally seek to earn profits in their ongoing operations as do stock companies. A mutual insurer needs profits to ensure the future financial health of the organization. A stock company may choose to share profits with its stockholders by the payment of dividends, which are a return on the stockholders' investment. Mutual insurers also may opt to share profits, but pay dividends instead to policyholders as a return of a portion of premiums paid.

Some mutual insurers have the right to charge insureds an assessment, or additional premium, after the policy has gone into effect. Such an assessment might be made after the insurer has endured a series of losses from a catastrophic event, such as a hurricane. These insurers are known as assessment mutual insurance companies, and they are less common than in the past.

From the perspective of the insured, differences between stock and mutual insurance companies are becoming less significant. Such things as potential assessments, which were a disadvantage, and dividends, which could be a competitive advantage, are less common features of mutual insurers today. In fact, the structure of mutual companies is gradually changing, making them more similar to stock companies. Some state laws now allow mutual insurers to sell stock to the public by creating a mutual holding company, and other states are considering the adoption of similar regulations. In recent years, some mutual companies have converted to stock companies through a process called **demutualization**. Some mutual companies have made these structural changes because they wanted to raise additional capital through the sale of stock to better compete with stock companies, which can benefit from favorable stock market conditions.

Reciprocal Insurance Exchanges

A **reciprocal insurance exchange**, or an **interinsurance exchange**, (also simply called a reciprocal) is an insurer owned by its policyholders, formed as an unincorporated association for the purpose of providing insurance coverage to its members (called subscribers), and managed by an attorney-in-fact. The term "reciprocal" comes from the reciprocity of responsibility of all **subscribers**, who agree to insure each other. Each member of the reciprocal is both an insured and an insurer. Because the subscribers are not experts in running an insurance operation, they contract with an individual or organization to operate the reciprocal; this manager is called an attorney-in-fact. The **attorney-in-fact** is the contractually authorized manager of the reciprocal who administers its affairs and carries out its insurance transactions. An agreement (known as a subscription agreement) authorizes the attorney-in-fact to act on behalf of the subscribers to market and underwrite insurance coverage, collect premiums, invest funds, and handle claims. The existence of an attorney-in-fact, empowered by the subscribers, is one of the main features that distinguishes a reciprocal from other types of insurers.

Reciprocals make up a small percentage of the total number of insurance companies in the U.S., but they do include some major national and international insurers. Small regional reciprocals also operate on a state-by-state basis.

Attorney-in-fact
In a reciprocal insurance exchange, the contractually authorized manager of the reciprocal who administers its affairs and carries out its insurance transactions.

Lloyd's

Although not technically an insurer, Lloyd's (formerly Lloyd's of London) is an association that provides the physical and procedural facilities for its members to write insurance. In other words, it is a marketplace, similar to a stock exchange. Members of Lloyd's do not take an active part in the day-to-day operation of Lloyd's. They are investors (companies, individuals, and Scottish Limited Partnerships) that hope to earn a profit from the insurance operations that occur at Lloyd's.

Each individual investor, called a "Name," of Lloyd's belongs to one or more groups called syndicates. A syndicate's underwriter or group of underwriters conducts its insurance operations and analyzes applications for insurance coverage. Depending on the nature and amount of insurance requested, the underwriters for a particular syndicate might accept only a portion of the total amount of insurance. The application is then taken to other syndicates for their evaluations.

The insurance written by each Name is backed by his or her entire personal fortune. However, each Name is liable only for the insurance he or she agrees to write, not for the obligations assumed by any other Name. In 1994, Lloyd's began admitting corporations as members. Unlike its individual members, corporate members of Lloyd's have limited liability. Corporate members today make up the dominant share of Lloyd's members.[1]

Lloyd's has earned a reputation for accepting applications for very unusual types of insurance, such as insuring the legs of a famous football player against injury. These applications may be the subject of newspaper articles, but the bulk of Lloyd's business does not involve such unusual coverages. In fact, most of the insurance written through Lloyd's is commercial property-casualty insurance, such as marine, aviation, catastrophe, professional liability, and automobile insurance.[2]

Lloyd's has operated continuously for more than 300 years, and Lloyd's underwriters are considered to be among the world's leaders in their fields.

Over the years, despite serious natural disasters and occasional mistakes in underwriting judgment, Lloyd's members have had the financial resources to survive catastrophes, pay claims, and move forward to more profitable times. For most of its history, many members have received an excellent return on their investments, and Lloyd's has had little trouble attracting new members. More recently, large losses over several years have created a strain on some of Lloyd's syndicate members. Nevertheless, Lloyd's remains one of the world's most important sources of insurance.

American Lloyds

American Lloyds associations are much smaller than Lloyd's, and most are domiciled in Texas, with a few in other states. Most of the Texas Lloyds associations were formed or have been acquired by insurance companies. Unlike the individual Names of Lloyd's, members (called underwriters) of American Lloyds have limited liability. The liability of underwriters at American Lloyds is limited to their investment in the Lloyds association. State laws require a minimum number of underwriters (ten in Texas) for each Lloyds association. American Lloyds are usually small and operate as a single syndicate under the management of an attorney-in-fact.

Captive Insurers

Captive insurer, or **captive**
An insurer formed as a subsidiary of its parent company, organization, or group, for the purpose of providing all or part of the insurance on the parent company or companies.

When a company, an organization, or a group of affiliated organizations forms a subsidiary for the purpose of having the subsidiary provide all or part of the insurance on the parent company or companies, the subsidiary is known as a **captive insurer**, or simply a **captive**. Although captive insurers have been in existence since the early part of the twentieth century, the widespread use of captives is more recent, with the major growth occurring since the late 1970s.

Three factors have contributed to the growth of captives in recent years: (1) low insurance cost, (2) insurance availability, and (3) improved cash flow. First, captives might be able to provide insurance coverage at a lower cost than other private insurers because acquisition costs are eliminated. For example, captives might not have to pay producers' commissions or advertising expenses because they provide insurance primarily to the parent company.

Second, a captive helps to eliminate the problems some corporations might face because necessary or desired insurance coverage is unavailable or costs more than the corporation is willing or able to pay. Forming a captive insurer eases the problems of availability and affordability for a parent company that has loss exposures that may be difficult to insure.

The third and most important factor is improved cash flow. A premium paid to a captive remains within the corporate structure until it is used to pay claims. Instead of paying premiums to an unrelated insurer, the corporation is able to invest its funds until the time they are needed for claims. Thus, the corporation can receive a significant cash flow advantage by creating a captive. This advantage becomes even greater when interest rates are high, as was the case during the late 1970s and early 1980s, when the number of captives increased dramatically.

Captive insurers have become an important alternative in the insurance-buying decisions of corporations. The relative importance of the factors affecting the growth of captives changes over time, but it appears that captives will remain an important source of insurance.

Reinsurance Companies

Some private insurers provide **reinsurance**, which is a contractual agreement that transfers some or all of the potential costs of insured loss exposures from policies written by one insurer to another insurer. The insurer that transfers some or all of the potential costs of insured loss exposures is the **primary insurer** (also called the reinsured). The insurer that assumes some or all of the potential costs of insured loss exposures of the primary insurer is the **reinsurer**. Some reinsurers are companies or organizations that specialize in the reinsurance business. Other reinsurers are also primary insurers that enter into reinsurance arrangements with other insurers.

A primary insurer might buy reinsurance for a variety of reasons. One of the most important reasons is that reinsurance permits the primary insurer to transfer some of its loss exposures to the reinsurer. For example, an insurer that writes a large amount of property insurance in an area where tornadoes commonly occur can use reinsurance to reduce its exposure to windstorm losses.

Reinsurance also enables a small insurer to provide insurance for large accounts (such as large national or multinational corporations) whose insurance needs would otherwise exceed the insurer's capacity. For example, consider a primary insurer that writes a commercial liability policy for a large company that manufactures sports helmets. Because the potential for heavy liability losses resulting from injuries caused by defective helmets is great, the primary insurer might contract with a reinsurer to cover all of its liability losses for this insured over a certain amount, such as $1 million. Therefore, the primary insurer and the reinsurer are sharing the liability loss exposures for this insured.

Government Insurance Programs

Despite the size and diversity of private insurers in the U.S., private insurers do not provide all types of insurance. Some loss exposures do not possess the characteristics that make them commercially insurable, but a significant need for protection against the potential costs of losses resulting from loss exposures still exists. Both federal and state governments have developed insurance programs, such as Social Security, to meet these needs. These programs are discussed next.

Reinsurance
A contractual agreement that transfers some or all of the potential costs of insured loss exposures from policies written by one insurer to another insurer.

Primary insurer
The insurer that transfers some or all of the potential costs of its insured loss exposures to another insurer in a reinsurance contractual agreement.

Reinsurer
The insurer that assumes some or all of the potential costs of insured loss exposures of the primary insurer in a reinsurance contractual agreement.

Federal Government Insurance Programs

Some federal government insurance programs serve the public in a manner that only the government can. For example, only the government has the ability to tax in order to provide the financial resources needed to insure some loss exposures and the power to make the system viable by requiring mandatory participation. One federal government insurance program that requires such participation is the Social Security program.

The Social Security program, formally known as the Old Age, Survivors, Disability, and Health Insurance program (OASDHI), is a comprehensive program that provides benefits to millions of Americans. The Social Security Administration, a federal governmental agency, operates the program and provides the following four types of benefits to eligible citizens:

1. Retirement benefits for the elderly
2. Survivorship benefits for dependents of deceased workers
3. Disability payments for disabled workers
4. Medical benefits for the elderly (under the Medicare program)

Mandatory participation in the Social Security program for those eligible for coverage eliminates the need for individual underwriting and helps to generate premium revenues to operate the system. Private insurers provide similar benefits (retirement benefits, life insurance, disability insurance, and health insurance) to some insureds, but they cannot approach the scope of the Social Security program. Some private insurers provide insurance to supplement specific Social Security benefits.

Other federal government insurance programs provide coverage for loss exposures that private insurers have avoided largely because of the potential for catastrophic losses. Examples of such plans are the National Flood Insurance Program and the Federal Crop Insurance Program. The need for each of these programs is highly concentrated—only a specific portion of the population needs the coverage. Those who have property in areas exposed to flooding need flood protection, and farmers in areas subject to hailstorms have the greatest need for crop insurance. This concentration of exposure units generally makes private insurers reluctant to provide coverage for flood and crop losses. In other words, the exposure units are not independent and thus are subject to catastrophic losses that private insurers cannot insure economically.

State Government Insurance Programs

State governments are actively involved in providing insurance for their citizens. Among the most common types of insurance programs provided or operated by state governments are as follows:

-   Workers' compensation insurance funds
-   Unemployment insurance programs
-   Automobile insurance plans

- Fair Access to Insurance Requirements (FAIR) plans
- Beachfront and windstorm pools

In addition, all states have some type of insurance guaranty fund to pay for covered losses should an insurer become financially unable to meet its obligations to its insureds.

Many states provide workers' compensation insurance through a variety of funds. North Dakota, Ohio, Washington, West Virginia, and Wyoming operate **monopolistic state funds**, which means that the state fund is the only source of workers' compensation insurance allowed in that state. All employers in the state who need workers' compensation insurance must obtain it from this fund. Puerto Rico and the U.S. Virgin Islands operate territorial funds, which are similar to monopolistic state funds. Some states operate a **competitive state fund**, which is a plan that competes with private insurers to provide workers' compensation insurance. Employers may choose between the state fund and some other means of meeting their obligations under workers' compensation statutes. Still other states provide workers' compensation to some employers through residual market plans. A **residual market plan**, also known as a **shared market plan**, is a program that makes workers' compensation insurance available to those who cannot obtain voluntary coverage from private insurers. In some states, private insurers provide the coverage for the residual market; in other states, the residual market is served by the state fund. In this way, the state is performing the function of satisfying a demand for coverage that private insurers are unwilling or unable to meet.

Whether provided by a private insurer or a state fund, workers' compensation insurance covers lost wages only for a job-related injury. Five states (California, Rhode Island, New Jersey, Hawaii, and New York) provide workers with disability insurance that will replace wages lost because of pregnancy and injuries or sickness that are not job related.

All state governments operate unemployment insurance programs, but the benefits provided vary by state. Minimum federal standards, however, as well as some federal financing, ensure that eligible workers have some unemployment insurance protection. Private insurance covering the loss of income due to unemployment is not available because of the catastrophic potential of widespread unemployment.

Most states now require that owners of motor vehicles obtain auto liability insurance before registering an automobile. However, applicants with poor driving records or persons with little or no driving experience might have difficulty obtaining automobile insurance. As a result, all fifty states and the District of Columbia have implemented automobile insurance plans through a residual market system to make auto liability insurance available to nearly every licensed driver. The form and operation of these plans vary by state, but all of the plans spread the cost of operating the plan among all private insurance companies writing business in the state. In most cases, the state

Monopolistic state fund
A state workers' compensation insurance plan that is the only source of workers' compensation insurance allowed in that state.

Competitive state fund
A state workers' compensation insurance plan that competes with private insurers to provide workers' compensation insurance.

Residual market plan, or **shared market plan**
A program that makes workers' compensation insurance available to those who cannot obtain voluntary coverage from private insurers.

has mandated the creation of automobile insurance plans but has left the administration of the plans to private insurers, which then share the costs.

In most states, FAIR plans make property insurance available where it would otherwise be unavailable. These state-run plans spread the cost of operating the plan among all private insurers selling property insurance in the state. FAIR plans were originally created in response to the urban riots of the 1960s so that property owners in urban areas could have access to property insurance. These plans now make property insurance more readily available to property owners who have exposures to loss over which they have no control. Therefore, eligible property includes, for example, property in urban areas as well as property exposed to brush fires.

Beachfront and windstorm insurance pools are residual market plans similar to FAIR plans. These plans exist in states along the Atlantic and Gulf Coasts and provide insurance to property owners against wind damage from hurricanes and other windstorms. Because these states have been severely affected by hurricanes in recent years, some property owners along the coasts have had difficulty obtaining windstorm coverage from private insurers. In beachfront states without such pools, property insurance is usually available through a FAIR plan.

Guaranty fund
A state fund that provides a system to pay the claims of insolvent insurers, generally funded by assessments collected from all insurers licensed in the state.

Each state, as well as the District of Columbia, has a property-casualty insurance **guaranty fund** that provides a system to pay the claims of insolvent insurers licensed in the state. The money to pay the claims generally comes from assessments made against all private insurers licensed in the state. In most states, licensed insurers operating in that state are assessed for their proportionate share of the estimated obligation only after an insurer has become insolvent. In New York, licensed insurers are assessed in advance to ensure the solvency of the guaranty fund.

INSURANCE REGULATION

The possibility that an insurer might not be able to pay legitimate claims to or for its policyholders is the primary concern of insurance regulators. This scrutiny helps to protect the public from irresponsible, unwise, or dishonest activities that could leave consumers with worthless insurance policies.

Historically, state governments for the most part have regulated the insurance business, beginning when state legislatures granted charters to new insurers and specified certain conditions regarding their minimum capital requirements, their investments, and their financial reports. State insurance departments were first established to monitor the operations of insurers and to investigate complaints from insureds. These departments generally have broad powers to regulate the insurance business in the public interest.

Insurance regulations vary by state. Despite the differences among the states, the primary objectives of insurance regulation are as follows:

- Rate regulation
- Solvency surveillance
- Consumer protection

Although many insurance professionals believe that state regulation of insurance has advantages over federal regulation, inefficiency can result when over fifty different insurance departments separately perform similar tasks and address the same issues and problems. Before examining rate regulation, solvency surveillance, and consumer protection, it is useful to understand the role of the National Association of Insurance Commissioners (NAIC) in fostering cooperation among these departments, which may help to mitigate some inefficiency.

National Association of Insurance Commissioners (NAIC)

The **National Association of Insurance Commissioners (NAIC)** was established to encourage coordination and cooperation among the various state insurance departments. The members of the NAIC are the heads (usually called commissioners) of the insurance departments of each of the fifty states and the District of Columbia. The commissioners of Puerto Rico, Guam, American Samoa, and the U.S. Virgin Islands also belong to the NAIC. The NAIC facilitates cooperation, coordination, and uniformity in insurance regulation among the states, but has no direct regulatory authority.

The NAIC meets quarterly, but it functions throughout the year with the assistance of its staff. NAIC standing committees meet periodically during the year and report to the NAIC at its regularly scheduled meetings.

When a new problem or issue arises, the NAIC studies the matter and issues a statement describing its position. In many cases, the NAIC drafts a **model law**, written in a style similar to that of a state statute, that reflects the NAIC's proposed solution to a given problem or issue. Each state legislature then considers the model law for possible enactment. A model law might not be passed in its exact form by every state legislature, but it provides a common basis for drafting state laws that affect the insurance industry. In this way, certain aspects of insurance regulation have a degree of uniformity among states.

The NAIC has also created a uniform financial statement for property-casualty insurers. Each insurer completes an annual financial statement in the prescribed manner and submits it to the insurance department of each state in which it is licensed to satisfy the financial reporting requirements of that state. This uniformity not only lessens the reporting burden for insurers, but also simplifies the insurance department's task of comparing the financial reports of many different insurers.

National Association of Insurance Commissioners (NAIC)
An association of the commissioners of the insurance departments of each state, the District of Columbia, and the U.S. territories and possessions, whose purpose is to coordinate insurance regulation activities among the various state insurance departments.

Model law
A document drafted by the NAIC, in a style similar to a state statute, that reflects the NAIC's proposed solution to a given problem or issue and provides a common basis to the states for drafting laws that affect the insurance industry.

In a further effort to help states monitor insurers' financial condition, the NAIC has implemented an accreditation program to increase uniformity and improve state regulation of insurance. The program's purpose is to ensure that states have the appropriate legislation and authority to regulate the solvency of the insurance industry. It also attempts to ensure that states apply the required legislation consistently. Under this program, states that have been accredited by the NAIC cannot accept the results of insurer examinations performed by states that have not been accredited.

Through its various programs and committees, the NAIC enables state regulators to pool their resources while preserving state regulation. The NAIC encourages uniformity, but each state can tailor its regulatory approach to meet the state's unique needs.

Rate Regulation

Because insurers develop insurance rates that affect most people, the laws of nearly all states give the state insurance commissioner the power to enforce regulation of insurance rates. Acting in the interest of insureds, regulators try to ensure that rates are adequate, not excessive, and not unfairly discriminatory.

Ratemaking

An insurer must collect sufficient premiums to pay for the insured losses that occur, to cover the costs of operating the company, and to allow a reasonable profit. Typically, the profit comes not from an excess of premiums over losses and operating costs, but from the investment of those premiums until losses are paid. Determining the proper rate to charge each insured for coverage involves ratemaking.

Ratemaking

The process insurers use to calculate the rates that determine the premium to charge for insurance coverage.

Rate

The amount per exposure unit for insurance coverage, used to arrive at a premium when multiplied by the number of exposure units.

Premium

The price of the insurance coverage provided for a specified period.

Ratemaking is the process insurers use to calculate the rates that determine the premium to charge for insurance coverage. The **rate** is the amount per exposure unit for insurance coverage (for example, $100 worth of coverage). The **premium** is the price of the insurance coverage provided for a specified period. To arrive at the premium (a process called rating), the rate is multiplied by the number of exposure units purchased. For example, if an insurer charges a rate of $1.20 per $100 of coverage on jewelry, the premium for a ring insured for $1,000 would be $12, according to the following formula:

$$
\begin{aligned}
\text{Premium} \ &= \ \text{Rate} \times \text{Number of exposure units} \\
&= \ \$1.20 \times 10 \text{ units} \\
&= \ \$12.
\end{aligned}
$$

This is a simplified rating example, but in fact it is a complex process to develop a final rate. For example, the $1.20 rate may reflect the expected cost of future losses, adjustments for factors such as territory and past loss history, and projections of the effects of inflation. Developing rates that accurately reflect each insured's share of predicted losses is one of the most important operations performed by insurance organizations. Because a given rate is the basis of an insured's premium, it is important to both the insured and the insurer that the rate, and therefore the premium, be a fair measure of the insured's exposure to loss.

To determine the premiums to charge, insurers predict, as accurately as possible, the expenses they will incur to pay for losses, recognizing that this prediction is uncertain. Insurers add an amount sufficient to cover the expected administrative costs of company operations to the predicted claim expenses. In addition, the premium includes a charge for profits and contingencies, such as possible catastrophic losses. This amount is often modified to reflect the investment income that can be earned on the funds held for future claim payments.

Insurers use rate classification systems that differentiate among insureds based on each insured's loss potential. For example, insureds with frame houses are placed in one classification for fire insurance, and insureds with brick houses are placed in another, because the probable severity of a fire loss is greater for a frame house. Similarly, where permitted, insurers group drivers into separate classifications so that young, inexperienced drivers are charged more than experienced drivers, and insureds who use their cars for business are charged more than insureds who do not. Insureds with similar characteristics are placed in the same class and charged the same rate.

An **actuary** analyzes data on past losses and the expenses associated with losses and, combining this with other information, develops insurance rates. Actuaries are usually educated in mathematics and statistics and have other specialized training. They use complex mathematical methods and technology to develop systems for determining insurance rates.

Actuary
A person who uses complex mathematical methods and technology to analyze loss data and other statistics and to develop systems for determining insurance rates.

One goal of an insurer's actuarial staff is to develop a ratemaking system that generates fair, equitable rates and meets corporate objectives. Attaining this goal requires actuaries to constantly monitor and update loss data to develop rates that state regulatory authorities will approve.

Objectives of Rate Regulation

Rate regulation serves the following three general objectives:

1. To ensure that rates are adequate
2. To ensure that rates are not excessive
3. To ensure that rates are not unfairly discriminatory

The first objective of rate regulation is to ensure that rates are adequate. When rates are adequate, the price charged for a given type of insurance coverage should be high enough to meet all anticipated losses and expenses associated with that coverage while generating a reasonable profit for the insurer. Rate adequacy helps insurers remain solvent so that they can meet obligations to policyholders. Therefore, rate regulation attempts to ensure that rates are adequate.

Adequacy is not always easy to achieve. It is virtually impossible to guarantee that premiums paid by insureds will be adequate to cover insured losses. Even when a large group of similar exposure units is covered, unexpected events—such as a natural disaster—might lead to losses significantly higher than those predicted when rates were originally set. For example, when Hurricane Andrew hit the southeastern U.S. in 1992, the resulting unexpected losses exceeded the predictions that had been used to rate the policies that covered these losses.

The goal of rate adequacy conflicts with pressures to keep insurance premiums at a reasonable level. An insurer might have difficulty competing if its rates are substantially higher than those charged by other insurers providing similar coverage and service. Also, although insurance regulators desire rate adequacy to maintain insurer solvency, other pressures encourage regulators to keep rates low.

The second objective of rate regulation is to ensure that rates are not excessive. States also require that insurance rates not be excessive. Excessive rates could cause insurers to earn profits that regulators deem to be unreasonable. Determining whether rates are either excessive or inadequate is difficult, especially because insurers must price insurance policies long before the results of the pricing decision are known. Nevertheless, when regulators determine that insurers have earned substantial profits in a particular type of insurance, they may require insurers to reduce rates or to return the "excess profit" to policyholders.

The third objective of rate regulation is to ensure that rates are not unfairly discriminatory. Because insurance is a system of sharing the costs of losses, each insured should pay a fair share of all policyholders' losses. Some disagreement exists as to how this fair share should be determined.

Actuarial equity
A ratemaking concept through which actuaries base rates on calculated loss experience to place insureds with similar characteristics in the same rating class.

One concept involves **actuarial equity**—basing rates on actuarially calculated costs of losses. Under this concept, actuaries define rate classifications and calculate rates based on the loss experience of each given class. Insureds with similar characteristics are placed in the same rating class and charged the same rate. Thus, the premium should accurately reflect each insured's expected contribution to the losses of a group of similar insureds.

Social equity
A rating concept that holds that rate structures discriminate unfairly if they impose a higher rate on an insured for factors beyond the insured's control, such as age or gender.

On the other hand, **social equity** holds that rate structures discriminate unfairly if they impose a higher rate on an insured for factors beyond the insured's control, such as age or gender. The notion of social equity is also used to suppress rates for classes of insureds when affordability is a concern or when insurance rates can be used to further public policy. For example, regulators may believe that employed people need cars to drive to work, but that high insurance rates may prohibit them from owning a vehicle or compel them to drive uninsured. The concept of social equity is applied in such cases when regulators enforce rate caps for inexperienced or urban drivers. In certain states, age and gender are no longer allowed as factors in rating auto insurance on the grounds that they are unfairly discriminatory.

Rate regulation attempts to balance the concepts of actuarial equity and social equity in determining whether a particular rating plan involves **unfair discrimination**.

Insurance Rating Laws

States have developed a variety of laws to regulate insurance rates in an attempt to balance conflicting objectives. Rate regulation varies by state, and different laws might apply to different types of insurance within a state. Despite these differences, the various insurance rating laws fall into the following categories:

- **Prior-approval laws.** These laws are used in many states and require that rates be approved by the state insurance department before they can be used. Insurers must also provide data that show that the rates are not excessive, inadequate, or unfairly discriminatory. The commissioner has a certain time period, typically thirty to ninety days, to approve or reject the filing. Some states have a "deemer provision" (or "delayed effect" clause) that deems the rates approved if the commissioner does not respond to a rate filing within the specified time period.

- **Flex rating laws.** Under these laws, prior approval is required only if the new rates are a specified percentage above or below previously filed rates. Insurers are permitted to increase or reduce their rates within the specified range without prior approval. Percentage ranges vary by state and by type of insurance, but they are generally between 3 percent and 25 percent.

- **File-and-use laws.** These laws require insurers to file rates with the state insurance department before the rates become effective. However, insurers are not required to wait for approval before using the rates.

- **Use-and-file laws.** These laws require that rates be filed within a specified period, often fifteen or thirty days, after they are first used in the state.

- **Open competition**, or **no-file laws.** In some states, insurers are not required to file rates or rating plans with the state insurance department. This approach is called open competition, because it permits insurers to compete with one another by quickly changing rates without review by state regulators. Market forces rather than administrative action determine rates under this approach. Advocates of open competition often cite the Illinois private passenger auto insurance market, free of rate regulation since the early 1970s, yet with lower rates, fewer uninsured drivers, higher numbers of competing insurers, and a smaller residual market than other states with comparable urban areas.

- **State-mandated rates.** These laws require all insurers to adhere to rates established by the state insurance department for a particular type of insurance, such as workers' compensation.

Modified versions of these laws also exist. For example, modified prior-approval laws permit an insurer to revise rates without prior approval if the revision is based solely on a change in the insurer's loss experience.

Unfair discrimination
Applying different standards or methods of treatment to insureds who have the same basic characteristics and loss potential, such as charging higher-than-normal rates for an auto insurance applicant based solely on the applicant's race, religion, or ethnic background.

Prior-approval law
An insurance rating law that requires rates to be approved by the state insurance department before they can be used.

Flex rating law
An insurance rating law that requires prior approval only if the new rates are a specified percentage above or below previously filed rates.

File-and-use law
An insurance rating law that requires insurers to file rates with the state insurance department but does not require insurers to wait for approval before using the rates.

Use-and-file law
An insurance rating law that requires rates to be filed within a specified period after they are first used in the state.

Open competition, or **no-file law**
An insurance rating law that does not require rates to be filed with the state.

State-mandated rates
An insurance rating law that requires all insurers to adhere to rates established by the state insurance department for a particular type of insurance.

Another example is a modified open competition law, which allows open competition as long as certain tests are met, such as evidence of competitive markets or rate increases of less than a certain percentage per year.

Insurance rating laws that do not require prior approval of rates do not relieve insurers of their obligation to use rates that are adequate, not excessive, and not unfairly discriminatory. State insurance departments can and do exercise their legal right to request, at a later date, the statistics that support the fairness of the new rate.

The following are three broad exceptions to these insurance rating laws:

Exempt commercial policyholders
An organization with sufficient size and sophistication to be permitted to buy property, liability, and automobile insurance using rates and/or policy forms not filed with state insurance departments.

1. **Exempt commercial policyholders**. These are organizations of sufficient size and sophistication that they are permitted to buy property, liability, and automobile insurance using rates and/or policy forms not filed with state insurance departments. Many states adopted such a concept in the late 1990s.

2. **Non-filed inland marine**. Many classes of inland marine insurance (which covers a wide range of usually land-based risks associated with transportation or communication) are exempt from filing requirements. Such exemptions differ by state. The justification is that the types of exposures qualifying as non-filed can vary greatly from one insured to the next, such that using standard forms and rates is impractical.

Non-filed inland marine
Classes of inland marine insurance that are exempt from filing requirements.

3. Excess and surplus lines insurance. When needed insurance is not available in the standard market, coverage may be provided by insurers that are exempt from rate and form regulation. These coverages and insurers are discussed in greater detail later in this chapter.

Solvency Surveillance

Solvency
The ability of an insurer to meet its financial obligations as they become due, even those resulting from insured losses that may be claimed several years in the future.

Solvency is an insurer's ability to meet its financial obligations as they become due, even those resulting from insured losses that may be claimed several years in the future. In an effort to ensure solvency, insurance regulators carefully monitor insurers' financial condition. This process is called **solvency surveillance** and involves determining whether an insurer's financial condition is sufficient for it to meet its financial obligations and remain in business. Two major aspects of solvency surveillance are insurer examinations and the Insurance Regulatory Information System (IRIS).

Solvency surveillance
The process, conducted by state insurance regulators, of verifying the solvency of insurers and determining whether their financial condition enables them to meet their financial obligations and to remain in business.

Insurer Examinations

Regulatory authorities periodically examine insurers. An examination consists of a thorough analysis of an insurer's operations and financial condition. This analysis usually occurs every few years under the direction of the insurance department of the state where the insurer's home office is located. During an examination a team of state examiners reviews a wide range of activities, including claim, underwriting, marketing, and accounting procedures. In addition, the insurer's financial records are carefully analyzed to ensure that the company is meeting all state financial reporting requirements and to determine whether the insurer has the ability to meet its obligations. If the examination uncovers problems, the insurance department usually has broad powers to take control of the situation to correct whatever problems are identified.

Insurance Regulatory Information System (IRIS)

The **Insurance Regulatory Information System (IRIS)** is an information and early-warning system established and operated by the NAIC to monitor insurers' financial soundness. IRIS uses data from an insurer's financial statements to develop twelve financial ratios that determine the insurer's overall financial condition. If the insurer has ratios that are outside predetermined norms, IRIS identifies the company for regulatory attention.

IRIS provides all state insurance departments with a timely and objective method of identifying companies that might have financial problems. Although the system does not always identify a problem before a financial crisis occurs, it is an important tool for solvency surveillance.

Consumer Protection

In addition to rate regulation and solvency surveillance, the activities that regulators undertake to protect insurance consumers include:

- Licensing insurers
- Licensing insurer representatives
- Approving policy forms
- Examining market conduct
- Investigating consumer complaints

Licensing Insurers

Most insurers must be licensed by the state insurance department before they are authorized to write insurance policies in that state. A **licensed insurer** (also called an **admitted insurer**) is one that the state insurance department has authorized to sell insurance in that state. An insurer that is incorporated in the same state in which it is writing insurance is known as a **domestic insurer**. An insurer that is licensed to operate in a state but is incorporated under the laws of another state is known as a **foreign insurer**. A licensed insurer that is incorporated in another country is called an **alien insurer**.

For example, an insurer that is incorporated in Massachusetts is considered a *domestic* insurer in that state. However, if the same insurer is also licensed to operate in New Hampshire and Vermont, it is considered a *foreign* insurer in those two states. An insurer that is incorporated in London, England, is considered an *alien* insurer in the U.S.

A primary requirement for obtaining an insurance license involves tests of financial strength. Each state has specific requirements concerning the

Insurance Regulatory Information System (IRIS)
An information and early-warning system established and operated by the NAIC to monitor the financial soundness of insurers.

Licensed insurer, or **admitted insurer**
An insurer authorized by the state insurance department to sell insurance within that state.

Domestic insurer
An insurer incorporated in the same state in which it is writing insurance.

Foreign insurer
An insurer licensed to operate in a state but incorporated in another state.

Alien insurer
An insurer licensed in a U.S. state but incorporated in another country.

minimum amount of surplus an insurer must have to be licensed in the state. Surplus, in its simplest form, is assets (property owned such as money, stocks, bonds, buildings, land, and accounts receivable) minus liabilities (financial obligations or debts). The required amount of surplus varies, depending on the state and the type of insurance for which the company wants to be licensed. If an insurer fails to meet financial standards or fails to operate in a manner consistent with state insurance laws, state regulators have the authority to revoke or suspend the company's license in order to protect consumers' interests.

Licensing Insurer Representatives

In addition to licensing insurers, all states have licensing requirements for certain insurer representatives. All states require insurance agents to be licensed to transact insurance business in the state. A license is usually granted only after the applicant passes an examination on insurance laws and practices. Most states have similar requirements for insurance brokers. Claim representatives (also known as adjusters) are also required to be licensed in some states before they are allowed to handle claims. (Later chapters explain the roles of insurance agents and brokers and the duties of claim representatives.)

In most states, the agent, broker, or claim representative must complete a prescribed amount of continuing education during a specified period before renewing a license. Licensing and continuing education laws vary widely by state, but all attempt to ensure that insurer representatives have a prescribed minimum level of insurance knowledge.

Approving Policy Forms

Many states require insurers to file their policy forms with the state insurance department in a manner similar to the method used for rate filings. Whenever an insurer wants to change the language of a particular policy in these states, it must submit the new form for approval. Such a requirement is waived for exempt commercial policyholders in states that have deregulated commercial insurance.

By regulating policy language, the state insurance department prevents insurers from including unfair or unreasonable provisions in insurance policies. Although the possibility always exists that an insured might misinterpret the policy, regulatory approval of policy forms reduces the possibility of misleading wording. Having clear and readable insurance policies is a goal of most regulators. In many cases, states also prescribe specific wording that must be included in insurance policies, such as cancellation requirements and procedures.

Examining Market Conduct

Regulators also scrutinize specific insurer practices. **Market conduct regulation** focuses on the practices of insurers in regard to four areas of operation: sales practices, underwriting practices, claim practices, and bad-faith actions.

Most states have statutes, usually called unfair trade practices laws, that identify certain practices that are considered unfair to the public. State regulators could suspend or revoke the licenses of insurance agents or brokers who engage in any of these unfair trade practices. Similarly, an insurer guilty of unfair underwriting practices could be fined or have its operating license suspended or revoked in the state. Most states also have statutes that prohibit unfair claim practices and assess fines against claim representatives and insurers that engage in such practices.

Market conduct regulation
Regulation of the practices of insurers in regard to four areas of operation: sales practices, underwriting practices, claim practices, and bad-faith actions.

Investigating Consumer Complaints

Regulatory examinations of insurers identify some of the abuses mentioned previously, but other abuses are exposed only when an insured or a claimant lodges a complaint. Every state insurance department has a consumer complaints division to investigate consumer complaints and help insureds deal with problems they have encountered with insurers and their representatives.

EXCESS AND SURPLUS LINES INSURANCE

Most property-casualty insurance policies are standardized, and many insurers use essentially the same policy forms. Insurers who voluntarily offer insurance coverages at rates designed for customers with average or better-than-average loss exposures are known collectively as the **standard market**. Such insurers write the majority of commercial property-casualty insurance in the U.S.

In most cases, the standard market provides the policies necessary to meet the property-casualty insurance needs of the public. But what about the unique or unusual exposures that the standard market is unwilling or unable to insure? Poor loss experience or expected losses associated with certain classes of business might not meet standard insurers' underwriting requirements. Changes in business practices or technology might create new loss exposures not contemplated in traditional insurance policies. These exposures require a creative, nontraditional insurance market. The term "excess and surplus lines" is often used to identify this nontraditional market. Likewise, **excess and surplus lines (E&S) insurance** consists of insurance coverages unavailable in the standard market.

Standard market
Collectively, insurers who voluntarily offer insurance coverages at rates designed for customers with average or better-than-average loss exposures.

Excess and surplus lines (E&S) insurance
Insurance coverages unavailable in the standard market that are written by nonadmitted insurers.

Classes of E&S Business

The following classes of business are often insured in the E&S market:

- Unusual or unique loss exposures
- Nonstandard business
- Insureds needing high limits of coverage
- Insureds needing unusually broad coverage
- Loss exposures that require new forms

Unusual or Unique Loss Exposures

One of the usual requirements of a commercially insurable loss exposure is that a large number of similar exposure units should exist. If an exposure does not meet this requirement, the coverage is difficult to price and therefore standard insurers are often unwilling to provide coverage. For example, suppose a singer does not show up for a concert. The sponsors of the concert can suffer a financial loss if they have to refund money to ticket holders. A coverage known as "non-appearance insurance," written by E&S insurers, covers the losses of the show sponsors if the performer named in the policy fails to appear because of a covered cause, such as injury, illness, or death.

Nonstandard Business

Sometimes loss exposures do not meet the underwriting requirements of the standard insurance market. There may be evidence of poor loss experience that cannot be adequately controlled. Perhaps the premiums that standard insurers normally charge are not adequate to cover these exposures. For example, consider the case of a restaurant that has a history of grease fires in its kitchen. Its standard insurer has decided not to renew its policy because of poor loss experience. An E&S insurer may be willing to write insurance for this restaurant with a premium substantially higher than a standard insurer would charge.

Insureds Needing High Limits of Coverage

Some businesses demand very high limits of coverage, especially for liability insurance. For example, a corporation involved in shipping oil in large tankers needs higher liability limits than those available in the standard market. A standard insurer may not be willing to offer limits as high as an insured needs. The E&S market often provides the needed limits in excess of the limits written by a standard insurer.

Insureds Needing Unusually Broad Coverage

The traditional insurance market uses standard coverage forms developed through advisory organizations, such as Insurance Services Office (ISO) and the American Association of Insurance Services (AAIS). When broader coverage is necessary, however, producers and insureds often seek such coverage from the E&S market.

Loss Exposures That Require New Forms

Creativity has long been a distinguishing characteristic of the E&S market. As new insurance needs arise, the E&S market is usually quick to respond. Producers and consumers often turn to the E&S market when they have an immediate need for a new type of coverage, such as coverage for media liability, including the insured's Web site.

Excess and Surplus Lines Regulation

Excess and surplus lines insurance is usually written by **nonadmitted insurers** (also called **unlicensed insurers**), which are not licensed in many of the states in which they operate. Nonadmitted insurers are not required to file their rates and policy forms with state insurance departments, providing them with more flexibility than that of standard insurers.

Nonadmitted insurer, or **unlicensed insurer**
An insurer that is not licensed in many of the states in which it operates and that writes E&S insurance coverages.

Although nonadmitted insurers are exempt from rate and form filing laws and regulations, the E&S market is subject to regulation. Some states maintain lists of E&S insurers that are approved to do business in the state; others keep lists of those insurers that are not approved. Most states have surplus lines laws that require that all E&S business be placed through an E&S broker. When an insurance producer seeks to insure a customer with a nonadmitted insurer, he or she must arrange for an E&S broker to handle the transaction.

E&S insurers and brokers provide a valuable service to the insurance industry and to the public. They provide insurance to many insureds who might otherwise be unable to obtain coverage. They find solutions to problems created by unusual or unique loss exposures.

SUMMARY

In the U.S., private insurers provide most property-casualty insurance, but both federal and state governments also provide some types of insurance. Most private insurers are either stock or mutual companies. Other types of private companies or groups that provide insurance include reciprocal insurance exchanges, Lloyd's, American Lloyds, captive insurers, and reinsurance companies.

Private insurers are generally reluctant to insure loss exposures that do not possess most of the characteristics of an ideally insurable loss exposure. In some instances, state and federal governments have intervened to make certain types of insurance available to the public. Government insurance programs address needs for insurance coverage that are not satisfied by private insurers. Examples of federal government insurance programs include the Social Security program, the National Flood Insurance Program, and the Federal Crop Insurance Program. State governments also provide various insurance programs, including state workers' compensation funds, unemployment insurance programs, automobile insurance plans, FAIR plans, and beachfront and windstorm pools. In addition, all states have insurance guaranty funds that cover insolvent insurers' unpaid claims.

Because insurance is a business that affects the public, state governments are heavily involved in the regulation of the insurance industry. State insurance departments are responsible for most insurance regulation. The NAIC provides coordination among insurance departments, but has no regulatory authority of its own. Insurance departments regulate insurance rates to ensure they are adequate, not excessive, and not unfairly discriminatory. Insurers and their actuaries develop insurance rates in a process called ratemaking. However, these rates are subject to various state insurance rating laws.

Solvency is another major concern of insurance regulators. Through periodic examinations of insurers' financial condition and use of IRIS, regulators conduct solvency surveillance to monitor insurers' financial soundness.

Regulators also try to protect consumers by licensing qualified insurers and their representatives, approving policy forms, examining market conduct, and investigating consumer complaints. Through the licensing of E&S brokers, state insurance regulators also regulate the E&S market, which provides insurance coverages that are unavailable in the standard market.

CHAPTER NOTES

1. Lloyd's, www.lloyds.com (accessed January 11, 2005).
2. Lloyd's, www.lloyds.com (accessed January 11, 2005).

Chapter 3

Direct Your Learning

Measuring the Financial Performance of Insurers

After learning the content of this chapter and completing the corresponding course guide assignment, you should be able to:

- Describe the sources of income for a property-casualty insurer.

- Describe the types of expenses that a property-casualty insurer incurs.

- Explain how an insurer's gain or loss from operations is determined.

- Distinguish between the admitted and nonadmitted assets of insurers.

- Describe the three types of liabilities found on the financial statements of insurers.

- Describe the typical items found on the balance sheet of a property-casualty insurer.

- Describe the typical items found on the income statement of a property-casualty insurer.

- Given an insurer's financial statements, calculate and explain the significance of the following profitability ratios:

  - Loss ratio

  - Expense ratio

  - Dividend ratio

  - Combined ratio

  - Investment income ratio

  - Overall operating ratio

- Given an insurer's financial statements, calculate and explain the significance of an insurer's capacity ratio.

- Define or describe each of the Key Words and Phrases for this chapter.

Develop Your Perspective

What are the main topics covered in the chapter?

Insurers must pay careful attention to their financial performance, in terms of both profitability and solvency. Standard sources of income and expenses as well as standard ratios create a uniform method of tracking financial performance over time and comparing the results of one insurer to another.

Describe the sources of income and types of expenses that are common for all insurers.

- How do common reporting requirements help regulators determine insurer solvency?

Why is it important to learn about these topics?

Profitability ratios are the shorthand language of the insurance industry. Large amounts of data are compressed into numbers to convey significant information. By understanding these ratios and their components, you will understand how the ratios and their changes over time can reflect improvements or problems in an insurer's results.

Consider profitability ratios in comparison to each other.

- Why do loss ratios and expense ratios provide only a limited view of an insurer's results?

- Why are combined ratios often used to compare one insurer's results to other insurers' results?

How can you use what you will learn?

Evaluate the profitability ratios of an insurer.

- How do the insurer's losses compare to its income?

- Is the insurer profitable? If so, how profitable?

- Are the insurer's results improving or deteriorating?

Chapter 3

Measuring the Financial Performance of Insurers

Sound management of an insurer requires careful attention to its financial performance. One concern about any insurer's financial performance is its profitability: Does the insurer generate enough profit to survive? A related concern is the insurer's solvency: Does the insurer have adequate resources to meet all of its financial obligations? Insurers prepare and analyze financial statements to monitor and report on their financial performance. Other interested parties also analyze the financial statements of insurers. For example, state insurance regulators want to monitor insurers' financial performance over time to identify any financial difficulties; insureds want to select insurers that have the financial resources to promptly pay covered losses; and investors want to determine the insurers' potential for growth and profitability.

INSURER PROFITABILITY

To survive long term, an insurer must generate more money than it spends, that is, the insurer's revenue must exceed its expenses. In a given month or year, an insurer's expenses might exceed its revenues, requiring the insurer to pay some of those expenses with accumulated funds. Such a pattern, however, will eventually deplete accumulated funds, and the insurer will fail. Like any other business, an insurer must manage its revenue and expenses to produce an overall income (revenue minus expenses) gain from its operations and to ensure the profitability on which its survival depends.

Insurers receive income from two major sources: (1) the sale of insurance and (2) the investment of funds. The first source generates underwriting income. Underwriting income (gain or loss) is the amount remaining after underwriting losses and expenses are subtracted from premiums. The second source generates investment income. Investment income (gain or loss) is the amount remaining after investment expenses are subtracted from the gross amount earned on investments during the period. While some insurers receive other income from the sale of specialized services or other incidental activities, most of the income an insurer receives is either underwriting income or investment income.

During a particular calendar year, an insurer calculates its written premiums by totaling the premiums charged on all policies written with effective dates of January 1 through December 31 of that year. Written premiums are the total premiums on all policies put into effect, or "written," during a given period. For example, when a policy is written to become effective on July 1 for a premium of $600, that entire $600 is counted as written premiums on July 1, even though it may not have yet been collected by the insurer. If the policy is changed on September 12 and a $75 refund is generated, the insurer's written premiums are reduced by $75 on September 12. Although written premiums provide a source of cash for insurers, rules of accounting allow insurers to recognize only earned premiums on the income statement.

Earned premiums are the portion of the written premiums that apply to the part of the policy period that has already occurred. The remaining portion of written premiums apply to the part of the policy period that has not yet occurred and is therefore called unearned premiums, representing insurance coverage yet to be provided.

The concept of earned and unearned premiums can be compared to how a magazine subscription might operate. When a subscriber pays a $24 annual subscription fee for a monthly magazine, the publisher does not "earn" the entire $24 subscription amount until the magazine has been provided for twelve months. If the subscriber cancels the subscription after receiving only six monthly issues, the publisher might refund $12, or half of the subscription amount (the "unearned" portion).

Likewise, when an insured pays a premium of $600 on July 1 for a one-year policy, the $600 premium is not fully "earned" until the end of the twelve-month coverage period. The entire $600, however, is considered written premiums for the current calendar year. As Exhibit 3-1 shows, only half of the $600 annual premium paid on July 1 is earned as of the end of the calendar year because only six months, or half of the protection period, has passed. Therefore, at the end of the calendar year, the insurer calculates $300 of earned premiums for this policy and $300 of unearned premiums. During the next calendar year, between January 1 and July 1, the unearned portion of the premium is earned as coverage provided by the insurer. If this policy is not renewed on July 1 of the second year, the insurer records *no* written premiums for this policy in the second year (remember that the entire $600 was considered to be written during the first year). The insurer records only the earned premiums of $300 from the previous year's written premium. See Exhibit 3-2 for two cases showing written premiums, earned premiums, and unearned premiums.

Underwriting Income

As mentioned, underwriting income is the amount of income (gain or loss) after losses and expenses are subtracted from premiums that are earned. Premiums are the money an insurer receives from its policyholders in return for the insurance coverage provided. In effect, premiums are the revenue from the insurer's underwriting operations. The losses paid by the insurers' policies plus the expenses associated with controlling and adjusting those losses are the primary underwriting expenses.

When calculating underwriting income for the year, or for any other period, an insurer must determine the portion of its total policy premiums generated during the period (written premiums) that it earned (earned premiums) and the portion it did not yet earn (unearned premiums).

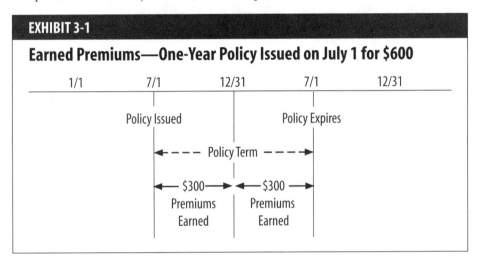

EXHIBIT 3-1

Earned Premiums—One-Year Policy Issued on July 1 for $600

Investment Income

Because an insurer collects premiums from its policyholders and pays claims for its policyholders, the insurer handles large amounts of money. Insurers invest available funds to generate additional income. Investment income can be substantial, particularly during periods of high interest rates or high returns in the stock market.

An insurer has investment funds available for two reasons. First, the insurer is legally required to maintain a certain amount of funds, called policyholders' surplus, so it can meet its obligations even after catastrophic losses. (Policyholders' surplus is discussed later in this chapter.) Provided that the insurer is operating profitably, its policyholders' surplus is generally available for investment. Second, the insurer usually receives premiums before it pays claims on the corresponding policies. Thus, an insurer can invest premiums and earn additional income until those funds are needed to pay claims. However, when an insurer settles claims, it must have funds readily available to meet its obligations. Similarly, if a policy is canceled before the end of the policy period, the insurer must be able to refund the unearned premiums.

Insurers have investment departments whose objective is to earn the highest possible return from investments while ensuring that funds are always available to meet the insurer's obligations. Thus, the investment department must select high-quality investments that are relatively secure and that can be readily converted to cash. One investment strategy may involve buying long-term bonds that are scheduled for maturity to match expected claim payment needs.

For an insurer to be profitable, its combined revenue from earned premiums and investment income must exceed its total loss payments and other expenses. Loss payments, as well as the various other types of expenses that an insurer incurs, are discussed next.

EXHIBIT 3-2

Examples of Written Premiums, Earned Premiums, and Unearned Premiums

Case 1

Annual policy with $600 premium is effective July 1.

    At the end of Calendar Year 1:

        Written premiums   = $600.

        Earned premiums   = $300 (6 of the 12 months of coverage have elapsed).

        Unearned premiums   = $300 (6 of the 12 months of coverage have not elapsed).

    At the end of Calendar Year 2 (assuming the policy is not renewed):

        Written premiums   = $0.

        Earned premiums   = $300 (the remaining 6 months of coverage have elapsed).

        Unearned premiums   = $0 (there is no more coverage; all the premium is earned).

Case 2

Annual policy with $600 premium is effective December 1.

    At the end of Calendar Year 1:

        Written premiums   = $600.

        Earned premiums   = $50 (1 of the 12 months of coverage have elapsed).

        Unearned premiums   = $550 (11 of the 12 months of coverage have not elapsed).

    At the end of Calendar Year 2 (assuming the policy is not renewed):

        Written premiums   = $0.

        Earned premiums   = $550 (the remaining 11 months of coverage have elapsed).

        Unearned premiums   = $0 (there is no more coverage; all the premium is earned).

In each case, the written premiums and the earned premiums total $600 by the time the coverage has expired. However, all of the written premiums are recorded immediately, while the earned premiums are counted as they are earned over time. In both cases, the unearned premiums disappear by the expiration date of the policy because all of the written premiums have been earned by the time the policy period ends.

Expenses

An insurer's expenses fall into two broad categories: (1) expenses associated with underwriting activities and (2) expenses associated with investment activities. Expenses associated with underwriting activity include payment for losses, loss adjustment expenses, and other underwriting expenses. Some insurers also pay dividends to their policyholders. Expenses associated with investment activities include salaries and other general expenses related to running the investment department.

Losses

The major expense category for most insurers is payment for losses arising from claims. Claims are demands for payment made by insureds based on the conditions specified in their insurance policies. For property-casualty insurers, loss payments often represent 70 to 80 percent of their total costs.

Claims are not necessarily settled immediately after a loss occurs. Sometimes the loss is not reported right away. When the loss is reported, the insurer's claim representative investigates the loss and verifies whether the loss is covered before the insurer pays the claim. Liability claims may involve lengthy legal proceedings. Some losses occur in one year but are settled in a later year. In any given year, an insurer knows only the amount of losses it has paid so far, but not a definite amount it will ultimately have to pay. To compare revenue and expenses, an insurer must calculate not only its paid losses but also its incurred losses for the period.

A **paid loss** is a claim payment that an insurer has made. Because it has been paid, a paid loss is a definite amount. Paid losses, however, do not include those losses in the process of settlement or losses that are incurred but not reported (IBNR). Therefore, another method to measure losses is to calculate incurred losses for a particular period. **Incurred losses** are the sum of paid losses and changes in loss reserves for a particular period and are calculated as follows:

Incurred losses = Paid losses + Changes in loss reserves.

Loss reserves are amounts designated by insurers to pay claims for losses that have already occurred but are not yet settled. Changes in loss reserves are calculated as follows:

Changes in loss reserves = Loss reserves at end of period − Loss reserves at beginning of period.

Because setting loss reserves for individual claims is an important part of the claim process, it is discussed in more detail later in this text.

Loss Adjustment Expenses

Insurers also incur loss adjustment expenses related to investigating and settling insurance claims. For property insurance claims, the claim representative must identify the cause of the loss and decide whether the loss is covered by the policy. If the loss is covered, the claim representative must determine the covered amount.

For liability claims, the claim representative must determine whether the insured is legally responsible for the bodily injury or property damage that is the basis of the claim and, if so, for how much. Determining the legal

Paid loss
A claim payment that an insurer has made.

Incurred losses
The sum of paid losses and changes in loss reserves for a particular period.

Loss reserves
Amounts designated by insurers to pay claims for losses that have already occurred but are not yet settled.

responsibility of the insured for a loss might require a complex and costly investigation. In addition to paying covered losses, liability insurers often pay the costs to defend the insured in the event of a lawsuit, regardless of whether the insured is ultimately held responsible for the damages. Thus, loss adjustment expenses associated with a liability claim can be substantial.

Other Underwriting Expenses

In addition to losses and loss adjustment expenses, the costs of providing insurance include other significant underwriting expenses, which can be categorized as follows:

- Acquisition expenses
- General expenses
- Premium taxes, licenses, and fees

The expenses associated with acquiring new business are significant. All property-casualty insurers have a marketing system to market and distribute their products. This system includes individuals involved directly with sales (usually called agents, brokers, producers, or sales representatives) and the administrative staff that manages and supports the sales effort. Many people who directly generate insurance sales for insurers receive a commission, which is usually a percentage of the premiums written by the salesperson. Others receive a salary, or a combination of salary and commission, and sometimes also a bonus based on sales, profit, or some other measure of productivity. While some insurers operate without salespeople (usually through direct response systems such as mail, telephone, and the Internet), these insurers must still employ and pay staff to manage and administer their marketing operations. Advertising expenses can also be a significant component of acquisition expenses for most insurers.

Insurers incur still other expenses in the process of underwriting and issuing insurance policies. They need staff and computer systems to review and analyze applications for insurance, assemble and issue insurance policies, generate billing statements, collect premiums, and record necessary information.

Like other businesses, insurers incur various general expenses. While these expenses do not relate directly to activities such as claims, marketing, and underwriting, they are crucial to the insurers' operations. These general expenses are associated with staffing and maintaining departments such as accounting, legal, statistical and data management, actuarial, customer service, information technology, and building maintenance. In addition, insurers must provide office space, telephones, computers, and other utility services, as well as other office equipment and supplies for these necessary support functions.

In the United States, states levy premium taxes, which are usually between 2 and 4 percent of all premiums generated by the insurer in a particular state.

Unless they function as excess and surplus lines insurers, insurers must hold and pay for licenses in each state in which they operate. In addition, insurers must participate in various state insurance programs, such as guaranty funds and automobile insurance plans. Insurers are typically assessed to fund or subsidize these state insurance programs.

Dividends

Some insurers choose to return a portion of premiums to policyholders as dividends, which may be paid out on a regular basis or may be associated with a special circumstance. Mutual insurers may pay a dividend to policyholders when operating results have been good. Dividends may also be paid by any insurer as a marketing technique. Insurers who want to provide the lowest cost to their policyholders may prefer to accomplish that by paying dividends only after their operating results warrant such payments. In this way, the insurer's solvency is better protected than it would be by charging low rates up front with little margin for error.

Investment Expenses

An insurer's investment department includes a staff of professional investment managers who oversee the company's investment program. In addition to devising investment strategy and implementing it through the purchase and sale of stocks, bonds, and other investments, the investment department is responsible for a careful and thorough accounting of all invested funds. Investment expenses include staff salaries and all other expenses related to the activities of the investment department. Insurers deduct these expenses from investment income on their financial statements to calculate the net income from investments, as shown in the following:

Net investment income = Investment income − Investment expenses.

Gains or losses realized from the sale of invested assets are added to net investment income resulting in **net investment gain or loss**, which represents the total results from investment activities.

Net investment gain or loss
An insurer's gains or losses from the sale of invested assets plus net investment income.

Gain or Loss From Operations

An insurer's **net underwriting gain or loss** is its earned premiums minus its losses and underwriting expenses for a specific period. Adding net investment gain or loss to net underwriting gain or loss shows an insurer's **overall gain or loss from operations** and is reported by the following formula:

Overall gain or loss from operations = Net investment gain or loss + Net underwriting gain or loss.

This overall figure gives a more complete picture of an insurer's profitability than net underwriting gain or loss because net investment gains generally help to offset underwriting losses.

Net underwriting gain or loss
An insurer's earned premiums minus its losses and underwriting expenses for a specific period.

Overall gain or loss from operations
Net investment gain or loss plus net underwriting gain or loss.

Net Income Before Taxes

An insurer's net income before taxes is its total earned premiums and investment income minus its total losses and other expenses in the corresponding period. Some adjustments for other income items might be necessary. For example, the insurer might have to write off some uncollected premiums, or it might have to add premiums that were written off during the previous period but were ultimately collected during the current period. Adjustments might also be necessary for a gain or loss on the sale of equipment or other items. Mutual insurers would also deduct dividends to policyholders from their income.

Income Taxes

Like other businesses, insurers pay income taxes on their taxable income. Taxable income might differ from net income before taxes because of the special requirements of the tax code. For example, a portion of interest earnings from qualified municipal bonds are not taxed, and deductions for certain expenses are limited. Insurers often adjust their investment strategy in response to changing tax laws.

Net Income or Loss

After an insurer has paid losses and reserved money to pay additional losses, expenses, and income taxes, the remainder is net income, which belongs to the owners of the company. The owners may receive a portion of this remainder as dividends. For a publicly held company, such dividends are payable to the shareholders. The amount that is left after dividends are paid becomes an addition to the insurer's surplus, which enables the insurer to expand its operations in the future. When evaluating insurers' rates, regulators permit an allowance for profits and contingencies that should provide the owners with an adequate return on their investment. Unless the insurer generates an adequate return or profit, it will not attract and maintain the investment funds it needs to survive.

INSURER SOLVENCY

To serve its policyholders in the long term, a property-casualty insurer must remain financially sound. Although comparing an insurer's revenue to its expenses in a single year reveals whether the company produced an income gain or a loss, this information alone does not indicate the insurer's financial condition. The financial position of an insurer at any particular time is measured by its assets, liabilities, and policyholders' surplus. Exhibit 3-3, later in this text, shows the balance sheet relationship of assets, liabilities, and policyholders' surplus. These are discussed next.

Assets

Insurers accumulate funds when they receive premium and investment income. As stated previously, insurers do not immediately need all of their premium income to pay claims and operating expenses. In the meantime, insurers invest them in income-producing assets.

Assets are types of property, both tangible and intangible, owned by an entity. Assets typically accumulated by an insurer include cash, stocks, and bonds; property, such as buildings, office furniture, and equipment; and accounts receivable from policyholders, agents, brokers, and reinsurers.

For the purposes of filing financial reports with state insurance regulators, an insurer's assets are classified as either admitted assets or nonadmitted assets.

Assets
Types of property, both tangible and intangible, owned by an entity.

Admitted Assets

Admitted assets are types of property, such as cash and stocks, that regulators allow insurers to show as assets on their financial statements. Regulators allow admitted assets to be shown on insurers' financial statements because these assets could easily be liquidated, or converted to cash, at or near the property's market value. In addition to cash, admitted assets include stocks, bonds, mortgages, real estate, certain computer equipment, and premium balances due in less than ninety days.

Admitted assets
Types of property, such as cash and stocks, that regulators allow insurers to show as assets on their financial statements.

Nonadmitted Assets

Nonadmitted assets are types of property that cannot be readily converted to cash at or near their market value if the insurer were to liquidate its holdings. For this reason, regulators do not allow insurers to show them as assets on their financial statements. Nonadmitted assets include office equipment, furniture and supplies, and premiums that are more than ninety days overdue.

The creation of the two categories of assets—admitted and nonadmitted—reflects the conservative view that insurance regulators take when evaluating an insurer's financial strength. Regulators do not want insurers to overstate their true financial condition. Therefore, certain types of assets are deemed nonadmitted and cannot be counted toward the value of an insurer's holdings or its financial strength.

Nonadmitted assets
Types of property, such as office furniture and equipment, that regulators do not allow insurers to show as assets on financial statements because these assets cannot readily be converted to cash at or near their market value.

Liabilities

Liabilities are financial obligations, or debts, owed by a company to another entity. An insurer has a financial obligation to its policyholders: It must satisfy legitimate claims submitted by insureds and other parties. The major liabilities of an insurer arise from this financial obligation to pay claims. Three types of liabilities are found on an insurer's financial statements. The two major liabilities are the loss reserve and the loss expense reserve, and the unearned premium reserve. The third type is "all other" liabilities, typically small obligations that are considered miscellaneous liabilities.

Liabilities
Financial obligations, or debts, owed by a company to another entity, usually the policyholder in the case of an insurer.

Loss Reserve and Loss Expense Reserve

Loss reserve
The amount estimated and set aside by insurers to pay claims for losses that have already occurred but are not yet settled.

The **loss reserve** is the amount estimated and set aside by insurers to pay claims for losses that have already occurred but are not yet settled. The loss reserve is considered a liability because it represents a financial obligation owed by the insurer. It is the insurer's best estimate of the final settlement amount on all claims that have occurred but have not yet been settled. Although establishing loss reserves for claims whose value is not yet definite might seem impossible, insurers use their experience, the law of large numbers, and their actuarial and statistical expertise to make reliable estimates of future claim settlement values. Insurers also set up the loss expense reserve to estimate the cost of settling the claims included in the loss reserve.

Unearned Premium Reserve

Unearned premium reserve
The total of an insurer's unearned premiums on all policies at a particular time.

The **unearned premium reserve** is the total of an insurer's unearned premiums on all policies at a particular time. The unearned premium reserve is a liability because it represents insurance premiums prepaid by insureds for services that the insurer has not yet rendered. If the insurer ceased operations and canceled all of its policies, the unearned premium reserve would represent the total of premium refunds that the insurer would owe its current policyholders.

Other Liabilities

As mentioned, other liabilities on an insurer's financial statements are much smaller than the loss reserve and the loss expense reserve, and the unearned premium reserve. For some insurers, there may be a significant obligation reflected in the liability for reinsurance transactions.

Policyholders' Surplus

Policyholders' surplus
An insurer's total admitted assets minus its total liabilities.

Once the total value of an insurer's admitted assets (cash, stocks, bonds, real estate, and so forth) and liabilities (loss reserve and loss expense reserve, unearned premium reserve, and other liabilities) is known, the insurer can determine its **policyholders' surplus**. Policyholders' surplus equals the insurer's total admitted assets minus its total liabilities. Policyholders' surplus measures the difference between what the company *owns* (its admitted assets) and what it *owes* (its liabilities).

Policyholders' surplus provides a cushion that is available should the insurer have an adverse financial experience. While premiums may include a margin for error, that margin might not be sufficient to offset unexpected losses, particularly catastrophic losses. If losses exceed expectations, the insurer must draw on its surplus to make required claim payments. Policyholders' surplus also provides the necessary resources if the insurer decides to expand into a new territory or develop new insurance products. Thus, the amount of policyholders' surplus held by an insurer is an important measure of its financial condition.

Exhibit 3-3 summarizes the admitted assets, liabilities, and policyholders' surplus held by the property-casualty insurance industry in 2003.

EXHIBIT 3-3

Consolidated Balance Sheet for the Property-Casualty Industry (2,380 Companies)

Consolidated Property-Casualty Industry Totals
Balance Sheet December 31, 2003
(in millions of dollars)

Admitted Assets:	
Cash and short-term investments	$ 89,251
Bonds	642,839
Preferred stock	9,205
Common stock	126,560
Real estate	9,466
Other assets	297,007
Total Admitted Assets	$1,174,328
Liabilities:	
Loss reserve and loss expense reserve	$ 445,422
Unearned premium reserve	176,311
Conditional reserve funds	19,892
Other liabilities	178,854
Total Liabilities	$ 820,479
Policyholders' Surplus	353,849
Total Liabilities and Policyholders' Surplus	$1,174,328

Based on data from *Best's Aggregates and Averages: Property-Casualty.* © A.M. Best Company—used with permission.

MONITORING INSURER FINANCIAL PERFORMANCE

Because the objectives of most insurers include being profitable and remaining in business in the long term, insurers must carefully monitor their financial performance. Regulators, investors, and others also monitor the financial performance of insurers.

Insurers must record and report financial information in a consistent manner, using various financial statements. Interested parties can analyze these financial statements to evaluate the insurers' financial performance. Insurance buyers, agents, and brokers often use the reports and evaluations of financial rating organizations, such as A.M. Best Company and Standard & Poor's Corporation, to select insurers that are considered to be in strong and stable financial condition.

Financial Statements

Insurers must prepare accurate financial statements that describe the company's financial position in an objective, standardized format. The two financial statements that provide the most information concerning the financial condition of an insurer are the balance sheet and the income statement.

Balance Sheet

Balance sheet
A financial statement that shows a company's financial position at a particular point in time. For an insurer, it includes the insurer's admitted assets, liabilities, and policyholders' surplus.

The **balance sheet** shows an insurer's financial position at a particular point in time and includes the insurer's admitted assets, liabilities, and policyholders' surplus. Exhibit 3-4 shows a condensed balance sheet for Atwell Insurer, a fictitious insurer, on the last day of the year.

Although a balance sheet shows an insurer's assets and liabilities only as of a particular date, they change constantly. Insurers establish unearned premium reserves for premiums they receive. The unearned premium reserve for each policy declines with the passage of time. Also, losses occur and insurers establish loss reserves. New policies are written, and old policies expire or are renewed. Meanwhile, the insurer buys and sells stocks, bonds, and other investments as needed to meet its obligations while earning investment income. Therefore, an analysis of an insurer's assets and liabilities is only as current as the date of the balance sheet, which presents a snapshot of the financial position of the company at that point in time.

EXHIBIT 3-4

Atwell Insurer Balance Sheet as of December 31

Admitted Assets:	
Cash and short-term investments	$ 50,000
Bonds	1,100,000
Common stock	350,000
Total Admitted Assets	$1,500,000
Liabilities:	
Loss reserve and loss expense reserve	$ 550,000
Unearned premium reserve	250,000
Other liabilities	200,000
Total Liabilities	$1,000,000
Policyholders' Surplus	500,000
Total Liabilities and Policyholders' Surplus	$1,500,000

Income Statement

An insurer's **income statement** shows its revenues, expenses, and net income for a particular period, usually one year. Exhibit 3-5 shows a condensed income statement for Atwell Insurer.

During the year, Atwell Insurer's revenues from earned premiums totaled $1,000,000. In the same year, the company's expenses totaled $1,080,000. These expenses included incurred losses, loss adjustment expenses, acquisition expenses, general expenses, premium taxes, licenses, and fees. Because losses and underwriting expenses exceeded earned premiums, Atwell Insurer experienced a net underwriting loss of $80,000. However, Atwell also earned net investment income of $100,000 during the year. Therefore, Atwell Insurer realized a net income gain of $20,000, before income taxes.

Income statement
A financial statement that shows a company's revenues, expenses, and net income for a particular period, usually one year.

EXHIBIT 3-5

Atwell Insurer Income Statement for the Year Ending December 31

Revenues:	
Earned Premiums	$1,000,000
Expenses:	
Incurred losses	$ 650,000
Loss adjustment expenses	100,000
Other underwriting expenses:	
Acquisition expenses	220,000
General expenses	90,000
Premium taxes, licenses, and fees	20,000
Total Expenses	$1,080,000
Net Underwriting Gain (Loss)	$ (80,000)
Net Investment Income	100,000
Net Income Before Income Taxes	$ 20,000

Financial Statement Analysis

Analyzing the relationship of different items that appear on insurers' financial statements helps determine how well insurers are performing. Comparing two items produces a ratio that highlights a particular aspect of financial performance. Several such ratios are widely used in the insurance industry by many people and organizations. Insurers use them to identify strengths and weaknesses in their companies' operations. Investors analyze the ratios to identify the insurers that are most attractive as investments. Regulators also examine the ratios to determine whether insurers have the financial strength to remain viable in the long term and to meet their financial obligations to policyholders and other parties.

These ratios are important to insurance agents and brokers as well. The financial condition of an insurer should be one of the factors considered when producers select the companies with which they place business. Producers should be reasonably sure that an insurer is financially sound and that it will be able to meet its financial obligations.

Profitability Ratios

There are several ratios for measuring the profitability of an insurer, including the following:

- Loss ratio
- Expense ratio
- Dividend ratio
- Combined ratio
- Investment income ratio
- Overall operating ratio

Profitability ratios are usually converted into percentages for easier analysis of financial performance.

Loss ratio

An insurer's incurred losses (including loss adjustment expenses) for a given period divided by its earned premiums for the same period.

The **loss ratio** compares an insurer's incurred losses to its earned premiums for a specific time period. The figure for incurred losses includes loss adjustment expenses. The loss ratio is calculated as follows:

$$\text{Loss ratio} = \frac{\text{Incurred losses (including loss adjustment expenses)}}{\text{Earned premiums}}.$$

When converted into a percentage, the loss ratio indicates what proportion of earned premiums is being used to fund losses and their settlement. By looking at this percentage, insurers, regulators, investors, and others can determine how closely actual loss experience compares to expected loss experience. For example, at the beginning of the year, management might have decided that an 85 percent loss ratio is the target for the coming year. As each month progresses, the loss ratio is recalculated based on the company's experience to date to determine whether the insurer is meeting the targeted 85 percent ratio.

Expense ratio

An insurer's incurred underwriting expenses for a given period divided by its written premiums for the same period.

The **expense ratio** compares the insurer's incurred underwriting expenses to its written premiums in a specific time period. The expense ratio is calculated as follows:

$$\text{Expense ratio} = \frac{\text{Incurred underwriting expenses}}{\text{Written premiums}}.$$

When converted into a percentage, the expense ratio indicates what proportion of an insurer's written premiums is being used to pay acquisition costs, general expenses, and premium taxes. In other words, this ratio indicates the insurer's general cost of doing business as a proportion of the premiums it has written. (Investment income and investment expenses are not part of either the loss ratio or the expense ratio.) The expense ratio gives a general picture of how efficiently the insurer is operating. Insurers watch the expense ratio carefully over time and attempt to reduce it by managing cash flow and controlling expenses.

The **dividend ratio** applies to those insurers that pay dividends to policyholders. It indicates what proportion of an insurer's earned premiums (if any) is being returned to policyholders in the form of dividends. The dividend ratio is calculated as follows:

$$\text{Dividend ratio} = \frac{\text{Policyholder dividends}}{\text{Earned premiums}}.$$

The dividend ratio by itself is not a measure of profitability, but it is sometimes a component of the combined ratio, described next.

The **combined ratio** is the sum of the loss ratio and the expense ratio and is used to compare cash inflows and outflows from insurance operations. The combined ratio is calculated as follows:

$$\text{Combined ratio} = \text{Loss ratio} + \text{Expense ratio}.$$

Looking at the individual components of the loss ratio and the expense ratio would give the following formula for calculating the combined ratio:

$$\text{Combined ratio} = \frac{\text{Incurred losses (including loss adjustment expenses)}}{\text{Earned premiums}} + \frac{\text{Incurred underwriting expenses}}{\text{Written premiums}}.$$

Notice that both the numerators (top numbers) and the denominators (bottom numbers) in the loss ratio and the expense ratio are different. The loss ratio attempts to relate the level of losses as they are incurred to the corresponding earned premiums. Both the incurred losses and earned premiums reflect the insurance coverage provided over time. Because these two measurements represent corresponding cash inflows and outflows on an accrual basis, they provide the most informative basis for the loss ratio.

Expenses are a different matter. Many of the underwriting expenses incurred by insurers involve acquisition expenses, such as producers' commissions. Because these expenses occur at the beginning of the policy period, the use of written premiums, which recognizes the entire premium as soon as it is written, is appropriate for comparing expenses to revenues. Therefore, written premiums are used in lieu of earned premiums as the denominator in the expense ratio.

While the combined ratio is considered the accepted measure of an insurer's underwriting performance, this ratio does not take into account the insurer's investment income, and thus does not measure the insurer's overall financial performance. Overall financial performance includes the results from both the insurer's underwriting activities and its investment activities.

Dividend ratio
An insurer's policyholder dividends for a given period divided by its earned premiums for the same period.

Combined ratio
The sum of the loss ratio and the expense ratio.

For insurers that pay policyholder dividends (not stock dividends), the third component of the combined ratio is the dividend ratio. The ratio would then be calculated as follows:

Combined ratio = Loss ratio + Expense ratio + Dividend ratio.

For clarity, when the combined ratio is calculated using policyholder dividends, it is often called "combined ratio after policyholder dividends."

When loss ratios are calculated, the results are decimal expressions such as 0.90 (an insurer whose outflow equals 90 cents of each premium dollar) or 1.15 (an insurer whose outflow is $1.15 for each premium dollar). In the industry vernacular, these ratios are typically expressed without the decimals, such as "90" or "115," much as one might express that a baseball player is "batting 333" when the mathematical calculation of getting one hit in each three at-bats results in a batting average of 0.333.

The lower the combined ratio, the better. Most insurers consider a combined ratio under 100 to be acceptable, because it indicates a profit from underwriting, even before investment income is considered. In fact, many insurers regularly experience a combined ratio over 100 and attempt to offset underwriting losses with investment income.

Investment income ratio
Net investment income divided by earned premiums for a given period.

The **investment income ratio** compares the amount of net investment income (investment income minus investment expenses) with earned premiums over a specific period. It is calculated as follows:

$$\text{Investment income ratio} = \frac{\text{Net investment income}}{\text{Earned premiums}}.$$

The investment income ratio indicates the degree of success achieved in the insurer's investment activities. The higher the ratio, the more successful are the insurer's investment activities.

Overall operating ratio
The combined ratio minus the investment income ratio.

The **overall operating ratio** is the combined ratio (loss ratio plus expense ratio) minus the investment income ratio (net investment income divided by earned premiums) and can be used to provide an overall measure of the financial performance of the insurer for a specific period. It is calculated as follows:

Overall operating ratio = Combined ratio – Investment income ratio.

The investment income ratio must be *subtracted* from the combined ratio because investment income is used to *offset* the insurer's losses and underwriting expenses. Of all the commonly used ratios, the overall operating ratio is the most complete measure of insurer financial performance. To obtain a true picture of an insurer's profitability, overall operating ratios for a number of years should be analyzed, because any company might have a single bad year that is offset by a pattern of profitability over a longer period. Exhibit 3-6 shows how to calculate the various profitability ratios for the fictitious Atwell Insurer.

EXHIBIT 3-6

Profitability Ratios for Atwell Insurer

Earned premiums	$1,000,000
Written premiums	1,100,000
Incurred underwriting expenses	330,000
Incurred losses (including loss adjustment expenses)	750,000
Net investment income	100,000

$$\text{Loss ratio} = \frac{\text{Incurred losses (including loss adjustment expenses)}}{\text{Earned premiums}} = \frac{\$750,000}{\$1,000,000} = 0.75 \,(\text{or } 75\%).$$

$$\text{Expense ratio} = \frac{\text{Incurred underwriting expenses}}{\text{Written premiums}} = \frac{\$330,000}{\$1,100,000} = 0.30 \,(\text{or } 30\%).$$

Combined ratio = Loss ratio + Expense ratio = 0.30 + 0.75 = 1.05 (or 105%).

$$\text{Investment income ratio} = \frac{\text{Net investment income}}{\text{Earned premiums}} = \frac{\$100,000}{\$1,000,000} = 0.10 \,(\text{ or } 10\%).$$

Overall operating ratio = Combined ratio − Investment income ratio = 1.05 − 0.10 = 0.95 (or 95%).

Expressed as percentages, the expense ratio for Atwell Insurer is 30 percent, while its loss ratio is 75 percent. This creates a combined ratio of 105 percent. When the investment income ratio of 10 percent is subtracted, the overall operating ratio equals 95 percent. Using insurer jargon, the overall operating ratio would be expressed simply as "95."

An insurer with an overall operating ratio of 100 percent breaks even because revenue from all operations equals total expenses plus incurred losses. A ratio of less than 100 percent indicates an overall operating gain because revenues are greater than total expenses. Conversely, if the ratio is greater than 100 percent, an operating loss has occurred because total expenses are greater than revenue.

Although these ratios are the clearest indicators of insurer profitability, they should be used carefully and reexamined frequently. The loss ratio includes incurred losses as a key component. Because measuring incurred losses involves an estimate of the amount that will ultimately be paid on claims that were incurred during the current year, the loss ratio is subject to revision as losses develop. Likewise, because the loss ratio is part of the combined ratio and the overall operating ratio, these two ratios are also subject to change.

The insurer cannot know exactly how it performed in a specific period until all claims for incurred losses in that period are fully paid, which may not occur for several years. Monitoring financial results from past years helps to determine the accuracy of the insurer's loss reserve estimates.

Capacity Ratio

Capacity ratio, or premium-to-surplus ratio
Written premiums divided by policyholders' surplus.

In addition to profitability, an important concern for an insurer is its capacity to write new business and thus to grow. The measure of an insurer's capacity is its **capacity ratio**, also known as its **premium-to-surplus ratio**. It is calculated as follows:

$$\text{Capacity ratio} = \frac{\text{Written premiums}}{\text{Policyholders' surplus}}.$$

The capacity ratio compares an insurer's written premiums (which represent its exposure to potential claims) to its policyholders' surplus (which represents its cushion for absorbing adverse results). If losses and expenses exceed written premiums and investment income, an insurer must use its surplus to meet its obligations. Therefore, an insurer's new written premiums should not become too large relative to its policyholders' surplus.

Exhibit 3-7 shows the capacity ratio for Atwell Insurer, using data from Exhibits 3-4 and 3-6. The ratio of 2.2-to-1 is not unusual, because insurers often have a premium-to-surplus ratio close to 2-to-1. While it is not a magic figure, insurance regulators use the capacity ratio as a benchmark to determine whether an insurer may be headed toward financial difficulty. For example, a premium-to-surplus ratio above 3-to-1 could be a sign of financial weakness because the insurer may not have a sufficient cushion of policyholders' surplus to absorb its increased exposure to claims. However, regulators cannot determine an insurer's financial condition by this measure alone. In addition to the capacity ratio, regulators use many other measures of financial performance.

EXHIBIT 3-7

Capacity Ratio for Atwell Insurer

Written premiums	$1,100,000
Policyholders' surplus	500,000

$$\text{Capacity ratio} = \frac{\text{Written premiums}}{\text{Policyholders' surplus}} = \frac{\$1,100,000}{\$500,000} = \frac{2.2}{1}.$$

SUMMARY

Sound operation of an insurer requires that great care be given to its financial condition and performance. To survive long term, an insurer's revenue must exceed its expenses. Insurers must operate profitably, remain solvent, and provide financial statements so that their financial performance can be monitored by state insurance departments and others.

The profitability of an insurer is more difficult to measure than the profitability of many other businesses because of timing differences between the receipt of money (premiums) and the performance of the corresponding service (claim payments). Earned premiums are a better measure of premium revenue than written premiums during a specific period. Similarly, incurred losses are a better measure of losses during that period than are paid losses.

An insurer's income includes both underwriting income and investment income. Its expenses include losses, loss adjustment expenses, other underwriting expenses, and investment expenses. The company's overall gain or loss from operations is the sum of its net underwriting gain or loss and its net investment gain or loss for a specific period. Unless there is an overall gain—that is, a profit—the insurer's financial condition will deteriorate.

Solvency is the primary measure of an insurer's financial condition. Solvency indicates the insurer's ability to meet its obligations. Its assets, or what it owns, must exceed its liabilities, or what it owes. The difference between admitted assets and liabilities is policyholders' surplus. To be certain that insurers do not overstate their policyholders' surplus, regulators require insurers to follow conservative accounting procedures. These procedures allow insurers to show on their financial statements only admitted assets, which include defined categories of assets that can be readily converted to cash. These accounting procedures for insurers also require that insurers show as liabilities their loss reserve and loss expense reserve, and unearned premium reserve.

To monitor financial performance, regulators and others examine insurers' financial statements. The balance sheet, which measures an insurer's financial position, shows the insurer's assets, liabilities, and policyholders' surplus on a given date, such as the last day of the year. The income statement, which measures profitability, shows the company's revenues, expenses, and net income before taxes during a given period, such as a year. Analysis of these financial statements makes it possible to measure an insurer's financial performance over time, to compare one company to another, and to identify financially weak insurers.

Analyzing financial statements often involves using ratios to make these comparisons. Several different ratios measure various aspects of profitability. The most useful ratio for measuring profitability is the overall operating ratio, which is calculated as the combined ratio (loss ratio plus expense ratio plus dividend ratio) minus the investment income ratio (net investment income divided by earned premiums). The capacity ratio (written premiums divided by policyholders' surplus) is also important because it measures an insurer's capacity to write new business and thus to grow.

Segment B

Insurance Operations

Chapter 4

Direct Your Learning

Marketing

After learning the content of this chapter and completing the corresponding course guide assignment, you should be able to:

- Describe the legal relationship known as agency.

- Describe the responsibilities of the agent and the principal in any agency relationship.

- Describe each of the following types of insurance agents' authority:

  - Express authority

  - Implied authority

  - Apparent authority

- Summarize the various types of insurance marketing systems and alternative distribution channels.

- Describe typical compensation arrangements for insurance producers.

- Describe advertising methods used by insurers, producers, and producer trade associations.

- Describe the various aspects of marketing management.

- Describe how states regulate producers' activities.

- Discuss unfair trade practices as they relate to insurance.

- Define or describe each of the Keys Words and Phrases for this chapter.

Develop Your Perspective

What are the main topics covered in the chapter?

This chapter covers the marketing (distribution) systems used by insurers to identify potential customers, and then to create and supply the insurance products and services customers need.

Describe the legal relationship known as agency.

- What are the roles of the principal and the agent?
- What types of authority do insurance agents have?

Compare the commonly used insurance marketing (distribution) systems.

- How are the independent agency system and the exclusive agency system similar?
- How are they different?
- What are the roles of direct writing systems and alternative distribution channels?

Why is it important to learn about these topics?

The initial contact between an insurer and its policyholders is often through an agent or another type of producer. Therefore, the insurer's relationship with its producers is a major marketing concern.

Consider the duties of principals and agents, which form the insurer's relationship with its producers.

- What duties does the agent owe to the principal?
- What duties does the principal owe to the agent?
- How is producer performance monitored and regulated by insurer management and by state regulators?

How can you use what you will learn?

Consider the marketing (distribution) choices available to an insurer and to customers.

- What are the advantages and disadvantages of the independent and exclusive agency systems?
- Who may benefit by using a broker instead of an agent?
- Why do insurers sometimes use a mixed marketing system?

Chapter 4
Marketing

Marketing enables an insurer to determine which products meet customers' needs and then to create, promote, sell, and deliver those products to its customers. An insurer may have the best product at the best price available, but if customers are not aware of this, the insurer will sell few, if any, policies. Customers have many different insurance needs. One insurer may attempt to fill only a few of those needs; another may attempt to fill many.

Insurance marketing does not stop after the customer buys the product. People involved in insurance marketing also assist customers in dealings with insurers after a policy is issued. Insurers depend on their marketing personnel to keep them informed about the changing needs and desires of customers.

There are many insurance marketing systems and most involve a salesperson of some kind. Various terms, such as agent, broker, producer, solicitor, and sales representative, are used to refer to this salesperson. This book uses the terms **producer** and agent interchangeably to refer to any person who sells insurance (produces business) for one or more insurers. The terms broker and sales representative are also used for special categories of producers.

THE LEGAL ROLE OF THE INSURANCE AGENT

The legal relationship known as agency is not limited to insurance. An **agency** exists whenever one party, the **agent**, represents or acts on behalf of another party, the **principal**. The principal gives the agent authority to act as its representative within certain guidelines. The principal may authorize the agent to do anything the principal can do. For example, an insurer (the principal) can authorize its agent to collect premiums from insureds for new insurance policies and then require the agent to remit those premiums (sometimes after deducting a commission) to the insurer within a certain amount of time.

The agency relationship requires a high degree of trust between the principal and the agent because it imposes serious legal obligations on both parties. While the agent has authority to act for the principal, the principal has control over the agent's actions on the principal's behalf. This authority and control are the two essential elements of an agency relationship.

Producer
A person who sells insurance products for one or more insurers.

Agency
A legal relationship that exists when one party, the agent, represents or acts on behalf of another party, the principal.

Agent
In the agency relationship, the party that is authorized by the principal to act on the principal's behalf.

Principal
In the agency relationship, the party that authorizes the agent to act on its behalf.

Creation of the Agency Relationship

Insurance agent
A legal representative of one or more insurers for which the representative has a contractual agreement to sell insurance.

An agency relationship is usually created by a written contract between the principal and the agent. In insurance, the insurer is the principal that appoints **insurance agents** to serve as its representatives; a written agency contract specifying the agent's scope of authority formalizes this relationship. The **agency contract**, also known as an **agency agreement**, is a written agreement between an insurer and an agent that specifies the scope of the agent's authority to conduct business for the insurer. It gives the agent the right to represent the insurer and to sell insurance on the insurer's behalf. The contract specifies the compensation arrangement between the insurer and the agent. It also describes how the agency relationship can be terminated. Insurance agency contracts usually have no fixed expiration date and remain in force until one party cancels the contract after giving proper notice to the other party as required by the contract.

Agency contract, or **agency agreement**
A written agreement between an insurer and an agent that specifies, among other things, the scope of the agent's authority to conduct business for the insurer.

The agency relationship, which is based on mutual trust and confidence, empowers the agent to act on behalf of the principal and imposes significant responsibilities on both parties.

Responsibilities of the Agent to the Principal

In an agency relationship, the agent's fundamental responsibility is to act for the benefit of the principal. The laws of agency impose the following five duties on all agents, including insurance agents:

1. Loyalty
2. Obedience
3. Reasonable care
4. Accounting
5. Relaying information

Two of the agent's most important duties are to be loyal to the principal and to obey the principal's lawful instructions. In addition, an agent must exercise a reasonable degree of care in its actions on behalf of the principal; in other words, the agent must act as a reasonably prudent person would under the same or similar circumstances. Under the duty of accounting, the agent is responsible to the principal for all of the principal's money and property that comes into the agent's possession; the agent must account promptly for any of the principal's money that the agent holds. The duty of relaying information requires the agent to keep the principal informed of all facts relating to the agency relationship.

In insurance, an agency contract specifically addresses certain rights and duties of the agent. For example, the contract explicitly describes the insurance agent's right to make insurance coverage effective and any limitations on that right. The contract also specifies how the agent is to handle funds, including stipulations on how and when the agent must remit premiums to the insurer. Insurance agency contracts usually give the agent the right to employ subagents who may act on behalf of the insurer according to the terms of the agency contract.

Responsibilities of the Principal to the Agent

Just as the agent owes duties to the principal, the principal legally owes certain duties to the agent. The principal's primary duty is to pay the agent for the services performed. In the case of an insurance agent, this duty requires the insurer to pay commissions and other specified compensation to the agent for the insurance the agent sells or renews.

The principal also has a duty to indemnify, or reimburse, the agent for any losses or damages suffered without the agent's fault, but arising out of the agent's actions on behalf of the principal. If a third party sues the agent in connection with activities performed on behalf of the principal, the principal must reimburse the agent for any liability incurred, if the agent was not at fault. However, no reimbursement is due if the agent acted illegally or without the principal's authorization, even though the principal may be liable to others for those acts. An important factor involved in this duty is the exposure of insurance agents to **errors and omissions (E&O)** claims, which may arise from the agent's negligent actions. For example, when an insurance agent gives a customer misleading or incorrect advice regarding the customer's insurance, the customer could bring an E&O claim against the agent if the customer suffers damage due to the agent's advice.

Errors and omissions (E&O)
Negligent acts (errors) committed by a person conducting insurance business that give rise to legal liability for damages; a failure to act (omission) that creates legal liability.

Responsibilities of the Agent and the Principal to Third Parties

An agency relationship also creates responsibilities to third parties (parties other than the agent and the principal). The agent's authorized actions on behalf of the principal legally obligate the principal to third parties in the same way as if the principal acted alone. Therefore, from an insured's point of view, little distinction exists between the insurance agent and the insurer.

Because the agent represents the insurer, the law presumes that knowledge acquired by the agent is knowledge acquired by the insurer. If, for example, the agent visits the insured's premises and recognizes an exposure (such as vacancy of the building) that could suspend or void the insured's policy, the insurer cannot deny a claim to the insured merely because the agent failed to communicate that information to the insurer. According to agency law, the fact that the agent knew about the exposure means that the insurer is also presumed to know about it.

Authority of Agents

The principal is legally bound by any actions of the agent that are within the agent's authority. Insurance agents generally have the following three types of authority to transact business on behalf of insurers that they represent:

1. Express authority
2. Implied authority
3. Apparent authority

Express Authority

Express authority
The authority that the principal specifically grants to the agent.

The terms of the agency contract define the agent's **express authority**. For example, the contract will state that the agent has authority to sell the insurer's products or that the agent has authority to bind coverage up to a specified limit.

Binding authority
An insurance agent's authority to effect coverage on behalf of the insurer.

Binding authority, generally granted to the agent in the agency contract, is a form of express authority. **Binding authority** is the power to make insurance coverage effective on behalf of the insurer. Binding coverage is usually accomplished by issuing **binders**, which are agreements to provide temporary insurance coverage until a formal written policy is issued. Binders can be either written or oral.

Binder
An oral or written agreement to provide temporary insurance coverage until a formal written policy is issued.

For example, assume Christopher owns an old car for which he has an automobile policy with no collision coverage. Christopher purchases a new car and telephones his insurance agent, Lisa, to make sure the car is covered before he drives it away from the dealer's lot. Reminding Christopher that he has no collision coverage, Lisa gives him a quote for collision coverage on the new car. Lisa and Christopher agree that Lisa will immediately add the new car to Christopher's policy, including collision coverage with a $250 deductible. Christopher agrees to pay the premium when he receives an invoice, and Lisa assures Christopher that "coverage is bound." Lisa then begins to process the paperwork necessary to issue a policy change (called an endorsement) that includes collision and other coverages on Christopher's new car.

If Christopher should have an accident before receiving the policy endorsement, he would have collision coverage on his new car because Lisa issued an oral binder. The binder is temporary because it will be replaced by a policy endorsement.

As illustrated by the previous example, oral binders are often used until the paperwork necessary to have an endorsement or a new policy issued is completed. Such paperwork often includes a written binder completed on a standard form. A written binder provides a brief summary of who is insured, what is insured, and what coverages and limits apply.

Binding authority gives an agent the power to put specified types and limits of coverage in force at once rather than waiting for approval from the insurer.

When an insurance agent binds coverage for a new client, the agent commits the insurer to covering an exposure for, and possibly paying a claim to, a customer who is unknown to the insurer. Binding authority involves important responsibilities for the agent, and agents are expected to use their binding authority carefully.

Implied Authority

The scope of an agent's authority, however, can go beyond the terms of the agency contract. In addition to express authority, the agent may have **implied authority** to perform other tasks necessary to accomplish the purpose of the agency relationship. For example, assume that XYZ Insurer's agency contract with Atwell Insurance Agency does not give Atwell's agents express authority to collect premiums from XYZ's insureds. Atwell's agents would have implied authority to do so because collecting premiums is an act that is reasonably necessary for Atwell to accomplish the sale of XYZ's policies, and the sale of XYZ's policies is expressly authorized in the agency contract.

Implied authority
The authority implicitly conferred on an agent by custom, usage, or a principal's conduct indicating intention to confer such authority.

Apparent Authority

An agent can also have **apparent authority** to act on behalf of the principal in ways that the principal does not intend. Usually, an insurance agent has broadly defined powers to represent an insurer and to transact the company's business. Without actual notice or reason to believe otherwise, a third party cannot be expected to know about any unusual limitations on the agent's authority. The insurer is bound by all acts within the agent's apparent authority, unless the insurer takes steps to prevent that outcome.

Apparent authority
A third party's reasonable belief that an agent has authority to act on the principal's behalf.

For example, XYZ Insurer furnishes its agents with application forms showing the XYZ name and logo. XYZ grants its agents binding authority for routine applications for homeowners insurance. If XYZ terminates its agency agreement with Granton Insurance Agency but fails to retrieve the blank application forms, a Granton producer may inadvertently take Maria's application for homeowners insurance on an XYZ application form, accept Maria's check for the premium, and tell her that her coverage is bound effective that day. If a fire occurs in Maria's house the next day, XYZ Insurer would probably be required to pay the claim because it appeared to Maria that the Granton Insurance Agency had the authority to bind her coverage with XYZ. From Maria's standpoint, the Granton Insurance Agency *apparently* had the authority to bind coverage for XYZ. Maria would not be penalized because she did not know that XYZ had terminated its agency contract with Granton. XYZ, however, may attempt to recover the cost of the claim from Granton.

INSURANCE MARKETING SYSTEMS

Insurers use many types of marketing systems, which are also known as distribution systems, designed to meet their particular marketing objectives. Most insurers typically use one or more of the following marketing systems:

- Independent agency system
- Exclusive agency system
- Direct writing system
- Alternative distribution channels

Exhibit 4-1 shows some of the differences between these systems. It is important to note that these marketing systems are not mutually exclusive. Some insurers use a mixed marketing system, combining two or more distribution systems. In fact, combinations of marketing systems are becoming increasingly common among insurers.

Independent Agency System

Independent agency

A business, operated for the benefit of its owner (or owners) that sells insurance, usually as a representative of several unrelated insurers.

The independent agency system is used by insurers of all sizes. An **independent agency** is a business, operated for the benefit of its owner (or owners) that sells insurance, usually as a representative of several unrelated insurers. The agency can be organized as a sole proprietorship (owned by an individual), a partnership (owned by two or more individuals), or a corporation (owned by stockholders). Under the independent agency system, insurance sales are made through independent agents.

EXHIBIT 4-1

Differences Among Insurance Marketing Systems

Type of marketing (or distribution) system	What company or companies do the producers represent?	Are the producers employed by the insurer?	How are producers usually compensated?	Does the agency or agent own the expiration list(s)?	What methods of sales are usually used?
Independent agency system	Usually more than one insurer	No, the producers are employed by the agency	Sales commissions and contingent commissions	Usually, yes	Personal contact, phone, or Internet
Exclusive agency system	Only one insurer or group of related insurers	Usually, no; however, some producers begin as employees	Sales commissions (commissions on renewals may be lower than on new business) and bonus	Usually, no; but the agency contract may provide for the agent's right to sell the list to the insurer	Personal contact, phone, or Internet
Direct writing system	Only the producers' employer	Yes	Salary, bonus, commissions, or a combination	No	Personal contact, phone, or Internet
Alternative distribution channels	Only the producers' employer	Yes	Salary	No	Mail, phone, or Internet

Independent Agents

An **independent agent** is a producer who works for an independent agency and can be either the owner or an employee of the agency. In a small independent agency operated by a sole proprietor who is the only producer, the independent agent and the independent agency are the same. Larger independent agencies are usually corporations that employ many producers. Independent agencies enter into agency contracts with one or more insurers.

One of the main distinguishing features between independent agency systems and other marketing systems is the ownership of the **agency expiration list**, which is the record of present policyholders and the dates their policies expire. The typical independent agency contract specifies that the independent agency—not the insurer—owns the list of policyholders, the dates their existing policies expire, and, most importantly, the right to solicit these policyholders for insurance. If the insurer ceases to do business with a particular agency, the insurer cannot legally sell insurance to the agency's customers or give the expiration list to another agency. Under such circumstances, the independent agency has the right to continue doing business with its existing customers by selling them insurance with another insurer. The customers, however, are not obligated to keep their business with the agency, but may choose another agency or company.

Because of the independent agency's traditional exclusive right to solicit policyholders on an agency expiration list, the ownership of expiration lists is the agency's most valuable asset when an independent agency is bought or sold. The agency has the right to sell its expiration lists to another independent agent. For example, if the agency were to be sold, the new buyer would want to keep the agency's customers and would therefore want the agency's expiration lists.

Sometimes, an independent agent determines that a different insurer represented by the agency can better meet an existing customer's needs. Occasionally, an insurer may be unwilling to renew an insurance policy or may have rates that are not competitive. Therefore, the agent must select another insurer for the customer. In either case, the independent agency has the right to switch the coverage to another insurer, subject to the customer's approval.

Independent Agencies That Represent Only One Insurer

Generally, independent insurance agencies represent more than one, and sometimes a dozen or more, insurers. However, some independent agencies represent only one insurer or a group of related insurers. Such an agency may not find it practical to represent more than one insurer because the agency is small or just starting in business. Other reasons for representing only one insurer may be that the agency specializes in one type of coverage or has a special arrangement with a particular insurer.

Some independent agents agree to place all or most of their business with just one insurer because there may be advantages in doing a large volume of

Independent agent
A producer who works for an independent agency who can be either the owner or an employee of the agency.

Agency expiration list
The record of an insurance agency's present policyholders and the dates their policies expire.

business with one insurer rather than a smaller volume with each of several insurers. For example, some insurers offer independent agents incentives for special agency agreements. Those incentives may include computer systems, higher commission rates, or a more open market for the agent's customers.

Closely related to and often working with independent agencies are brokers and managing general agencies. These are discussed next.

Brokers

Insurance broker

An independent business owner or firm that sells insurance by representing customers rather than insurers.

An **insurance broker** is an independent business owner or firm that sells insurance by representing customers rather than insurers. Brokers shop among insurers to find the best coverage and value for their clients. Some insurers require that brokers purchase insurance through one of the company's agents who, in turn, pays a portion of the agent's commission to the broker. Other insurers have contracts with and regularly accept business directly from insurance brokers and pay them a fee or commission for the business. Because they are not legal representatives of the insurer, brokers are not likely to have authority to commit the insurer to write the policy by binding coverage, unlike agents, who generally have binding authority. An excess and surplus lines (E&S) broker is licensed by a state or states to transact insurance (for coverages usually unavailable in the standard market) through specialty nonadmitted insurers.

In practice, despite the technical distinctions between brokers and independent agents, the differences are quite limited. Both brokers and independent agents are intermediaries between insurers and insurance buyers, and both collect premiums from insureds and remit them to insurers. Both are in the business of finding people with insurance needs and selling insurance appropriate to those needs. In fact, the same person can act as an agent on one transaction and as a broker on another. A person acts as an agent when placing insurance with an insurer for which he or she is licensed as an agent but may act as a broker when placing insurance with other agents or insurers.

Large brokerage firms have many brokers who generally handle commercial insurance accounts that often require sophisticated knowledge and service. Many brokerage firms operate nationally, with offices in many states, and some operate internationally as well. In addition to insurance sales, large brokerage firms, as well as large agencies, may provide extensive loss control, appraisal, actuarial, risk management, and other insurance-related services that large businesses need.

Managing general agency (MGA)

An independent business or organization that appoints and supervises independent agents for insurers that use the independent agency system.

Managing General Agencies (MGAs)

A **managing general agency (MGA)** is an independent business or organization that appoints and supervises independent agents for insurers that use the independent agency system. MGAs serve as intermediaries between insurers and agents who sell insurance directly to the customer, in much the same position as wholesalers in the distribution system for tangible goods. The MGA's exact duties and responsibilities depend on its contracts with the insurers it represents. The MGA receives a managerial commission—often referred to as an override—which is a percentage of the premium or the profits on policies sold by producers placing business with the insurer through the MGA.

E&S brokers resemble MGAs in that they usually transact business primarily with other brokers and agents, not directly with customers. In fact, some firms operate as both MGAs and E&S brokers.

Exclusive Agency System

An **exclusive agent** sells insurance exclusively for one insurer or a group of related insurers. Like the independent agent, the exclusive agent's business operation is his or her own insurance sales agency. An agency agreement describes the exclusive agent's binding authority and compensation arrangements. Unlike the agency agreement in the independent agency system, the exclusive agency system limits the agent to selling insurance exclusively for one insurer or group of related insurers. If a desired type of insurance is not written by the insurer represented, some contracts allow the agent to place ("broker") the business with an independent agent or another exclusive agent.

Exclusive agent
An agent that has a contract to sell insurance exclusively for one insurer or a group of related insurers.

Generally, an exclusive agent is not an employee of the insurer but a self-employed representative of the company. With some exclusive agency insurers, agent trainees begin as employees and later make the transition to owning their own businesses.

Some exclusive agency contracts provide that the agent owns the agency expiration list and has the right to sell it to another party, but this is often not the case. Usually, the contract contains an agreement that, upon termination of the agency contract, the insurer will buy the expiration list from the exclusive agent using a predetermined formula to establish its value. An exclusive agent's expiration list—and the right to consider people on the list as customers of that agent—can become a valuable asset as an exclusive agent's business grows.

Direct Writing System

A **direct writing system** is a system of insurance marketing that uses sales representatives who are employees of the insurer. As with the exclusive agency system, agents in this system sell insurance for only one insurer or group of related insurers. Unlike most producers in the exclusive agency system, however, agents in the direct writing system are not self-employed. Rather, they are employees of the insurer and their job is to sell insurance for the company. Employees who work as insurance producers for a direct writing insurer are generally called sales representatives. A direct writing insurer's sales representatives are sometimes called agents, and they must possess agents' licenses. Legally, they function as agents of the insurer, and most insurance buyers would not distinguish between an agent and a sales representative.

Direct writing system
A system of insurance marketing that uses sales representatives who are employees of the insurer.

Like employees in general, a direct writing insurer's sales representatives work from offices or other business locations provided by the employer. The insurer in this system, unlike an insurer using the independent or exclusive agency system, pays office expenses as well. Employees can be transferred from job to job and from office to office to meet the overall needs of the insurer. Increasingly, these sales representatives can also work from their homes, using their own or company-provided computers and phone services.

Because the direct writing insurer's sales representative is an employee of the insurer, the expiration list belongs not to the sales representative but to the insurer, which can use the customer information as a source of prospects for follow-up sales by its other sales representatives.

Sometimes a customer needs a type of policy not available from an insurer that the agent represents. When this happens, the agent may contact an agent who represents another insurer and apply for insurance through that agent. The agent who represents the insurer usually shares the commission with the agent who has the customer.

In this situation, the original agent acts as a broker—the agent shops for insurance on behalf of the customer. The act of placing the insurance for this customer through another agent is called brokering. The insurance sold in this manner is referred to as brokered business.

Exclusive agents and direct writing insurers' sales representatives, as well as independent agents, may occasionally broker business for an account whose other coverages are handled by the producer's insurer. Authority for such transactions would be specified in the agency or employment contract.

Alternative Distribution Channels

In addition to the three marketing systems just described, insurers as well as producers use the following alternative distribution channels to sell insurance:

- Direct response
- Internet
- Call centers
- Group marketing
- Financial institutions

Direct Response

Direct response

A system of insurance marketing that relies primarily on mail, phone, and/or Internet sales, without the services of an agent.

The **direct response** distribution channel markets directly to customers. No agent is involved; rather the direct response relies primarily on mail, phone, and/or Internet sales. Although this distribution channel is also called direct mail, customers can also contact insurers via telephone and the Internet. Direct response relies heavily on advertising and targeting specific groups of affiliated customers.

Internet

As a distribution channel, the Internet can be used at various times to varying degrees by all parties to the insurance transaction: the insurer, the producer, and the customer. Interaction can occur between the producer and the customer, the producer and the insurer, and the customer and the insurer. Interactions can range from exchanges of e-mail to multiple policy quoting, billing, and policy issuance. Customers also interact with insurers on the Internet via Web-based insurance distributors, also called insurance portals or aggregators. These portals deliver leads to the insurers whose products they offer through their Web sites.

Call Centers

Call centers sell insurance products and services through telemarketing. The best-equipped call centers can replicate the activities of producers. In addition to making product sales, call centers staff can also respond to general inquiries, handle claim processing, answer billing questions, and process policy endorsements. Call centers operate with customer service representatives, touch-tone service, or speech-enabled (voice response) service.

Group Marketing

Group marketing sells insurance products and services to individuals or businesses that are all members of the same organization. Group marketing includes affinity marketing, mass marketing, and worksite marketing.

Affinity marketing targets various customer groups based on profession, interests, or hobbies. Mass marketing, also called mass merchandising, offers insurance to large numbers of targeted individuals or groups, such as senior citizens. Worksite marketing markets insurance (most commonly life, health, and disability) to employees of a particular company or organization. Insurance premiums are usually discounted and deducted on an after-tax basis from employee paychecks through payroll deduction.

Financial Institutions

Insurers and producers can also elect to market their products and services through a bank or other financial services institution. Marketing arrangements can range from simple to complex. For example, a small insurance agency may place an agent at a desk in a local bank, or a large insurer may form a strategic alliance with a regional or national financial holding company to solicit customers.

Mixed Marketing System

Traditionally, each insurer used just one of the marketing systems or distribution channels previously described, however many insurers have departed from this practice. The term **mixed marketing system** refers to an

Mixed marketing system
An insurer's use of more than one marketing system or distribution channel.

insurer's use of more than one marketing system or distribution channel. For example, some insurers that traditionally sold insurance only through independent agents are now also using direct response, developing business without producers and without paying commissions to producers. These insurers generally argue that advertisements and direct mail enable them to reach customers they would not reach through an independent agent.

Conversely, some direct writing insurers, seeking to expand their business, have entered into agency agreements with independent agents in some areas. These direct writing insurers have turned to independent agents as a distribution system partly because they have found it relatively expensive to establish offices and develop trained employees, especially in small communities.

PRODUCER COMPENSATION

While some producers receive a salary, commissions provide the primary form of compensation for producers. Producers typically earn two types of commissions—sales commissions and contingent commissions.

Sales Commissions

An independent agency or an exclusive agency receives commissions from the insurer for all insurance premiums the agency generates. A **sales commission** (or simply, **commission**) is a percentage of the premium that the insurer pays to the agency or producer for new policies sold or existing policies renewed. An insurance broker may receive a sales commission or fee directly from the insurer or may receive a portion of the commission from the agent who placed the insurance.

Sales commission, or **commission**
A percentage of the premium that the insurer pays to the agency or producer for new policies sold or existing policies renewed.

For insurance agents, the method of premium collection determines how sales commissions are received. If the insurer handles billings and collections (direct billing), the insurer periodically mails a commission check to the agency. If the agency collects the premiums (agency billing or producer billing), it subtracts its commission on each policy and remits the balance of collected premiums to the insurer, usually on a monthly basis.

In a small agency with only one agent, the entire commission goes to that agent. In a larger agency, a portion of the commission typically goes to the producer who made the sale, and the remainder goes to the agency to cover other expenses.

Usually, commissions are not fully earned at the time of a sale. If policies are canceled or premiums are returned to an insured for some other reason (such as deleting or reducing coverage), the producer must also return the unearned portion of the commission to the insurer.

The commission compensates the agency not only for making the sale but also for providing service before and after the sale. Service provided before the sale includes locating and screening insurance prospects, conducting a successful sales solicitation, getting the necessary information to complete an application, preparing a submission to the insurer, and presenting a proposal or quote to the prospect. To make a sale, the agent must also evaluate a prospect's insurance needs and recommend appropriate coverages for the prospect to select. After the sale, the agency often handles the paperwork that accompanies policy changes, billing, and claim handling. When it is time for the policy to be renewed, the agency must again analyze coverage needs and consider any changes in insurance coverage that have become available.

The producer who is an employee of a direct writing insurer generally receives a salary and perhaps also a bonus that relates to the premiums of the policies the producer sells. The compensation arrangements of direct writing insurers tend to emphasize sales to new customers, because these companies generally assign service after the sale to employees who specialize in the applicable areas, such as claims. With some insurers, drive-in claim service offices and other customer service centers handle most of the services required after the sale, including policy changes and billing issues.

Contingent Commissions

In addition to commissions based on a percentage of premiums, some agencies receive a **contingent commission**, which is based on the premium volume and profitability level of the agency's business with that insurer. The insurer compares the premiums received for policies sold by the agency with the losses incurred under those policies to determine whether the agency's business has earned a profit. If the business sold by the agency attains a certain volume of premium and level of profitability, the company shares a portion of the profit with the agency.

Contingent commissions encourage agencies to sell only policies that will be profitable for the insurer. Agencies that practice careful selection can earn sizable contingent commissions as a result. An independent agency is typically eligible to receive a contingent commission annually from each insurer for which the agency's business has been profitable.

Insurers that use the exclusive agency or direct writing system may offer higher sales commissions, rather than contingent commissions, for agents whose sales generate a given level of profit. Alternatively, these companies sometimes offer bonuses or other forms of compensation to agents whose business is profitable.

Contingent commission
A commission that an insurer pays, usually annually, to an independent agency that is based on the premium volume and profitability level of the agency's business with that insurer.

ADVERTISING

An independent agency uses advertising to attract customers to the agency; therefore local advertising often stresses the agency rather than the various insurers it represents. On the other hand, many insurers marketing through the independent agency system use national advertising programs intended to enhance the company image. With many products including insurance, name brands tend to be most readily accepted by customers. Accordingly, insurers design advertising symbols and slogans to increase their public recognition.

Independent agents sometimes identify with national symbols or repeat slogans from national advertising campaigns in their local advertisements. At other times, their ads focus on the agency itself—its quality of service, reputation, personnel and their qualifications, range of services, or similar themes that may attract an insurance buyer.

In the exclusive agency system, advertising programs emphasize the names of both the insurer and the agent. Sometimes an insurer's advertisement lists every agent in the area with a photo of each. Advertising for direct writing insurers tends to emphasize the company itself rather than individual producers or office locations.

Because they do not have producers, insurers using direct response marketing must use other ways to attract new customers. Some insurers using the direct response system advertise heavily—an activity that can be quite costly. Others, working from an established customer base, have traditionally relied successfully on free word-of-mouth advertising.

In addition to the traditional types of advertising—television, radio, magazines, newspapers, and direct mail—insurers and agents of all types use the Internet for advertising. Nearly all insurers and agents have Web sites that provide information about their company or agency and its products and services.

Producers' Trade Associations

Trade associations serve their members through activities such as education, political lobbying, research, and advertising. The advertising programs are intended to create a favorable image of association members as a group and to make the public familiar with the logos and other association symbols.

Independent Agents' Trade Associations

Most independent agents are members of the Independent Insurance Agents & Brokers of America (IIABA), the National Association of Professional Insurance Agents (PIA), or both. The IIABA is often called the "Big I" because of the prominent letter "I" in its advertising logo. (In some states, IIABA and PIA have consolidated to form one state insurance agents' association.)

Agents' and Brokers' Trade Association

The Council of Insurance Agents and Brokers (CIAB) includes independent agents and brokers associated with large agencies or brokerage firms that primarily handle commercial insurance.

Managing General Agents' Association

Many managing general agents are members of the American Association of Managing General Agents (AAMGA), which, like agents' and brokers' associations, also provides various services to its members.

MARKETING MANAGEMENT

All insurers need some means of managing the activities of producers. This includes systems to supervise and motivate producers, and to provide them with insurance products they can sell. Marketing management also involves monitoring agency sales and underwriting results to ensure that both the company's and the agency's sales and profit objectives are met.

Producer Supervision

Although selling insurance is essentially a one-on-one activity that often occurs away from the producer's office and the insurer's home office, insurers do supervise their producers. An insurer using independent agents typically employs marketing representatives who visit the independent agents representing the company. The role of the **marketing representative** is to develop and maintain a sound working relationship with the insurer's agents and to motivate the agents to produce a satisfactory volume of profitable business for the insurer. Marketing representatives also have the responsibility of finding and "appointing" (entering into agency contracts with) new independent agents who can potentially produce profitable business for the company. Some marketing representatives operate from their homes and spend most of their time traveling among agencies in their marketing territories, maintaining a close personal contact with the insurer's agents.

Other insurers have **production underwriters**, who spend most of their time inside the insurer's office but also travel to maintain rapport with agents and to meet with clients in special situations. Insurers using the direct writing system may use an agency manager or district manager to supervise a group of producers, directing their activities rather closely.

Depending on how an insurer is structured, producer supervision and support can be provided from either the insurer's home office or a branch or regional office. Small insurers, or those doing business in a limited geographic area, may have only one office. When this is the case, producers interact directly with personnel in the home office.

Insurers conducting business nationally or over a widespread geographic area usually find it beneficial to establish field offices close to producers' offices, and producers usually work closely with a local field office rather than the home office. A small field office, perhaps with only one marketing manager or marketing representative, may be called a service office. A larger office, containing management personnel, underwriters, and claim representatives may be called a branch or regional office.

Marketing representative
An insurer employee who visits agents representing the insurer, develops and maintains sound working relationships with those agents, and motivates the agents to produce a satisfactory volume of profitable business for the insurer.

Production underwriter
An insurer employee who works in the insurer's office in an underwriting position but also travels to visit and maintain rapport with agents and sometimes clients.

Producer Motivation

Insurers also need to motivate their producers to sell the types of insurance the companies want sold. Some producer motivation results from personal relationships and encouragement by marketing representatives, regional managers, and other people working in field offices. Other motivation comes from marketing programs developed in the home office.

The financial incentives that producers receive for selling can affect their sales performance. The insurer's marketing department considers this motivational effect when recommending salaries, bonuses, or commissions to be paid to producers.

Some insurers may also develop sales contests to encourage specific production activities, such as selling a particular type of policy or reaching a particular level of sales activity. Sales contests can lead to awards or special recognition.

Product Management and Development

Insurance production is most successful when producers have a desirable product to sell at a competitive price. The insurer's marketing department— usually at the home office level—strives to give producers the products and pricing they need. The home office marketing department bases many of its decisions on information provided by producers and by other insurer personnel in the field. An insurer's product management involves maintaining an ongoing relationship with producers.

People involved with sales are often the first to identify a need that could be addressed by either a new policy or modification of an existing policy. Those involved in marketing are acutely aware of what the competition is doing in regard to product management and development. The response to new product development by competitors is often critical to satisfying changing market demands.

The home office marketing department cooperates with other departments to determine what coverages the insurer's insurance policies should provide, what price to charge, and what other services the insurer should offer. Decisions in those matters are based partly on claim costs for the particular insurer or for the industry as a whole and on information about the coverages, prices, and services of competing insurers.

PRODUCER REGULATION

State insurance departments regulate both insurer and producer activities. Producer regulation occurs primarily through agent and broker licensing laws and other state laws dealing with insurance, such as unfair trade practices laws.

Licensing Laws

To function legally as an insurance agent, a producer must be licensed by the state or states in which he or she wants to sell insurance. Producers' licensing laws vary by state and change periodically. Some states have several different licenses, including licenses for agents, brokers, and solicitors. The exact titles and the authority that goes with the licenses vary somewhat by state. Generally, insurance agents are defined legally as representatives of the insurer(s) for which they sell insurance. Brokers, as stated previously, are representatives of the insurance purchasers rather than of the insurers.

Some states, such as California, have separate licenses for solicitors, who work for and are representatives of agents or brokers, often as office employees, but have less authority than agents. Generally, solicitors can solicit prospects but cannot bind insurance coverage. In other states, such office employees who solicit insurance must secure an agent's license; they are often called customer service representatives (CSRs) or customer service agents (CSAs).

To obtain a state agent's license, a candidate must meet several requirements. Usually, the candidate must pass an examination and meet other qualifications of the state insurance department to receive a state insurance license. These examinations typically deal with insurance principles, insurance coverages, and insurance laws and regulations. Some states mandate a certain number of hours of classroom study before a candidate can take a license examination. In some states, completing a recognized professional designation program allows the candidate to waive the classroom and examination requirements for licensing. Once a state agent's license has been issued, the agent must seek to be appointed by one or more insurers before the agent can sell insurance.

Producers' licenses generally have a specified term, such as one or two years, and can be renewed by paying a fee specified by the state. Most states also impose a continuing education requirement, requiring that producers periodically complete a specified number of hours of educational study related to the insurance business. Producers in those states must provide evidence that they have completed approved continuing education courses before the state will renew their licenses.

Licensed producers are required to adhere to all laws regulating insurance sales in the state or states in which they conduct business. The state can suspend or revoke licenses under certain circumstances, such as engaging in unfair trade practices.

Unfair Trade Practices Laws

Many states have adopted **unfair trade practices laws** that specify certain prohibited business practices. These laws are not specifically limited to the activities of insurance producers; underwriters, claim representatives, and

Unfair trade practices law
State law that specifies certain prohibited business practices.

others could also be guilty of misconduct in these areas. Although they vary by state, these laws typically prohibit various unfair trade practices, such as the following:

- Misrepresentation and false advertising
- Tie-in sales
- Rebating
- Other deceptive practices

Misrepresentation and False Advertising

It is an unfair trade practice for insurance agents or other insurance personnel to make, issue, or circulate information that does any of the following:

- Misrepresents the benefits, advantages, conditions, or terms of any insurance policy
- Misrepresents the dividends to be received on any insurance policy
- Makes false or misleading statements about dividends previously paid on any insurance policy
- Uses a name or title of insurance policies that misrepresents the true nature of the policies

It is also considered an unfair trade practice to make untrue, deceptive, or misleading advertisements, announcements, or statements about insurance or about any person in the insurance business.

Tie-In Sales

It is an unfair trade practice for a producer to require that the purchase of insurance be "tied" to some other sale or financial arrangement—a practice referred to as a tie-in sale. It is also an unfair trade practice for a lender to require that a borrower purchase insurance from the lender or from any insurer or producer recommended by the lender. Each transaction must stand on its own. For example, assume that Richard, a salesman with a car dealership, also holds an insurance agent's license with XYZ Insurer. If Julia purchases a car from Richard, Richard cannot require that Julia purchase insurance on the car from XYZ Insurer. Julia is free to purchase insurance from any company or agency she chooses. If Richard told Julia that the loan on her new car would be denied unless she purchases a policy from XYZ, Richard would be guilty of an unfair trade practice because he would be requiring a tie-in sale—tying the sale of insurance to the financing of the car.

Rebating
A practice, prohibited in most states, of offering a cash payment or something of value to an applicant as an inducement to buy or maintain insurance.

Rebating

The prohibition of **rebating** means that producers are not allowed to pay a portion of the premium or give any commission to a policyholder. This prohibition also means that producers are not permitted to offer to do other business with the policyholder in exchange for the purchase of a policy.

Most states have enacted anti-rebating laws. The rationale behind anti-rebating laws is that the practice is unfair to customers who do not get a rebate. Further, some feel that rebating undermines the principles of insurance pricing regulations that most states enforce. Insurance regulators in many states pay close attention to rates not only to make sure that the insurance customer is not overcharged, but also to make sure that rates are adequate to protect the insurer from financial failure. Some feel that rebating allows insurance customers to pay a rate that is below that needed to safely maintain the insurer's solvency.

However, rebating is permitted in at least one state, California, under limited circumstances. Proposition 103, which was passed by California voters in 1988, repealed the law that prohibited insurance agents from rebating part of their commission to clients. As a result, rebates may now be made to California insureds, unless specifically prohibited by sections of the state's Insurance Code. California's civil rights laws impose further restrictions by prohibiting insurance producers from offering rebates, or varying the size of rebates, if the practice unfairly discriminates among individuals.

Opponents of anti-rebating laws in other states continue to argue that such laws inhibit competition in the insurance marketplace. These laws may be challenged further in the future.

Other Deceptive Practices

Unfair trade practices laws also prohibit other practices of insurers that are deceptive or unfair to applicants and insureds. For example, these laws prohibit an insurer and its producers from making false statements about the financial condition of another insurer. For example, an agent for one insurer cannot mislead his client by saying that another insurer has a poor financial rating in the hope of discouraging the client from purchasing insurance from the competing insurer.

It is also an unfair trade practice to put false information on an insurance application to earn a commission from the insurance sale. Occasionally, some information may cause the insurer to reject the application, which would deny the producer a commission. Producers are required to be honest in the information they enter on application forms. Both insurers and policyholders count on insurance transactions being conducted in utmost good faith.

SUMMARY

Insurance marketing is the process of identifying potential customers and then creating, promoting, selling, and delivering the insurance products and services they need. Although there are many aspects of this process, the initial contact between an insurer and its policyholders is typically through an agent or another type of producer. Therefore, a major marketing concern is the insurer's relationship with its producers.

The legal relationship of agency empowers the insurance producer—the agent—to act on behalf of the insurer—the principal. Normally, insurers make very specific agency contracts with their producers. An agent owes specific duties, such as loyalty and obedience, to the principal in acting for the principal's benefit; and the principal owes certain duties to the agent, such as compensation for services. The principal is legally bound by any acts of the agent that are within the agent's authority. The agent's authority includes the express authority stated in the agency contract, the implied authority that is not expressly granted, and the apparent authority a third party may reasonably expect the agent to have.

The specific relationship an insurer has with its producers reflects the type of marketing system the insurer uses to sell its products. Insurance marketing systems include the independent agency system, the exclusive agency system, and the direct writing system. Independent agents are in business for themselves, they usually represent several different insurers, and they own their expiration lists. Exclusive agents represent only one insurer and adhere to the insurer's programs and procedures, even though they are also in business for themselves. The sales representatives of direct writing insurers are the insurers' own employees. Beyond these three marketing systems, insurers and producers also use alternative distribution channels, including direct response, Internet, call centers, group marketing, and financial institutions.

The compensation of insurance producers includes commissions and salaries. The sales commissions paid to agents and brokers are a percentage of the insurance premiums they produce. Sales commissions are often supplemented by contingent commissions, which reflect the volume and profitability of that business for the insurer. The sales representatives of direct writing insurers receive a salary, which may be supplemented by a bonus reflecting sales performance.

Advertising, another aspect of insurance marketing, reflects the marketing system used. Insurers relying on independent agents usually advertise to promote the company image, while independent agents try to attract local customers to their offices. Joint advertising campaigns are often used to serve the needs of both the agent and the insurer. Exclusive agency companies tend to emphasize both the company name and the local service. Direct writing insurers advertise primarily to promote the company's name and products with the public. Insurers using alternative distribution channels rely heavily on advertising to bring customers to them.

An insurer's marketing management activities include producer supervision, producer motivation, and product management and development. Insurers motivate producers through personal contact and through incentive programs developed in the home office. Through product management and development activities, insurers provide producers with the products needed to produce business for the insurer.

State regulators oversee the marketing activities of insurers and their producers. Insurance producers must meet specific requirements to obtain and maintain a license in the state or states in which they transact business. States prohibit unfair trade practices such as misrepresentation and false advertising, tie-in sales, rebating, and other deceptive practices.

Chapter 5

Direct

Direct Your Learning

Underwriting

After learning the content of this chapter and completing the corresponding course guide assignment, you should be able to:

- Describe the purpose of underwriting and an insurer's major underwriting activities to achieve that purpose.

- Explain how underwriters protect an insurer's available capacity.

- Explain which type of insurance rates would be more appropriate in a given situation:

  - Class rates

  - Individual rates

- Describe the responsibilities of underwriting management.

- Describe the steps in the underwriting process that an underwriter follows in selecting policyholders.

- Describe information sources that underwriters use in the underwriting process.

- Describe four categories of hazards that underwriters must evaluate in reviewing an application for insurance.

- Describe an underwriter's options when evaluating an application for insurance.

- Explain how states regulate underwriting activities through restrictions on unfair discrimination, cancellation, and nonrenewal.

- Define or describe each of the Key Words and Phrases for this chapter.

Develop Your Perspective

What are the main topics covered in the chapter?

Within an insurer, underwriters have responsibility for establishing products, pricing those products, and selecting customers to whom the products will be sold. This chapter describes the processes underwriters apply in performing these functions.

For each of the underwriting functions, describe the tasks required.

- When are class rates and individual rates applied?
- How are policyholders selected among applicants?

Why is it important to learn about these topics?

An insurer's profitability often relies on the success of the underwriting department in performing its functions. However, underwriters have limited resources available for their use in policyholder selection, and they are limited in their activities by regulatory restrictions.

Examine the restrictions placed on underwriters performing policyholder selection.

- How do underwriting limitations restrict policyholder selection activity?
- How do regulatory limitations also protect policyholders?

How can you use what you will learn?

Analyze why some insurers select limited products, markets, or geographic areas in which they offer products.

- How would the limitation of products offered by an insurer make the underwriting process easier?
- How would a company benefit by offering insurance policies only in a limited geographic area?

Chapter 5
Underwriting

Underwriting is the process of selecting insureds, pricing coverage, determining insurance policy terms and conditions, and then monitoring the underwriting decisions made. To a large extent, an insurer's success in achieving its goals depends on the effectiveness of its underwriting.

Insurers themselves, rather than their employees, are sometimes called underwriters. However, the term **underwriter** is usually reserved for an insurer employee who evaluates applicants for insurance, selects those that are acceptable to the insurer, prices coverage, and determines policy terms and conditions.

UNDERWRITING ACTIVITIES

Underwriting consists of the following activities:

- Selecting insureds
- Pricing coverage
- Determining policy terms and conditions
- Monitoring underwriting decisions

The first three activities are not performed in sequence but occur simultaneously. The last activity, monitoring underwriting decisions, is ongoing. Underwriters try to select insureds to whom the insurer can offer insurance coverage under reasonable conditions. Of course, the price charged for coverage must be high enough to enable the insurer to pay claims and to provide the insurer with a reasonable profit.

Selecting Insureds

Insurers must carefully screen applicants to determine which ones to insure. If insurers do not properly select policyholders and price coverages, some insureds might be able to purchase insurance at prices that do not adequately reflect their loss exposures. Underwriters, producers, and underwriting managers all participate in selecting policyholders.

Underwriting
The process of selecting insureds, pricing coverage, determining insurance policy terms and conditions, and then monitoring the underwriting decisions made.

Underwriter
An insurer employee who evaluates applicants for insurance, selects those that are acceptable to the insurer, prices coverage, and determines policy terms and conditions.

Most insurers receive more insurance applications than they accept. An insurer cannot accept all applicants for the following two basic reasons:

1. The insurer can succeed only if it selects applicants who, as a group, present loss exposures that are proportionate to the premiums that will be collected. In other words, insurers try to avoid adverse selection.
2. An insurer's ability to provide insurance is limited by its capacity to write new policies.

Adverse Selection Considerations

Adverse selection

A situation that occurs because people with the greatest probability of loss are the ones most likely to purchase insurance.

Insurers expect to pay claims. Without claims, insurance would be unnecessary. However, insurers try to select applicants who are not likely to have covered losses greater than the insurer anticipated in its insurance rates. On the other hand, people with the greatest probability of loss are often more likely to purchase insurance, a situation called **adverse selection**. Poor underwriting results might occur if too many of the applicants accepted for insurance are those most likely to incur serious losses. Underwriters minimize adverse selection by screening applicants to avoid those who present loss potentials not adequately reflected in the insurance rates.

An extreme example of adverse selection involves a burning building. No insurer would knowingly write fire insurance to cover a building that is already burning, but the owner of an uninsured building that is on fire would probably be glad to purchase fire insurance on the building.

Adverse selection is particularly prevalent with some kinds of insurance. For example, owners of property next to a river are more likely to purchase flood insurance than are those who own property on a hilltop with no flood exposure.

Capacity Considerations

Capacity

The amount of business an insurer is able to write, usually based on a comparison of the insurer's written premiums to its policyholders' surplus.

Capacity refers to the amount of business an insurer is able to write and is often measured by comparing the insurer's written premiums to its policy-holders' surplus (the insurer's total admitted assets minus its total liabilities). An insurer must have adequate policyholders' surplus to increase the volume of insurance it writes.

Insurers often impose voluntary capacity constraints that are more conservative than those used by regulators. This restriction on capacity provides a cushion to allow for variability in the insurer's underwriting and investment results.

An insurer's capacity limits its ability to write new business. Selling new policies creates insurer expenses, such as producers' commissions, that reduce the policyholders' surplus in the short term. Reduced policyholders' surplus leads to reduced capacity. Yet, in the long term, if the new policies generate premiums that exceed losses and expenses, the new policies will increase the policyholders' surplus. Barring serious underwriting or investment losses, an insurer can increase its capacity through steady, orderly growth in sales of policies that contribute to the insurer's profits. Planned growth is generally one of the goals of an insurer.

Insurers attempt to protect their available capacity in the following three primary ways:

1. By maintaining a spread of risk
2. By optimizing use of available resources
3. By securing reinsurance

The first way insurers protect their available capacity is by maintaining a spread of risk. Because every insurer has limited capacity, insurers must allocate their available capacity. Insurers prefer to spread their risk among various types of insurance and different geographic areas. Consequently, insurers reduce the chances that overall underwriting results will be adversely affected by a large number of losses in one type of insurance or one territory. For example, a tornado might require an insurer to pay extensive property claims in one community, but these claims would be balanced against premiums from other communities that do not experience a tornado in the same year, as well as premiums from other types of insurance the insurer writes.

Insurers also allocate capacity by setting limitations on the amount of insurance they write for any one insured. Generally, limitations are more restrictive for some types of business than for others, depending on the exposures presented. For example, an insurer might place a lower limit on the maximum amount of fire insurance it will provide on a rural home with no fire hydrants nearby and no fire department within ten miles than on a home located within a city with excellent public fire protection.

The second way insurers protect their capacity is by optimizing the use of available resources. In addition to its financial resources, every insurer depends on other resources. Among these are physical resources, which include offices and equipment, and human resources, which include underwriters, claim representatives, producers, and service personnel.

Underwriting and servicing some kinds of insurance require special skills or experience. Consequently, some insurers do not offer those types of insurance. For example, an insurer might avoid applications for insurance on farms if it does not have personnel experienced in handling farm business. Without appropriate underwriting expertise, an insurer will be unable to recognize unusual loss exposures in a farm operation and price coverage accordingly. Without experienced farm claim representatives, it can be very difficult and expensive to settle such claims. Conversely, another insurer might have personnel capable of handling farm business, and that insurer might want to use its available capacity to increase the amount of insurance it writes for farmers.

The third way insurers protect their available capacity is by securing reinsurance. In reinsurance, the reinsurer receives a portion of the premiums from the primary insurer's policies and assumes some of the financial consequences of loss exposures on those policies. The primary insurer usually retains a portion of the premiums, pays the insured losses, and is then reimbursed by the reinsurer for the portion of losses for which the reinsurer is contractually responsible. If reinsurance is readily available, insurers can increase the number of new policies they write by transferring some of the premium and financial consequences of loss exposures to reinsurers. Thus, securing reinsurance can affect an insurer's capacity to write business.

Pricing Coverage

The underwriting pricing goal is to charge a premium that is commensurate with the loss exposure. In other words, each insured's premium should be set at a level that is adequate to enable the total premiums paid by a large group of similar insureds to pay the losses and expenses of that group and to allow the insurer to achieve a reasonable profit. Basically, pricing insurance involves classifying the applicant by category of loss exposure and then determining a premium by applying an appropriate rate to the applicant's exposure units.

Premium Determination

As discussed in previous chapters, the rate is the price of insurance charged per exposure unit, and an exposure unit is a unit measure of loss potential used in rating insurance. The exposure unit used depends on the type of insurance, as follows:

Type of Insurance	Exposure Unit
Workers' compensation	Each $100 of payroll
Property insurance	Each $100 of insurance
Auto liability insurance	Each car month insured (one car insured for one year would be 12 exposure units)

The premium is determined by multiplying the rate by the number of exposure units. For example, the premium for property insurance with a limit of $250,000 at a rate of $0.40 per $100 of insurance is $1,000, calculated as follows:

$$\text{Premium} = \frac{\$250,000}{\$100} = 2,500 \text{ units} \times \$0.40 \text{ per unit} = \$1,000.$$

The premium is the total amount of money an insured pays the insurer for a particular policy or coverage for a stated period. For example, an insurer may charge a premium of $750 to provide a one-year property insurance policy with a $500 deductible for a $200,000 brick home located in Anytown, U.S.A. The same insurer may charge $750 to provide identical coverage on a $160,000 brick home located five miles outside Anytown. While the total premium would be the same in both cases, the rate per $100 of insurance is different, probably reflecting a difference in fire protection in the two locations.

Of course, accurately predicting what losses a particular insured will have during a given policy period is difficult. An excellent driver may have several auto accidents in a year because of a streak of bad luck. A careless driver may get through the same year without any accidents. However, according to the law of large numbers, prediction becomes more accurate as the number of similar insureds increases. Although one excellent driver may have a worse year than one careless driver, it is highly unlikely that a group of one hundred cautious drivers will have more insured losses than a group of one hundred careless drivers. Each group of drivers should be charged a premium commensurate with their loss exposure. Therefore, drivers with good driving records are generally charged less than those with poor driving records.

In determining the appropriate premium to charge for coverage, insurers use either class rates or individual rates, which are discussed next.

Class Rates

Class rates are common in property and liability insurance. Personal insurance and commercial insurance often involve large numbers of insureds with similar loss exposures grouped into rating classes. Each insured in a given rating class has approximately the same exposures to loss and would therefore be charged approximately the same rate for insurance coverage. **Class rates** are sometimes called **manual rates** because they have traditionally been published in rating manuals—loose-leaf binders used by underwriters, raters, and producers in pricing individual policies. Most insurers have replaced rating manuals with computerized rating systems based on class rates formerly published in rating manuals. The rating of most personal insurance and a growing amount of commercial insurance is computerized. Class rates are based on the loss statistics of the large number of insureds that constitute a rating class. In many different situations, the use of class rates provides a uniform approach to pricing coverage for similar insureds.

Class rate, or manual rate
A type of insurance rate that applies to all insureds in the same rating category or rating class.

Many insureds within a rating class have loss characteristics that may not be fully reflected in class rates. **Merit rating plans** modify class rates to reflect these loss characteristics. A merit rating plan serves the following two purposes:

Merit rating plan
A rating plan that modifies class rates to reflect loss characteristics of a particular insured.

1. It enables the insurer to fine-tune the class rate to reflect certain identifiable characteristics of a given insured.
2. It encourages loss control activity by rewarding safety-conscious insureds with a lower rate than that for those who do not practice loss control.

The following examples illustrate the use of merit rating plans:

*   *Safe driver insurance plans.* In personal auto insurance, insurers use safe driver insurance plans (rating plans in which premiums are based on the insured's driving record) to lower the premiums for drivers with a history of accident-free driving and no major traffic convictions.
*   *Premium discounts.* In homeowners insurance, insurers typically provide premium discounts for insureds whose homes have fire alarms or burglar alarms.
*   *Experience rating.* In commercial insurance, insurers often use experience rating. In this type of rating, premiums are increased for insureds whose loss experience has been worse than average, and premiums are decreased for insureds whose loss experience has been better than average.

- *Schedule rating.* In commercial insurance, schedule rating allows an underwriter to consult a schedule of credits or debits based on criteria that are not reflected in the class rate, and then modify the rate by the applicable credits. An example of such a characteristic is the attitude of the insured's management toward loss control. If the insured's management encourages loss control activities, the insurer could apply a schedule credit to the property insurance rate. Schedule debits or credits are expressed as percentage increases or decreases from the class rate.

Individual Rates

Individual rate, or **specific rate**
A type of insurance rate that reflects the unique characteristics of an insured or the insured's property.

Class rates are not suitable for some types of insurance. For example, an underwriter would not be able to use a rating manual or rating system to determine the rate for fire insurance on a factory building that has an unusual construction and is occupied for a unique purpose. An individual rate, or a specific rate, would be used in such a situation, and it is developed only after a detailed inspection of the structure and its contents. Each **individual rate** reflects the building's unique characteristics, such as its construction (for example, brick or frame), its occupancy (for example, warehouse or manufacturing), public and private fire protection (such as distance to the fire department and existence of a sprinkler system), and external exposures (for example, proximity to other buildings or to brush that could spread a fire to the building).

Judgment rate
A type of individual rate that is used to develop a premium for a unique exposure for which there is no established rate.

The pricing of insurance coverage for one-of-a-kind exposures must often be based primarily on an underwriter's experience and judgment. An underwriter may examine rates for comparable exposures to determine appropriate rates before arriving at the premium that will actually be charged for the unique exposure. A **judgment rate**, which is a type of individual rate, is not arbitrary but is based on the underwriter's experience in covering unique exposures for which there is no established rate. Judgment rating is often used in rating ocean marine insurance covering many types of cargo being transported to ports worldwide.

Determining Policy Terms and Conditions

Selection and pricing are intertwined with a third underwriting activity—determining policy terms and conditions. The insurer must decide exactly what types of coverage it will provide to each applicant and then charge a premium appropriate to that coverage.

Standard form
A policy form that contains standard insurance wording; it is used by insurers that subscribe to the services of insurance advisory organizations.

In addition to developing loss costs, insurance advisory organizations develop policy forms using standard insurance wording. These policy forms, called **standard forms**, can be used by insurers that subscribe to (pay for) the services of the advisory organization. Because many insurers use standard forms, the policy issued by one insurer is often identical to the policy that would be issued by a competing insurer.

For each type of insurance it handles, an insurer needs to decide whether to use standard forms developed by the advisory organizations or to develop its own policy language, possibly providing coverages that differ in some ways from coverages provided by other insurers. Some types of insurance, such as professional liability insurance, have no standard form because many coverage differences exist among policies.

When advisory organizations develop insurance policies, they also develop rules specifying what kinds of insureds will be eligible for certain policies. Insurers need to decide whether they will adhere to these rules or modify them.

Monitoring Underwriting Decisions

Underwriters periodically monitor the **hazards** (conditions that increase the frequency or severity of a loss), loss experience, and other conditions of specific insureds for significant changes. Because underwriting decisions involve an assessment of loss potential, hazards and other conditions must be reviewed periodically.

Hazard
A condition that increases the frequency or severity of a loss.

If an underwriter made loss control recommendations (such as installing fire extinguishers) to a particular insured, follow-up is necessary to ensure that the insured has implemented the recommendations. An increase in hazards might change an acceptable insured into an unacceptable one for the coverage and premium charged. For example, if an insured converts a garage into a laboratory for producing toxic chemicals, the coverage and premium would have to be changed to reflect the increase in hazard, or continued coverage might be denied. Monitoring helps underwriters discover such changes and alter coverage and premium as necessary.

Monitoring also applies to underwriting decisions on an entire book of business. A **book of business**, or a **portfolio**, is a group of policies with a common characteristic, such as territory or type of coverage. A book of business can also refer to all policies written by a particular insurer or agency.

Book of business, or portfolio
A group of policies with a common characteristic, such as territory or type of coverage. A book of business can also refer to all policies written by a particular insurer or agency.

Underwriters might also be responsible for maintaining the profitability of a book of business by achieving written premium and loss ratio goals for that book. This is especially true for insurers that underwrite policies, such as personal auto or homeowners applications, through the use of computerized systems. Such systems screen the applications using a scoring system that measures the acceptability of the loss exposures. Underwriters then monitor the results for the entire book of business to ensure that the screening system is making selections that achieve the goals established for the book of business. An underwriter can make recommendations to adjust the screening to achieve the desired results.

UNDERWRITING MANAGEMENT

An insurer's underwriting management has many responsibilities, including the following:

- Participating in the insurer's overall management
- Arranging reinsurance
- Delegating underwriting authority
- Developing and enforcing underwriting guidelines
- Monitoring underwriting results

Only by constantly adjusting to a changing environment can an insurer meet its goals. Insurers change underwriting rules and standards as business conditions change. Underwriting management has the responsibility for implementing these changes.

Participating in Insurer Management

An insurer's senior management team generally includes officers responsible for marketing, product development, claims, finance, actuarial services, and other functions, as well as underwriting. The head of an insurer's underwriting department participates with other members of the insurer's management team in making broad business decisions about the insurer's goals, including annual written premium and loss ratio goals, and plans to meet those goals. Decisions at this level might determine what type of marketing system will be used, where offices will be located, what emphasis will be placed on personal and commercial insurance, and so forth. Given senior management consensus on the insurer's broad goals and how its capacity should be allocated, underwriting management must decide how underwriting activities can contribute to these goals. An insurer's underwriting management must then develop underwriting goals that complement or support the company's overall goals.

Arranging Reinsurance

Another aspect of underwriting management is arranging reinsurance. The two broad categories of reinsurance are treaty reinsurance and facultative reinsurance.

Treaty reinsurance
An arrangement whereby a reinsurer agrees to automatically reinsure a portion of all eligible insurance of the primary insurer.

Treaty reinsurance is an arrangement whereby a reinsurer agrees to automatically reinsure a portion of all eligible insurance of the primary insurer. The treaty is a contract that defines the eligible insurance. The primary insurer is required to reinsure, and the reinsurer must accept, all business covered by the treaty. Policies are not selected individually.

Primary insurers and reinsurers periodically renegotiate the reinsurance treaty. Before entering into a treaty and agreeing on pricing, the reinsurer carefully evaluates the primary insurer's past performance and expected future underwriting results. Because the treaty is based on all eligible insurance written by the primary insurer, the reinsurer is more concerned with the group of insureds as a whole than with the individual accounts that compose the group.

Facultative reinsurance in an arrangement whereby the primary insurer chooses which policies to submit to the reinsurer and the reinsurer can accept or reject any policies submitted. It is not automatic but involves a separate transaction for each reinsured policy. That is, the reinsurer evaluates each policy it is asked to reinsure. Underwriters for the primary insurer decide which policies to submit for reinsurance, and underwriters for the reinsurer decide which policies to reinsure. Pricing, terms, and conditions of each policy are individually negotiated.

Facultative reinsurance
An arrangement whereby the primary insurer chooses which policies to submit to the reinsurer and the reinsurer can accept or reject any policies submitted.

Delegating Underwriting Authority

Underwriting management focuses on the entire group of insureds while underwriters who usually work in field offices must deal with individual applications. Underwriting management must determine how much underwriting authority to grant to those underwriters. **Underwriting authority** establishes the types of decisions an underwriter can make without needing approval from someone at a higher level. The amount of authority given to each underwriter usually reflects the underwriter's experience, responsibilities, and the types of insurance handled.

Underwriting authority
The scope of decisions that an underwriter can make without receiving approval from someone at a higher level.

With some insurers, underwriting authority is highly decentralized; that is, underwriting management delegates extensive underwriting authority to personnel in the field offices. Other insurers are highly centralized, with many or all final underwriting decisions being made in the home office. For insurers with centralized underwriting authority, field offices serve as a point of contact where insurer personnel gather information, accept applications, and provide policyholder services. Many insurers are neither completely centralized nor completely decentralized; these insurers strive to maintain a balance between the underwriting authority given to underwriters in field offices and the underwriting authority reserved for home office underwriters.

Many insurers also grant some underwriting authority to the agents who represent the company. Called front-line underwriters, these agents make the initial underwriting decision about applications and then forward those applications that meet underwriting guidelines to the company underwriter. Agents usually have the authority to accept applications and bind coverage for the insurer if the applicant clearly meets the guidelines and if the limit of insurance is within a predetermined amount. The extent of the authority granted to an agent generally depends on the agent's premium volume and loss experience with the insurer.

Developing and Enforcing Underwriting Guidelines

Underwriting management develops the guidelines that underwriters use in the underwriting process. Companywide rules guide underwriters toward consistent decisions that enable the insurer to meet its overall underwriting goals.

Underwriting guidelines and bulletins explain how underwriters should approach each application. The guidelines list the factors that should be considered by the underwriter for each type of insurance, the desirable and undesirable characteristics of applicants relative to those factors, and the insurer's overall attitude toward applicants that exhibit those characteristics. Based on the guidelines, underwriters evaluate the applications they receive, decide how to handle the applications, and act on those decisions.

Underwriting management activity does not end with the development of underwriting guidelines. The guidelines must be clearly communicated to all underwriters, which may require training programs. In addition, underwriting management must prepare and distribute bulletins or guideline revisions whenever changes are made.

Monitoring Underwriting Results

Underwriting audit
A process in which members of the home office underwriting department examine files to see whether underwriters are following underwriting guidelines.

Underwriting management must also monitor the underwriting results to see whether underwriting guidelines have had the desired effect. Monitoring includes steps to ensure that underwriters are following underwriting guidelines and that underwriting goals are being met. If the guidelines are not followed, there is no evidence about whether they are effective. Periodically, underwriting management sends underwriting audit teams to visit field offices to examine underwriting files, a process called an **underwriting audit**. If the audit reveals that guidelines are being followed, it is then necessary to determine whether they are having the desired results. For example, assume an insurer has broadened its homeowners insurance policies by adding extra coverages, such as an additional theft limit on jewelry, in an attempt to attract new customers. Monitoring would reveal the extent to which insured losses increase because of the coverage addition, whether sales have increased, and whether revenues from the increased sales more than offset the costs of claims.

Many factors affect an insurer's success. Constant monitoring of underwriting results enables underwriting management to adjust underwriting guidelines to accommodate changing conditions, goals, and results.

THE UNDERWRITING PROCESS

An underwriting decision must be made on every new insurance application, as well as on renewal policies and on many policy changes, such as adding a car or increasing policy limits. The underwriting process consists of the following four steps:

1. Gathering underwriting information
2. Making the underwriting decision
3. Implementing the underwriting decision
4. Monitoring the underwriting decision

Traditionally, underwriting was a nonautomated process that depended on human judgment. Increasingly, however, portions of the underwriting process, particularly in personal insurance, are computerized. Computerized underwriting processes use software that emulates the steps an underwriter would take. Computerized underwriting is most common with high-volume types of insurance such as personal auto or homeowners insurance. In this type of underwriting, the computer screens applications and accepts those that clearly meet all criteria and rejects those that clearly do not. Questionable applications are referred to an underwriter for evaluation.

Some insurers now use **expert systems**, also known as **knowledge-based systems**, to assist underwriters in the underwriting process. These computerized systems are programmed to emulate the underwriting decision-making process as it would be performed by "expert" (usually senior) underwriters. The expert system asks for the information necessary to make an underwriting decision, thereby ensuring that no information is overlooked. Although expert underwriting systems are capable of making an underwriting decision (usually by assigning a grade on a scale of one to ten or one to one hundred), most are used to supplement an underwriter's decision making, not to replace the underwriter.

Inexperienced underwriters can use the expert system to determine why a certain grade was assigned. The ability of the expert system to interact with the underwriter also makes the system an excellent training tool.

Expert systems, or **knowledge-based systems** Computer software programs that supplement the underwriting decision-making process. These systems ask for the information necessary to make an underwriting decision, ensuring that no information is overlooked.

Gathering Underwriting Information

Underwriters base their decisions about individual applications on a combination of information and judgment. To make a decision, underwriters need adequate information to analyze the potential losses each applicant represents. Underwriters derive information from several sources, including the following:

- *Producers.* In addition to completing and submitting applications, producers might supply additional information not included on applications, such as a personal evaluation of the applicant.

- *Consumer investigation reports.* Various independent reporting services investigate and provide background information on prospective insureds. Insurance applications generally inform the applicant that he or she may be investigated.

- *Government records.* Motor vehicle records (MVRs) are commonly used in underwriting auto insurance. Underwriters can also seek underwriting information in court records and public information relating to property ownership.

- *Financial rating services.* Firms such as Dun & Bradstreet (D&B) and Standard & Poor's provide data on the credit rating and financial stability of specific businesses. In personal insurance, insurance credit reports are often used to examine an individual's financial history. Some insurers use insurance scoring, which is a statistical analysis of credit report information that identifies the relative likelihood of an insurance loss based on the actual loss experience of individuals with similar financial patterns.

- *Inspection reports.* Many insurers employ loss control representatives whose duties include inspecting the premises and operations of insurance applicants and preparing reports for underwriters.

- *Field marketing personnel.* Many insurers have marketing representatives or other employees who spend much of their time in the field working with producers. These field personnel can often provide additional insights regarding an applicant based on personal observations.

- *Claim files.* After a policy has been issued, the insured may have claims. Significant information about the insured may thus appear in the insurer's claim files, and additional information may be available from the claim representatives who handled the claims.

- *Production records.* In evaluating applications, underwriters generally consider the track record of the producer who submits the application. If the producer has consistently generated profitable business, the underwriter may be willing to accept an applicant that may not meet all of the underwriting standards.

- *Premium audit reports.* Rates for some kinds of commercial insurance are applied to estimated payroll, sales, or some other exposure unit whose final measure is not determined until the end of the policy year. Insurers employ premium auditors to obtain the final figures from insureds' accounting records to compute the final premium on such policies. In addition to providing this exact information, a premium auditor can provide other information about an insured, especially because the premium auditor has probably visited the insured's premises and seen the operations.

- *Applicant's or insured's records.* Underwriters can sometimes obtain information from the applicant's or insured's records, including copies of appraisals of jewelry (for valuation purposes) and bills of sale. For businesses, the annual report, which describes the firm's operations and future plans and includes its financial statements (balance sheet and income statement), provides much useful underwriting information. Most businesses now have Web sites that could also be a source of valuable information to an underwriter.

Making the Underwriting Decision

As discussed earlier in this chapter, conditions that increase the frequency or severity of a loss are called hazards. Examples of hazards include an untrained driver in regard to auto insurance and the poor maintenance of fire extinguishers in regard to insurance on a building. Once the underwriter has gathered the necessary information, he or she must analyze the information to determine what hazards the applicant presents. To make an underwriting decision, the underwriter must then evaluate underwriting options and choose the best one.

Analyzing Hazards

An applicant with hazards that are greater than normal may not be acceptable as an insured, unless the hazards can be eliminated, controlled, or offset by a substantially increased premium. In contrast, an applicant presenting normal or less-than-normal hazards is generally desirable from an underwriting standpoint. An underwriter must evaluate the following four categories of hazards:

1. Moral hazards
2. Attitudinal (morale) hazards
3. Physical hazards
4. Legal hazards

Moral hazards are conditions that may lead a person to intentionally cause or exaggerate a loss. The threat from a moral hazard is the possibility that the insured may intentionally cause a loss or file a false claim. For example, an insured may intentionally cause a fire or an auto accident to collect a claim payment on a building or car and unjustly enrich himself or herself. A moral hazard may be indicated by a weak financial condition (which could be detected in a financial report) or questionable moral character (which could be indicated by a police record).

One of the characteristics of an ideally insurable loss exposure is that losses be accidental. Insurance is intended to deal with losses that are unexpected from the insured's standpoint; it is not feasible to insure against events within the insured's control. The prudent underwriter rejects applicants presenting a significant moral hazard.

Attitudinal hazards, also known as **morale hazards**, involve carelessness about, or indifference to, potential loss on the part of an insured or applicant. Such hazards are more subtle and thus more difficult to detect than are moral hazards. A particularly dangerous attitudinal hazard is an insured's attitude that "I don't need to be careful because I have insurance." Evidence of an attitudinal hazard may be found in personality traits (some people are naturally careless and therefore accident-prone regardless of insurance), poor management (tolerance of dangerous conditions and practices), or past loss experience (a history of losses caused by carelessness).

Moral hazards and morale hazards are often confused, which is why the term "attitudinal" is more often used to refer to morale hazards. Someone who represents a moral hazard may, for example, set a fire to collect an insurance settlement. Someone who represents a morale (attitudinal) hazard may be careless in allowing smoking in hazardous areas or permit combustible supplies to be piled in a furnace room.

In evaluating an application for property insurance on a building, the underwriter considers possible physical hazards, such as those inherent in the building's construction, occupancy, protection, and external exposures.

Moral hazard
A condition that may lead a person to intentionally cause or exaggerate a loss.

Attitudinal hazard, or **morale hazard**
A hazard that involves carelessness about, or indifference to, potential loss on the part of an insured or applicant.

Physical hazard
A tangible characteristic of property, persons, or operations that tends to increase the frequency or severity of loss.

Legal hazard
A characteristic of the legal or regulatory environment that hampers an insurer's ability to collect a premium commensurate with the exposure to loss.

Physical hazards are tangible characteristics of property, persons, or operations that tend to increase frequency or severity of loss. An office building located next to a restaurant without adequate fire protection clearly represents a greater fire hazard than an office building located next to a retail store with excellent fire protection.

Legal hazards are characteristics of the legal or regulatory environment that hamper an insurer's ability to collect a premium commensurate with the exposure to loss. Hazards in the legal environment might include court decisions that interpret policy language in a way unfavorable to insurers. For example, commercial liability policies at one time provided coverage for pollution losses that were sudden or accidental, but court decisions applied coverage in cases in which insurers thought the pollution was clearly not sudden or accidental but gradual. Because of this legal hazard (courts mandating coverage broader than insurers intended), insurers ceased to provide pollution liability coverage in many cases or started charging an additional premium for pollution liability coverage.

The regulatory environment presents legal hazards when it forces underwriters to charge premiums that are too low for the exposures or to provide coverages that are too broad. Legal hazards are also presented when regulatory authorities unduly restrict insurers' ability to cancel or nonrenew policies.

Evaluating Underwriting Options

In evaluating each application, an underwriter has the following three options:

1. Accept the application without modification
2. Reject the application
3. Accept the application with modification

The application may be so desirable that the underwriter will accept it with no changes. Conversely, the application may be so undesirable that the underwriter will reject it. The third option requires the greatest amount of underwriting creativity. Often an applicant that is not acceptable for the insurance originally requested can become acceptable if some aspect of coverage is changed or if methods to reduce the frequency or severity of loss are implemented. Generally, the underwriter, producer, and applicant all want the insurance policy to be issued. If the particular coverage requested cannot be provided, the underwriter might be able to offer an alternative that satisfies all parties.

Frequently, a policy can be issued if the applicant agrees to implement loss control measures. For example, an underwriter may agree to write property insurance for the owner of a particular bookstore, provided the store owner installs and maintains an appropriate fire alarm system.

Another possibility may be to modify the rate charged for the coverage. A producer may have quoted auto insurance using the insurer's preferred risk rate, a lower rate offered to substantially better-than-average applicants. The underwriter may determine that the applicant does not qualify as a preferred risk but would be acceptable for coverage at standard class rates.

Coverage may also be modified—that is, the underwriter may offer terms and conditions that are somewhat different from those that the applicant has requested. For example, an underwriter may be asked to provide an auto policy, including coverage with a $100 deductible for an applicant who has had several claims for windshield damage. The applicant may be a preferred risk except for this one coverage. The underwriter could offer the desired coverage with a $500 deductible and thus avoid rejecting the applicant. This modification would turn a standard risk into a preferred risk. If the applicant agrees, the underwriter has succeeded in making an application acceptable through coverage modification.

Facultative reinsurance is a common underwriting alternative in cases in which an otherwise acceptable application exceeds the limit in the underwriting guidelines. For example, suppose an insurer is asked to provide $10 million of property insurance on a building, but the insurer's acceptable limit on a single building is $500,000. After checking with underwriting management, an underwriter may determine that facultative reinsurance could be obtained to handle the remaining $9.5 million of coverage. By arranging reinsurance in the amount of $9.5 million, the underwriter can accept the application for the limit of $10 million requested by the applicant.

After carefully analyzing hazards and underwriting options, the best underwriting decision for a particular application usually becomes obvious. Each alternative, such as following loss control recommendations or accepting modified coverage, requires the agreement of the applicant and may involve further negotiation. In such situations, the underwriter normally contacts the producer to negotiate the modified terms, price, or conditions with the applicant.

Implementing the Underwriting Decision

If the underwriting decision is within the underwriter's authority and consistent with underwriting guidelines, the underwriter can approve the policy and submit the file for processing and policy issuance. This approach is typical with routine applications for auto insurance, homeowners insurance, and small commercial accounts. In more complex cases, the insurer must communicate the underwriter's decision to the producer, along with a quote showing the premium to be charged and the terms and conditions to be offered. After the producer discusses this information with the applicant, and possibly compares it with quotes from other insurers, the underwriter may be asked to issue the policy or may learn that the applicant has decided to do business with another insurer.

To accept an application for coverage exceeding the underwriter's authority, an underwriter must seek a supervisor's approval. The supervisor may simply approve or reject the underwriter's recommendation, or the entire application may be referred to a more specialized or experienced senior underwriter.

Monitoring the Underwriting Decision

The underwriter's job does not end when a policy is issued. The underwriter must also monitor the results of the initial underwriting decision. Among other things, the underwriter needs to reevaluate his or her underwriting decisions by considering claims that develop from accounts that were accepted. The nature and number of losses in a given period may indicate that some other underwriting action is required.

The fact that an insured has a serious loss or several losses does not necessarily indicate that the underwriter made a bad decision. Conversely, a lack of serious losses on an account does not necessarily mean that the underwriter made a good decision in accepting the account. The lack of losses may have been a matter of chance. Despite these variations in the loss experience of individual accounts, the entire group of accounts handled by an underwriter is expected to meet the loss ratio goals established for that portfolio. Each account contributes to the underwriter's record in the long term.

If serious problems develop with an account, the underwriter may need to take corrective action. Such action may include recommending additional loss control measures, modifying the terms of coverage, canceling coverage (if permitted), or marking the policy for nonrenewal at the end of the present policy term.

During the policy term, the underwriter may also receive one or more requests for coverage changes. Each request must be carefully considered and implemented as appropriate. Some changes present no increased hazard, while others may increase the potential for losses. For example, a change of vehicles on an automobile policy from a five-year-old sedan to a newer model does not necessarily represent an increased hazard, but it may if, at the same time, a young driver is added as an additional operator.

Finally, as the expiration date of a policy approaches, the underwriter may need to repeat the underwriting process before agreeing to renew the policy for another term. Renewal underwriting can generally be accomplished more quickly than underwriting new business because the insured is already known, to some degree, and claim reports or loss control reports may provide additional information. However, the underwriter must determine whether any changes in the exposures have occurred, and, if so, carefully go through the underwriting process again.

Many insurers do not repeat the entire underwriting process for existing personal insurance policies, such as auto and homeowners, at every renewal. Instead, they continue to renew these policies until something triggers an underwriting review. Claims, requests for coverage changes, or the passage of a certain amount of time may prompt the insurer to repeat the underwriting process.

REGULATION OF UNDERWRITING ACTIVITIES

In the interest of protecting the public, every state regulates insurers' underwriting activities and places some constraints on the terms and conditions that insurers offer. Two important examples of underwriting activity regulation are as follows:

1. Prohibition of unfair discrimination
2. Restrictions on cancellation and nonrenewal

Prohibition of Unfair Discrimination

The ability to discriminate fairly among applicants is one of the most important elements of underwriting. However, state insurance regulations prohibit unfair discrimination in insurance. This prohibition also applies to insurance underwriting activities. The challenge lies in distinguishing between fair discrimination and unfair discrimination.

With the attention given to topics such as racial and sexual discrimination, it is easy to forget that discrimination itself can be a neutral word. Dictionary definitions of discrimination include "The quality or power of finely distinguishing" and "The act or practice of discriminating categorically rather than individually."

Teachers discriminate—that is, they finely distinguish—when they assign different grades to students with different levels of performance. Schools discriminate categorically when they admit kindergarten students based on age rather than rating them individually on the basis of physical or mental maturity.

Similarly, underwriting involves distinguishing among properties, businesses, and people and grouping them into categories. An insurer's ability to discriminate fairly is essential if insureds are to be charged a premium commensurate with their loss exposures.

According to state insurance laws, unfair discrimination is prohibited as an unfair trade practice. Examples of unfair discrimination include the following:

- *Geographic location.* Refusing to issue, canceling, or nonrenewing coverage for an applicant or an insured solely on the basis of geographic location. This prohibited practice is sometimes called redlining—suggesting a bright red line on a map surrounding a prohibited area.
- *Gender or marital status.* Refusing to issue, canceling, or nonrenewing coverage for an applicant or an insured solely on the basis of that person's gender or marital status.
- *Race.* Refusing to issue, canceling, or nonrenewing a policy solely because of the applicant's or the insured's race.

These examples of unfair discrimination all include some kind of prejudice: judging, with no further information, that property in a given area, persons of a particular gender or marital status, or members of a certain race are likely to have unacceptable levels of losses. Further information in each case may indicate that the applicant or insured does not meet the insurer's underwriting standards, regardless of address, gender, marital status, or race. Therefore, if coverage is denied after objective underwriting criteria have been applied, it is not likely that unfair discrimination has occurred.

Restrictions on Cancellation and Nonrenewal

Most states require that insurers provide notification to the insured within a specified period, such as thirty days, before a policy is to be canceled or nonrenewed. This notice is intended to give the insured an opportunity to replace the coverage. Generally, restrictions of this kind help insurance to serve its purpose of providing protection for policyholders. However, such restrictions also limit the speed with which an underwriter can stop providing coverage for an insured who has become undesirable.

For example, after widely publicized claims involving allegations of child abuse caused insurers to become concerned about the legal hazards of operating daycare centers, some policies providing coverage to these centers were canceled or nonrenewed. At the same time, insurer capacity was severely restricted for other reasons as well, affecting many kinds of insurance. Insurers canceled or nonrenewed some policies in an attempt to reallocate their available capacity. In response, several states enacted laws prohibiting insurers from canceling insurance policies during the policy term and restricted insurers' rights to nonrenew policies. Even when such noncancellation laws had not been passed, underwriters became much more reluctant to exercise cancellation rights to avoid adverse reaction that could lead to further regulatory restrictions on underwriting activities.

SUMMARY

Underwriting is the process by which insurers evaluate applicants for insurance and those currently insured in order to maintain a profitable book of business. Underwriting consists of the following activities:

- Selecting those applicants who meet the company's underwriting guidelines
- Pricing the coverage to charge a premium commensurate with the loss exposure
- Determining the proper policy terms and conditions
- Monitoring underwriting decisions

While underwriters are responsible for day-to-day decisions, they must refer to the insurer's underwriting guidelines. Underwriting management sets the insurer's guidelines to make optimal use of the company's available capacity and avoid adverse selection. The role of underwriting management involves various responsibilities, including the following:

- Participating in the overall management of the insurer in making broad business decisions

- Arranging reinsurance, which can be either treaty reinsurance (on all eligible policies) or facultative reinsurance (involving a separate transaction for each reinsured policy)

- Delegating underwriting authority, which establishes the types of decisions a underwriter can make without receiving approval from someone at a higher level

- Developing and enforcing underwriting guidelines that reflect the company's overall underwriting objectives

- Monitoring the results of underwriting to see whether the underwriting guidelines have had the desired effect

In making decisions, underwriters follow four steps in the underwriting process:

1. Gathering the necessary information from various sources to evaluate applicants

2. Making the underwriting decision, which includes analyzing hazards (which can be moral, attitudinal, physical, or legal), evaluating underwriting options (accepting or rejecting the application or accepting it with modification), and choosing the best option

3. Implementing the underwriting decision

4. Monitoring the underwriting decision

In the interest of protecting the public, every state regulates insurers' underwriting activities by prohibiting unfair discrimination. In addition, most states require that insurers provide notification to the insured within a specified period before a policy can be canceled or nonrenewed.

Direct Your Learning

Claims

After learning the content of this chapter and completing the corresponding course guide assignment, you should be able to:

■ Describe the role performed by each of the following in the claim handling process:

- Staff claim representatives (inside and outside)

- Independent adjusters

- Producers

- Public adjusters

■ Describe the activities in the claim handling process.

■ Describe how the claim handling process applies to property insurance claims.

■ Describe how the claim handling process applies to liability insurance claims.

■ Describe the special considerations for catastrophe claims.

■ Describe the claim representative's role in establishing an insurer's loss reserves.

■ Describe the practices prohibited by unfair claim practices laws.

■ Define or describe each of the Key Words and Phrases for this chapter.

Develop Your Perspective

What are the main topics covered in the chapter?

Claim representatives are responsible for handling claims and performing activities to determine how much an insurer will pay for covered losses. Through this function, they fulfill the promise made in the insurance contract.

Identify the various types of claim representatives and their functions.

- How would the types of claims handled by staff adjusters differ from those handled by independent adjusters?

- When are public adjusters likely to be consulted on a claim?

Why is it important to learn about these topics?

In addition to handling claims, claim representatives also play an important role in establishing an insurer's loss reserves. Loss reserves are accounting liabilities for future claim payments.

Consider the financial results if claim representatives underreserve or overreserve large liability claims.

- How might the results of an insurance product be incorrect if the claim representative sets the value of the loss reserves too low or too high?

How can you use what you will learn?

Examine an insurance claim experienced by you, a family member, or a friend.

- How were the claim representative's actions controlled by unfair claim practices laws?

- How might the claim experience have been different if unfair claims practices laws were not in place?

Chapter 6
Claims

At 8:00 AM, Rajiv Gupta drove his two children to school, as he did each school day. Fifteen minutes earlier, he dropped off his wife at the train station for her commute to work. Leaving the school, he entered the expressway for the twenty minute ride to his office. As he accelerated to merge into the highway traffic, he glanced over his left shoulder to see if the lane was clear. It was, and he pressed on the gas pedal. However, the car in front of him had stopped in the merge lane, and Rajiv could not halt his car in time. He braced himself as his car slammed into the rear bumper of the stopped vehicle.

Steam poured from under his crumpled hood as traffic backed up behind him. His back hurt, but he was able to get out of the car and exchange insurance information with the other driver, who was shaken but showed no visible injury. The police were summoned, and Rajiv was cited for careless driving.

Rajiv had his car towed to a repair shop. That day he called his insurer. He learned that his auto insurance policy will pay for the towing bill and for a rental car while his vehicle is being repaired. His insurer will also pay to repair the damage to his car, less his $500 deductible, and will pay for the medical expenses he incurs from the accident. Because he was cited and at-fault in the accident, Rajiv's insurer will also pay for repairs to the other vehicle.

Three months later, the other driver filed a lawsuit demanding $250,000 for pain and suffering damages from the accident. Rajiv's insurer advised him that they will defend against this lawsuit, paying both the legal costs and any judgment up to his liability policy limit.

Property-casualty incurred insurance claims and loss settlement expenses approach $300 billion per year in the United States.[1] The responsibility for properly investigating, evaluating, and settling the hundreds of thousands of claims submitted annually to insurers rests with the people in claim departments.

Insurance is a promise. In return for the premium payment, the insurer promises to pay those claims that are covered by the policy provisions. An insurance claim payment is the fulfillment of the promise made by the insurer; this chapter discusses the people and the processes that enable insurers to keep that promise.

For insurance purposes, a **claim** is a demand by a person or business seeking to recover from an insurer for a loss that may be covered by an insurance policy.

Claim
A demand by a person or business seeking to recover from an insurer for a loss that may be covered by an insurance policy.

Claimant
Anyone who submits a claim to an insurer.

First party
The insured in an insurance contract.

Third party
A person or business who is not a party to the insurance contract but who asserts a claim against the insured.

A **claimant** is anyone who submits a claim to an insurer. Insurance claim professionals distinguish between first party and third party claimants. The **first party** is the insured. In some cases, particularly in liability claims, the claimant is a **third party** who has suffered a loss and who seeks to collect damages for that loss from an insured, as shown in Exhibit 6-1. This text uses the term claimant to refer both to a third-party claimant and to the insured who makes a claim.

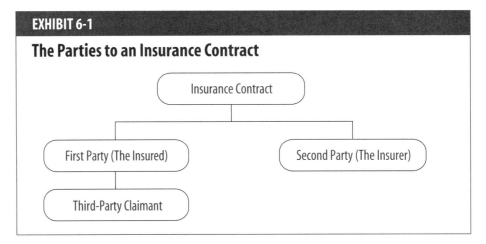

EXHIBIT 6-1

The Parties to an Insurance Contract

The primary purpose of the claim handling process is to satisfy the insurer's main obligation under the insurance policy: to pay claims for covered losses. To fulfill this obligation, the insurer's claim representative must respond promptly once a claim is submitted. **Claim representatives** (also called **adjusters**) verify coverage, determine the cause of loss and amount of damages, and settle or otherwise conclude the claim.

Claim representative, or **adjuster**
A person responsible for verifying coverage, determining the cause of loss, determining the amount of damages or extent of loss, and settling or otherwise concluding a claim.

The terms "claim adjusting" and "settlement" are often used when discussing claims. In a narrow sense, a settlement is a payment that satisfies the insurer's obligation to the claimant. It is important to note that within the property-casualty insurance industry, the term is frequently used in a broader sense to refer to the process of negotiating the amount of loss payment (if any), and closing the claim through payment or denial. This text uses the term "claim handling" to refer to the entire series of events that begins with the report of loss to the insurer and typically ends with payment (or denial of payment) to the claimant.

CLAIM HANDLING RESPONSIBILITY

If an insurer is handling claims, several different types of people can have claim handling responsibility, depending on the circumstances. These include the following:

- Staff claim representatives (inside and outside)
- Independent adjusters

- Producers
- Public adjusters

In addition, an organization that has established a self-insurance plan must make provisions to handle its own claims by using either an internal claim department or an outside administrator.

Staff Claim Representatives of Insurers

A **staff claim representative** is an insurer employee who performs some or all of the insurer's claim handling activities. Most insurers have at least two kinds of staff claim representatives: inside claim representatives, who work exclusively inside the office, and outside claim representatives, who travel to the site of the loss and elsewhere to perform claim investigations and evaluations.

Staff claim representative
An insurer employee who performs some or all of the insurer's claim handling activities.

Inside Claim Representatives

An **inside claim representative** is an insurer employee who handles claims that can be settled, usually by phone or mail, from inside the insurer's office. Some claim representatives also use e-mail and Internet-based communication to settle claims. The role of an inside claim representative is to gather information about a claim, verify coverage, determine the cause of loss, determine liability and damages (for liability claims), and make a timely settlement. Traditionally, the inside claim representative handled only relatively simple and straightforward cases. However, the inside representative may also handle complex claims by managing external independent claim adjusters. Often, the inside claim representative gathers the initial claim information from the claimant, insured, or the producer.

Inside claim representative
An insurer employee who handles claims that can be settled by phone, mail, or e-mail from inside the insurer's office.

The inside claim representative communicates with the insured or claimant to obtain information about how and when the loss occurred. If a third party is involved, the inside claim representative may use a tape recorder to take statements about the loss from the insured, the claimant, and any witnesses, after obtaining their permission to tape their statements. In many cases, the claimant's statement is taken first to get a record of the claimant's version of the occurrence.

For claims involving automobile accidents, the claim representative usually orders a police report and compares this report with the statements of the insured, the claimant, and any witnesses. The inside claim representative also requests repair estimates or assigns appraisers to inspect damaged automobiles and to estimate repair costs. Some insurers have drive-in claim facilities in which the claimant can obtain a damage appraisal and receive claim payment. For simple cases, such as a broken window or a minor automobile accident in which no one is injured, the inside claim representative can usually arrange for the insured or claimant to have repairs made or can otherwise settle the claim without involving anyone else. Many claims, however, require an outside claim representative or the services of an independent adjuster. Typically, the inside claim representative coordinates the activities of the outside representative or independent adjuster.

Outside Claim Representatives

Outside claim representative, or **field claim representative**
An insurer employee who handles claims that cannot be handled easily by phone, mail, or e-mail.

An **outside claim representative**, also called a **field claim representative**, is an insurer employee who handles claims that cannot be handled easily by phone, mail, or e-mail. Outside claim representatives spend much of their time visiting the scene of a loss, interviewing witnesses, evaluating damage, and meeting with insureds, claimants, attorneys, and other persons involved in the claim.

An outside claim representative is usually a member of the insurer's staff located in a branch office, regional office, or elsewhere, and is assigned to handle claims that occur in the area served by that location. An insurer assigns an outside claim representative when it is not practical to settle the claim by correspondence or when an inside claim representative needs investigative assistance. For example, if a claim involves significant property damage, an outside claim representative inspects the property to assess the damage. If a claim involves bodily injury, an outside claim representative usually gathers information in person by taking statements from the injured parties, inspecting the accident site, and interviewing witnesses, physicians, and others.

Independent Adjusters

Insurers usually find it efficient to locate staff claim representatives only in those areas where a significant number of policyholders may submit a large volume of claims. Generally, it is inefficient for an insurer to have a staff of claim representatives in an area where few claims are filed. To handle claims in areas where they do not have large numbers of policyholders, insurers often hire independent adjusters.

Independent adjuster
A claim representative who offers claim handling services to insurers for a fee.

Independent adjusters are claim representatives who offer claim handling services to insurers for a fee. While some independent adjusters are self-employed, many work for any of several large, national independent adjusting firms. These firms have offices located throughout the U.S. and handle all types of claims.

Although a particular insurer may not have enough policyholders to set up its own staff of claim representatives in a specific area, it is feasible for an independent adjusting firm to open an office as long as there is enough claim activity within a reasonable distance from the office. These firms offer their services to any insurer needing claim handling services in that geographic area.

In some situations, an insurer may hire independent adjusters even if the insurer has staff claim representatives in the area. A staff claim representative may work with an independent adjuster when a claim involves a unique or complex situation and the staff claim representative does not have sufficient expertise to handle the claim alone. Many insurers, for example, use independent adjusters to handle claims involving business income or ocean marine insurance. Independent adjusters offer the expertise for such special claim handling needs of insurers.

Insurers may also need independent adjusters after a natural disaster, such as a catastrophic hurricane. Because of the volume of claims generated by natural disasters, insurers not only send staff claim representatives to work with insureds and producers, but also hire independent adjusters to assist in handling claims. Special considerations for handling catastrophe claims are discussed later in this chapter.

Producers

In an independent or exclusive agency, the agency usually receives the first notification of a claim. Depending on the office size, the agency may have one person, several people, or an entire department responsible for handling claims.

Some agencies do little more than communicate the claim information to the insurer. Other agencies take a more active role in the claim handling process. The producer immediately sets up a claim file and collects information about the loss. For some claims, the producer then monitors the claim handling process and the insured's satisfaction with the insurer's claim service.

If the producer has settlement authority, the producer may actually settle claims. **Settlement authority** is authority expressly given to a producer by an insurer to settle and pay certain types of claims up to a specified limit. For example, an insurer may give a producer settlement authority up to a certain limit (such as $1,000 or $2,500) per claim for certain types of claims, such as homeowners or auto physical damage. This authority allows the producer to settle claims and make payments on behalf of the insurer in such cases.

Settlement authority
Authority expressly given to a producer by an insurer to settle and pay certain types of claims up to a specified limit.

Insurers have found that allowing producers to handle small or routine claims results in both expense savings and increased goodwill. Without the direct involvement of the insurer on small claims, the claim can be handled more quickly and with less expense to the insurer. Because agency personnel obtain the loss information, verify coverage, determine the cause of loss, determine the amount of damages or extent of loss, and issue the claim payment, delays and expenses involved in contacting the insurer's claim staff are eliminated. This reduction in claim handling expenses benefits both the producer and the insurer because it contributes to a more competitively priced product.

To ensure that the insurer's claim handling standards are met, staff claim representatives perform quality control reviews on some or all of the claims settled by producers. The insured benefits from the prompt claim payment, and the producer and the insurer also benefit from the goodwill created. The producer can give personal service to the insured, and both the insurer and the producer benefit from having a satisfied customer.

Public Adjusters

In some situations, insureds may decide to hire a public adjuster to represent their interests in the claim handling process. A **public adjuster** is a person hired by an insured to represent the insured in handling a claim.

Public adjuster
A person hired by an insured to represent the insured in handling a claim.

Often, an insured hires a public adjuster either because a claim is complex or because the loss negotiations are not progressing satisfactorily. The public adjuster acts as an advocate for the insured in negotiating the claim. The insured generally pays the public adjuster a percentage of the settlement as compensation for this assistance.

The insured may also hire an attorney for the same purpose. Once the insurer has received notice that the attorney or public adjuster will be representing the insured, the claim representative must communicate directly with that party.

Claim Handling Under Self-Insurance Plans

Self-insurance plan
An arrangement in which an organization pays for its losses with its own resources rather than by purchasing insurance.

Many organizations have self-insurance plans to cover part or all of their loss exposures. A **self-insurance plan** is an arrangement in which an organization pays for its losses with its own resources rather than by purchasing insurance. However, many organizations with self-insurance plans purchase insurance to pay losses that exceed a predetermined amount, called a retention. For example, a firm might self-insure all losses up to $2 million and then purchase insurance to cover losses over $2 million.

Organizations with self-insurance plans must make provisions for handling claims. Options for claim handling include using an internal claim department or a third-party administrator.

Internal Claim Departments

If the organization is large enough, it may establish its own claim department. A smaller organization may decide to hire one or two claim representatives to handle its claims. In either case, the organization uses its own personnel to investigate and settle claims.

Regardless of the number of claim representatives an organization employs, the internal claim staff should have the skill and experience necessary to handle many different types of claims. However, the employees of internal claim departments may have little or no experience in handling certain types of complex cases, such as products liability claims or workers' compensation injuries. Furthermore, in workers' compensation claims, a problem could occur if the injured employee and the claim representative cannot agree on a settlement. Because of the problems that can arise from the use of an internal claim department, many organizations with self-insurance plans hire third-party administrators to handle the claims associated with self-insured loss exposures.

Third-Party Administrators

Third-party administrator (TPA)
An organization that contracts to provide administrative services, including claim handling, to other businesses.

The growth of self-insurance has created a need for **third-party administrators (TPAs)**, which are organizations that contract to provide administrative services, including claim handling, to other businesses, particularly to businesses that have self-insurance plans. Large independent adjusting firms sometimes function as TPAs for self-insureds and also provide independent claim handling services to insurers. Many property-casualty insurers have established subsidiary companies that serve as TPAs. When a self-insuring organization hires a TPA, that organization generally purchases more than claim handling expertise. Most TPAs offer claim recordkeeping and statistical analysis in addition to claim handling services.

CLAIM HANDLING PROCESS

Claim handling procedures can vary widely depending on the type of claim involved. A minor, single-vehicle auto accident may require only verifying coverage and loss details, obtaining estimates of vehicle damage, and paying the claim. Little else is required as long as the accident involves no bodily injuries and no other vehicles. Once the claim representative verifies that coverage applies and determines the repair costs, the claim can be settled.

An auto accident that involves two or more autos and injures several people can take months or even years to settle. In such cases, different persons could provide conflicting testimony about the accident, and difficult questions regarding legal responsibility could arise. The claim representative may need the skills of a physician, a lawyer, an engineer, and a police officer to understand all the issues involved.

Despite the unique challenges and variations from case to case, the same four activities are involved in processing most claims (once the claim representative has acknowledged receipt of the insured's or claimant's loss report) as follows:

1. Verifying coverage
2. Determining the cause of loss
3. Determining the amount of damages or extent of loss
4. Negotiating and settling (or denying) the claim

Although the claim handling process generally involves these four steps, the sequence and the manner in which they are carried out varies by insurer and by the type of claim—property or liability.

Property Insurance Claims

In property insurance claims, two parties are usually involved in the claim negotiation process: the insured and the insurer. Claim representatives usually do not have to determine who was at fault (unless the insured is suspected of an intentional act, such as arson). When handling a property insurance claim, the claim representative rarely has to consider unforeseen side effects manifesting months or years after the claim has occurred, which is often the case when bodily injury is involved. Finally, valuing property is usually easier than placing a dollar value on the income-earning ability or the life of a person who has been disabled or killed in an accident.

Verifying Coverage

Once the insurer responds to the first report of the claim, the claim representative must verify whether the claim is covered under the insured's policy. If a question of coverage exists and the insurer plans to continue its investigation, the insurer might send a reservation of rights letter to the insured. A **reservation of rights letter** is a notice sent by the insurer advising the insured that the insurer is proceeding with a claim investigation but retains its right to deny coverage later. A reservation of rights letter serves two purposes: to inform the insured that a coverage problem might exist and to protect the insurer so that it can deny coverage later, if necessary.

Failure to reserve its rights while facts are gathered may prevent the insurer from denying coverage later. Examples of claims that may require a reservation of rights letter include occurrences that happened outside the policy period, intentional actions of the insured, and situations involving more than one insurer when there is a question of which insurer must pay first.

After receiving the initial report of a claim, the claim representative must gather further information to verify coverage. The initial verification involves confirming that a valid policy was in effect, determining that the date of the loss falls within the policy period, and establishing whether the damaged property is insured under the policy. Often, the claim representative uses a simple checklist, such as the one shown in Exhibit 6-2, to begin the verification process.

The claim representative must then determine whether the coverage provided by the policy will pay any or all of the claim submitted. For a property insurance claim, the claim representative must seek the answers to the following four questions to verify that the claim is covered:

1. Does the insured have an insurable interest in the property?
2. Is the damaged property covered by the policy?
3. Is the cause of loss covered by the policy?
4. Do any additional coverages, endorsements, or coverage limitations apply?

The first question determines whether the person or organization making a claim for the damaged property has an insurable interest in the property. In property insurance, an **insurable interest** exists if a person or other entity would suffer a financial loss if the property were damaged. In most property insurance losses, the insured is the property owner, so the question of insurable interest is easily answered.

Reservation of rights letter
A notice sent by the insurer advising the insured that the insurer is proceeding with a claim investigation but that the insurer retains its right to deny coverage later.

Insurable interest
A coverage verification criterion that exists when a person or other entity would suffer a financial loss if the subject property were damaged.

EXHIBIT 6-2

Sample Verification Checklist for Personal Automobile Liability Claims

Yes   No

☐   ☐   The insured's name and address listed on the claim matches the policy information.

☐   ☐   The loss occurred during the effective dates of the policy.

☐   ☐   The policy was in force at the time of the claim.

☐   ☐   The vehicle involved in the accident was listed on the policy at the time of the claim.

☐   ☐   The individual operating the vehicle is insured by the policy.

☐   ☐   The location of the accident is included within the policy territory.

Applicable liability limits: _____

Tort threshold does/does not apply: _____

However, others may also have an insurable interest in the property. For example, a mortgagee (such as a bank that has provided a home mortgage loan) has an insurable interest in real property to the extent of the outstanding mortgage. Under certain circumstances, the mortgagee has rights to collect under an insurance policy if the mortgaged property has been damaged or destroyed. The claim representative must identify who has an insurable interest in the property so that payment can be made according to the policy provisions.

The second question that the claim representative must answer is whether the damaged property is covered by the policy. In the case of a damaged home or commercial building, the answer may seem obvious. The answer, however, may not be as simple as it appears. For example, insurance coverage on a building usually includes any item permanently attached to the building and any outdoor equipment used to maintain the building. Although the building may be clearly insured, would a room air conditioner attached to a window frame be considered a part of the building? Would a toolshed connected to a dwelling by a fence be considered a part of the dwelling? These are the types of questions that the claim representative must answer according to the policy provisions.

The question of whether the damaged property is covered by the policy is equally important for personal property. Most property insurance policies exclude losses to certain types of property. For example, the homeowners policy generally does not cover losses to property of tenants or to most motorized vehicles.

The third question the claim representative must answer is whether the cause of loss is covered by the policy. Often, the cause of the loss, such as fire or lightning, is clearly covered under the policy. Disputes between the insured and the insurer are not likely to occur. However, disagreements may arise when the cause of loss is less obvious. Disputes can occur, for example, if there is more than one possible cause of loss, as in a hurricane when damage may have been caused either by wind or by flooding. Disputes may also arise about the meanings of terms used in the policy. In some cases, the insured has the burden of proving whether coverage exists under a particular property insurance policy. In other cases, the burden of establishing that the cause of loss is excluded rests with the insurer. This burden of proof issue is discussed further in a later chapter.

The fourth question the claim representative must answer is whether any additional coverages, endorsements, or coverage limitations apply. In many insurance policies, additional coverages and limitations modify the basic coverage provided. For example, under a homeowners policy, the definition of covered property does not include trees, shrubs, plants, or lawns. However, these items can be covered under an additional coverage, which specifically states that trees, shrubs, plants, and lawns are covered up to a specific dollar amount if damaged by certain specified causes of loss.

The insured might also have purchased an additional coverage, selected one or more optional policy coverages, or modified coverage through an endorsement (policy amendment). Such changes to the basic policy can eliminate or modify exclusions or limitations. The claim representative should recognize that such policy modifications might apply and must consider them when determining whether a property claim is covered.

Insurance policies contain important limitations on coverage. Although a homeowners policy covers most types of personal property, certain types of property, such as jewelry and furs, are covered for only a specified dollar amount when the loss is due to theft. Similarly, a homeowners policy does not cover losses caused by vandalism if the dwelling has been vacant for more than thirty consecutive days. Such policy limitations are important in verifying coverage.

The claim representative must also check the policy to see whether a deductible applies to the loss, which would reduce the amount of the loss payment. For an especially large deductible or a small loss, application of the deductible may indicate that no payment can be made. Before determining whether a given loss is covered, the claim representative must confirm that the loss occurred during the time period and within the territory described in the policy.

During the investigation, the claim representative should consider whether the final cost of the claim can be reduced by subrogation (recovering a claim payment from the party responsible for the loss) or salvage (the rights of the insurer to recover and sell or otherwise dispose of insured property on which the insurer has paid a total loss). Subrogation and salvage are discussed in detail later in this chapter.

Determining the Cause of Loss

As discussed, the cause of loss must be known to verify coverage. For a property insurance claim, investigation often involves visiting the loss site to inspect the damaged property. Whether it is real property, such as a house or an office building, or personal property, such as household furnishings or business inventory, the claim representative must inspect the property (except for smaller claims handled by inside adjusters) to determine the cause of the loss and to assess the damage. For some losses, the cause is obvious; in others, the cause is harder to determine.

The claim representative may also need to interview and take statements from any witnesses to the loss to better understand how and why the loss occurred. When a building is totally destroyed, the best information about how the loss occurred often comes from witnesses. This information can help determine the cause of loss, which could be especially important in situations in which someone other than the insured may be responsible.

Determining the Amount of Damages or Extent of Loss

Another fundamental aspect of a claim, particularly with regard to real property, is the physical condition of the property before the loss occurred. This information is difficult to obtain when a building has been completely destroyed. The claim representative must consult with the insured, examine the building remains, study pictures that may be available, and examine blueprints showing the building's dimensions.

For personal property, the most important information is what property was damaged or destroyed. Creating an inventory of damaged personal property can be an arduous task for some losses, such as serious fire losses. However, for the claim representative to determine the value of the loss, a detailed inventory is essential and specific information must be gathered. When the loss involves a business, historical valuation information often appears in the company's financial records. In addition, if a business income loss is involved, the financial records are useful in determining the proper valuation of the lost income.

For claim representatives, the valuation of loss can be the most difficult aspect of settling property insurance claims. In order to indemnify the insured according to the policy provisions, the claim representative must be able to answer the following two questions:

1. How does the policy specify that the property be valued?
2. Based on that specification, what is the value of the damaged property?

All property insurance policies include a valuation provision that specifies how to value covered property at the time of the loss. The most common property valuation methods are as follows:

- Actual cash value
- Replacement cost
- Agreed value

Actual cash value (ACV)
The cost to replace property minus an allowance for the property's depreciation.

Depreciation
The allowance for physical wear and tear or technological or economic obsolescence.

Actual cash value (ACV) is the cost to replace the property minus an allowance for the property's depreciation. (**Depreciation** is the allowance for physical wear and tear or technological or economic obsolescence). For example, assume a fire completely destroys a new television and a four-year-old sofa. The television has a replacement cost of $600 (its cost when it was purchased a week earlier), and the sofa would cost $800 to replace with a comparable (of like kind and quality) new sofa. (A sofa that is four years old probably cannot be replaced with exactly the same sofa because styles change. Therefore, the sofa's replacement cost would be the cost of a new sofa comparable to the one that was destroyed.) Under these circumstances, an ACV settlement includes $600 for the television because it has not yet had time to depreciate. For the sofa, however, the claim representative has to place a value on the used property.

The claim representative must determine the extent of depreciation that should be considered. This determination is usually made by estimating the property's expected useful life. If, under normal circumstances, a sofa might be used for ten years and it is now four years old, a good estimate of depreciation from normal wear and tear is 40 percent. Therefore, with a replacement cost of $800 and depreciation estimated at 40 percent, the ACV of the damaged sofa is $480. A payment of $480 would indemnify the insured for the loss of the four-year-old sofa. Certain types of property, such as computers, become obsolete after a certain amount of time, so obsolescence must also be estimated.

Replacement cost
The cost to repair or replace property using new materials of like kind and quality with no deduction for depreciation.

Another valuation method specified in some property insurance policies allows for valuation on a replacement cost basis. An item's **replacement cost** is the cost to repair or replace the property using new materials of like kind and quality with no deduction for depreciation. In this case, deduction for depreciation is not a part of the valuation, and the insured in the previous example would be paid $800 for the four-year-old sofa. Generally, a loss valued on a replacement cost basis is paid only after the property has been replaced. The insurer may pay the claim first on an ACV basis, and the insured then has 180 days to provide notice of the replacement cost.

Agreed value
A method of valuing property in which the insurer and the insured agree, at the time the policy is written, on the maximum amount that will be paid in the event of a total loss.

Still another method for valuing property losses is agreed value, which is used to insure property that is difficult to value, such as fine arts, antiques, and collections. Under the **agreed value** method, the insurer and the insured agree, at the time the policy is written, on the maximum amount that will be paid in the event of a total loss. This agreed value is often based on an appraisal, and that amount is stated in the policy declarations. If a total loss to the property occurs, the insurer will pay the agreed value, regardless of the property's exact value at the time of the loss.

In commercial insurance, there are various agreed value options for property insurance policies. In some policies, the term agreed value has a different meaning and relates to the amount of insurance that the insured must carry to avoid a penalty for underinsurance.

Once the claim representative has verified coverage and identified the valuation method specified in the policy, the valuation process begins. Claim representatives must use guidelines to determine both replacement cost and ACV. Personal property and real property present different valuation problems.

If the exact style and brand of the damaged personal property are available for purchase, obtaining the replacement cost is simple. If the particular item is no longer available, the claim representative identifies the closest substitute in style and quality and uses that substitute's value as the replacement cost.

For actual cash value, however, depreciation must be estimated. While claim representatives have attempted to develop straightforward methods, such as the useful life procedure described in the case of the damaged sofa, these procedures do not fit every circumstance. For example, if a sofa has an expected life of ten years, the claim representative makes a reasonable estimate in considering the four-year-old sofa to be 40 percent depreciated. But what if the sofa is fifteen years old? Is the sofa considered worthless? The fifteen-year-old sofa has some value as long as it is functional, so the depreciation procedure must make allowance for that fact. The claim representative may have guidelines stating that property still being used is no more than 75 percent depreciated, no matter how old it is. While such guidelines may be developed to treat most cases, it is impossible to anticipate every situation the claim representative may encounter. Therefore, the claim representative must use good judgment to determine depreciation.

The replacement cost of real property can usually be determined by using three factors as follows:

1. Square footage of the property
2. Type and quality of construction
3. Construction cost per square foot

The first factor is the square footage of the property. If the building has been badly damaged, its area can be determined from the original blueprints or by measuring the remains.

The second factor is the type and quality of construction. A one-family frame house with standard trim and fixtures costs far less to replace than the same size house built of stone with high-quality woodworking, skylights, and other features. The quality of the house or building is more apparent if part of the structure has escaped damage. Pictures of the house or building can be useful, particularly if the structure has been totally destroyed.

The final factor affecting replacement cost is the construction cost per square foot currently charged for the style and quality of the destroyed building. Contractors who do business in the general location of the damaged building can quote costs per square foot in various quality-of-construction categories, such as $65 per square foot for standard quality, $75 per square foot for medium quality, and $90 per square foot for superior quality. Multiplying the square footage by the appropriate cost per square foot yields the building's replacement cost.

If the building is only partially damaged, the claim representative usually prepares a repair estimate or obtains repair estimates from one or more contractors. Replacing the property when a partial loss has occurred involves restoring the property to its previous state as closely as possible.

Some policies specify that the ACV method should be used to measure loss to real property. For policies specifying ACV valuation, claim representatives estimate depreciation of real property using methods similar to those used for estimating depreciation of personal property. Other policies state that the insured can collect the replacement cost of damaged real property under certain circumstances. Often, however, these policies provide for immediate payment of the ACV of the property, and payment of the remainder of the replacement cost is made when actual repair or replacement is completed. Either type of policy requires a claim representative to calculate the ACV of damaged real property.

Negotiating and Settling the Claim

After verifying coverage, determining the cause of loss, and determining the amount of damage or extent of loss, the claim representative must settle the claim. This step usually requires that the claim representative and the insured discuss the details of the loss and the valuation of the damage to agree on an amount for the insurer to pay to settle the loss. The negotiation phase of claim handling can be relatively simple, as in the case of the fire-damaged television in a previous example. However, it may be complicated because of a large number of damaged items, property of high value, or disagreement between the insured and the claim representative regarding the value or circumstances of the loss. Whenever possible, questions of coverage, valuation, and other matters should be discussed and resolved as they arise. In addition, investigation and valuation often continue while the negotiation is in progress.

Subrogation and Salvage Rights

After the claim representative and the insured agree on the amount of the settlement, two other factors can affect the insurer's cost for property claims: subrogation and salvage rights.

Subrogation is the insurer's right to recover payment from a third party that is legally responsible for having caused the loss. When an insurer pays an insured for a loss, the insurer assumes the insured's right to collect damages from a third party responsible for the loss. Subrogation often applies in claims involving auto accidents. Once the insurer pays the insured for the repair or replacement of the damaged auto, the policy provides that any rights to collect from another party responsible for the damage to the auto belong to the insurer (up to the amount the insurer paid the insured for the claim). Subrogation prevents an insured from collecting from both the insurer and the party at fault for the same loss.

Subrogation
The insurer's right, assumed from the insured, to recover payment from a third party that is legally responsible for the loss.

The claim representative investigates whether another party involved in the accident is legally responsible for the damage paid by the insurer. If another party is responsible, the insurer can attempt to collect the repair or replacement cost from that person or that person's insurer. Formal legal proceedings may be necessary to determine who is legally responsible for the damage.

Salvage rights are the insurer's rights to recover and sell or otherwise dispose of insured property on which the insurer has paid a total loss or a constructive total loss. A **constructive total loss** exists when a vehicle (or other property) cannot be repaired for less than its actual cash value minus the anticipated salvage value. For example, if an auto damaged in an accident cannot be repaired for less than its ACV minus the anticipated salvage value, the auto is considered to be a constructive total loss. In this case, the insurer pays the auto's ACV to the insured (or finds an auto similar to the insured's auto before it was damaged).

Salvage rights
The insurer's rights to recover and sell or otherwise dispose of insured property on which the insurer has paid a total loss or a constructive total loss.

Constructive total loss
A loss such that property cannot be repaired for less than its actual cash value minus the anticipated salvage value.

Although the settlement with the insured is paid as a total loss, the insurer might be able to collect some salvage value for the damaged auto. Depending on the actual condition of the vehicle, an auto salvage dealer may be willing to pay for the auto to obtain scrap metal and undamaged parts that can be resold as used parts. In this way, the salvage value can offset some of the insurer's claim cost.

For example, assume the ACV of the insured's car at the time of an accident is $10,000, and the repairs will cost $9,000. If the car could be sold for $1,500 to a salvage dealer, the insurer would consider the car a constructive total loss because it would cost more for the insurer to pay the repair cost than to pay the insured the ACV of $10,000 and then sell the salvage for $1,500. ($10,000 ACV – $1,500 salvage value = $8,500, which is less than the $9,000 cost of repairing the car.)

Liability Insurance Claims

Liability claim adjusting is different from property claims adjusting because determining liability may be difficult. First, the claimant is a third party who has been injured or whose property has been damaged by the insured. The claimant may perceive the claim representative as an adversary, and this perception could cause the claimant to act in a hostile or unfriendly manner.

Second, a liability claim may involve bodily injury. It is not always easy to determine the amount of the loss in property damage liability claims, and determining the amount of loss is more difficult and complex when the loss involves bodily injury or death.

Liability claim settlement sometimes involves a claim for damage that the insured has allegedly caused to the property of others. The process for handling property damage liability claims resembles the claim handling process for property insurance claims, with the added difficulty of determining whether the insured is legally responsible for the property damage that has occurred. The following discussion concentrates on the issue of legal responsibility, which is central to the liability claim handling process.

Verifying Coverage

As in a property claim, the claim representative must gather information to verify coverage. The process includes checking that a valid policy was in effect, determining that the date of the loss falls within the policy period, and discovering whether any additional coverages, endorsements, or coverage limitations apply. In handling a liability claim, the key difference from a property claim is that the claim representative must determine if the insured is legally responsible for the loss; if not, coverage does not apply.

Determining the Cause of Loss

After receiving the first report of injury or damage and verifying coverage, the claim representative must gather detailed information relating to the liability claim. The question of how much damage occurred may be secondary because the amount of the loss is relevant only if the loss is covered under the insured's policy and if the insured is legally responsible for the loss. Therefore, the claim representative must first determine how and why the loss occurred and whether the insured appears to be responsible.

In investigating a liability claim, the claim representative often inspects the scene of the occurrence or accident. This inspection is particularly useful if a traumatic event has occurred, such as an auto accident, a building collapse, or a fire. By studying the scene and interviewing the insured, the claimant, and any witnesses, the claim representative attempts to reconstruct the events that led to the loss. This reconstruction helps to determine, as closely as possible, how the loss occurred and who is responsible. Additional details are needed to determine the extent of the bodily injury or property damage. At this point, the claim representative collects enough information to help determine whether the liability policy covers the loss and, if so, whether the insured may be legally responsible.

As soon as possible, the claim representative speaks directly with the injured party or the injured party's legal representative to hear that side of the story and to assess what bodily injury or property damage has been sustained. Many times the events surrounding an accident are difficult to reconstruct, so the claim representative often receives different interpretations from the injured party and the insured as to how the loss occurred. The claim representative also gathers reports from any available witnesses.

The injured party has the option of suing the insured, and the ensuing legal process could end in a legal decision determining who is responsible and to what extent. Because of the time, expense, and uncertainty involved in a lawsuit, insurers often prefer to settle claims out of court. If the claim does go to court, the insurer is obligated to provide and pay for the insured's defense for a covered claim (until the insurer has paid the full policy limit for the occurrence involved).

Liability policies usually cover the insured's liability arising from certain specified activities, such as owning or using an automobile or operating a business, subject to certain exclusions. Coverage depends on whether the activity leading to the claim is within the scope of the policy's coverage and whether any exclusions in the policy apply to the specific case. Based on the information gathered, the claim representative must determine whether coverage applies.

If the claim representative's investigation finds that no coverage applies, the insurer will deny the claim. For example, if the policy excludes injury intended by the insured and the insured purposely injures someone with a baseball bat, there would be no coverage unless the insured has evidence that the injury was careless but not intentional. In that case, the claim representative would need to investigate further to determine whether the injury was indeed intentional on the insured's part. If coverage does exist, the valuation aspect of liability claims settlement then becomes very important.

Valuation

Damages are money claimed by, or a monetary award to, a party who has suffered bodily injury or property damage for which another party is legally responsible. When bodily injury occurs, determining the amount of damages often depends on medical records and the reports and opinions of physicians. Properly evaluating medical information is important in determining the amount of damages and is a distinguishing factor in the loss settlement process for bodily injury liability claims. This aspect of bodily injury claims requires experience and skill.

Legal liability cases may involve the following types of damages:

- Compensatory damages (which include both special damages and general damages)
- Punitive damages

Compensatory damages are intended to compensate a victim for harm actually suffered. Compensatory damages include special damages and general damages.

Damages
Money claimed by, or a monetary award to, a party who has suffered bodily injury or property damage for which another party is legally responsible.

Compensatory damages
Damages intended to compensate a victim for actual harm suffered; these damages include special damages and general damages.

Special damages
Compensatory damages for specific, out-of-pocket expenses, such as doctor and hospital expenses.

General damages
Compensatory damages awarded for losses that do not have a specific economic value, such as pain and suffering.

Specific, out-of-pocket expenses are called **special damages**. In bodily injury cases, these damages usually include hospital expenses, doctor and miscellaneous medical expenses, ambulance charges, prescriptions, and lost wages for time spent away from the job during recovery. Because they are specific and identifiable, special damages are easier to calculate than general damages.

General damages are compensatory damages awarded for losses that do not have a specific economic value. Examples of general damages include compensation for any of the following: pain and suffering; disfigurement; loss of limbs, sight, or hearing; and loss of the ability to bear children. Because these losses do not involve specific and measurable expenses, estimating their dollar value requires considerable expertise. For the claim representative, the best guide is usually to analyze past cases similar to the case currently under investigation. For that purpose, the claim representative may use any of the following tools to estimate the bodily injury valuation of specific damages: supervisor's guidance, roundtable discussion with other claim representatives, or computer software.

There is usually no direct relationship between the amount of general damages and the amount of special damages. In some cases, such as when a claimant loses an eye, the amount of special damages may be relatively low, but the general damages may be quite high because of the pain and suffering involved and the change in the claimant's quality of life. In other cases, such as for whiplash injuries, general damages may be minimal, but special damages may be considerable because the claimant requires physical therapy or other medical treatment.

In recent years, courts have often made large awards for general damages, particularly for traumatic incidents like automobile accidents. Claim representatives must be aware of the awards for damages made in their jurisdictions, because these awards provide a guideline for negotiating with the injured party.

Punitive damages
Damages awarded by a court to punish wrongdoers who cause bodily injury or property damage to others and to deter others from committing similar wrongs.

When a court finds the defendant's conduct particularly malicious or outrageous, it might award punitive damages. The purpose of **punitive damages** is to punish the wrongdoer and to deter others from committing similar wrongs. In some states, the insurer's payment of an award for punitive damages is not permitted because such payment by an insurer would not punish the insured. Some policies expressly exclude the payment of punitive damages.

Negotiating and Settling the Claim

While the awards for damages described previously may result from court decisions, a large percentage of liability cases are settled out of court through negotiations between the claim representative and the claimant or the claimant's attorney. In most instances, neither party wishes to become involved in a formal legal action with the accompanying costs and delays. When negotiations do not result in a settlement, however, the claimant has the option of suing for the alleged damages. The court then decides who is responsible and determines the value of the bodily injury or property damage. Even after the claimant initiates a lawsuit, however, the claim negotiation process usually continues. Many out-of-court settlements have resulted after some or all of the courtroom testimony has been given. Negotiating with the claimant while simultaneously preparing for proceedings in court requires a great deal of skill, patience, and understanding on the part of the claim representative.

SPECIAL CONSIDERATIONS FOR CATASTROPHE CLAIMS

Although this chapter focuses on the day-to-day process of handling claims, the volume of claim handling activity reaches crisis proportions following catastrophic losses, as from a hurricane or a terrorist attack. For each insurer faced with a significant number of losses resulting from a catastrophe, activity originates from the following two sources:

1.   Processing the increased number of property claims
2.   Dealing with the increased scrutiny of the claim handling processes when media attention turns toward the victims

For these reasons, property insurers subject to catastrophic losses should prepare well in advance to handle the large number of losses should a catastrophic event occur.

Processing the Increased Number of Property Claims

After a catastrophe, policyholders and regulators expect an insurer to settle losses quickly, regardless of the volume of claims or any disruptions to the insurer's own resources. As noted previously, effective catastrophe response requires careful preparation. Contingency plans that are detailed and communicated throughout the organization serve the following purposes:

•   Identifying weaknesses, bottlenecks, and potential difficulties
•   Permitting staff to clearly understand their roles and responsibilities during a crisis in advance, so that they can react productively and not emotionally
•   Keeping the organization free to focus on handling claims without reallocating essential resources to resolve problems for which it was unprepared

Exhibit 6-3 presents some of the challenges involved in catastrophe response and illustrates how contingency planning can help an organization prepare to meet these challenges.

EXHIBIT 6-3

Challenges Involved in Catastrophe Response

Area	Potential Problems	Possible Responses
Staffing	Insufficient claim staff to handle volume of incoming claims. Staff unavailable as they deal with their own property damage.	Identify and train staff from other areas to assist. Establish relationships with independent adjusters to help manage overflow. Bring in catastrophe teams of claim representatives from other regions.
Premises	The insurer's premises are damaged or must be evacuated.	Identify and arrange for the use of alternative premises. Secure existing premises.
Systems	Records are destroyed or computer systems are down.	Maintain current backup at a remote location where information can be accessed.
Communication	Communication links are destroyed.	Identify public broadcasting services that may be used. Arrange for cellular phones.
Transportation	Roads and bridges are damaged.	Identify alternative routes and resources to move staff and materials into damaged areas.
Utilities	Utilities are suspended.	Arrange for generator-powered electricity, water tank services, portable toilets, and showers.
Material and labor	Available construction materials and labor are insufficient.	Arrange sources of materials and labor from nearby communities.
Mass evacuation	Policyholders are evacuated from an area.	Identify and secure temporary housing, including motels, mobile homes, and other temporary buildings.
Policyholder needs	Policyholders are confused, stressed, and anxious.	Prepare catastrophe kits, including sources of information and assistance, for distribution to policyholders.
Community needs	Efficient claim settlement depends on restoring resources and community services.	Coordinate with other insurers and community disaster relief agencies.
Employee stress	Employees' stress levels during catastrophes are high.	Train employees in stress management and have counselors available on site. Provide temporary daycare services and meals as other businesses are closed and employees work longer hours.
Security	Policyholders can become aggressive as they try to recover from their losses and payments are delayed. Insurers may become the target of violence when unfavorable rumors circulate. Criminals are attracted to post-catastrophe locations for temporary employment paid in cash.	Increase security at the insurer's premises and parking lots. Maintain visible security in lobby and public areas. Restrict access to work areas. In the event of a temporary curfew, arrange for travel passes for employees who work before or after curfew hours.

Dealing With Claim Handling Scrutiny

The human tragedy that follows a catastrophe cannot be overstated, but the relief delivered through the insurers' efficient claim handling can help enormously. Insurers can initiate certain activities to ensure that catastrophe losses are handled promptly, despite the huge volume of claims. These include the following modifications to normal operations:

- Developing and using abbreviated claim handling procedures to speed processing
- Temporarily increasing claim settlement authority to producers for the duration of the catastrophe response
- Temporarily transferring claim settlement authority to preselected independent adjusting firms
- Bringing in catastrophe teams of claim representatives from other regions
- Making advance payments to policyholders for expenses such as additional living expenses
- Immediately settling all questions of property valuation in favor of the policyholder
- Suspending all but the most essential recordkeeping
- Reallocating available employees in critical work areas

In addition, claimants are under enormous stress following a catastrophe. After claimants restore their lives to as normal as possible, claim payment by an insurer may be the only step remaining until they can begin repairing their homes and businesses. At this point, claimants may become aggressive in their pursuit of a settlement. Claim staff should be trained in dealing with aggressiveness without resorting to antagonistic responses. Media attention can easily be diverted to the plight of claimants with insurers painted in the role of the enemy. Such negative media can escalate aggressive behavior by other claimants who may perceive the need to assert their rights.

Finally, claim departments should prepare to assist claimants with problems that occur outside of normal claim-related issues. For example, some claim settlement checks for property losses are made both to the policyholders and their mortgagees. Mortgagees may withhold their signatures until they have evidence that repairs to the secured property have been completed. However, in post-catastrophe areas, repairs may require payment in advance. A staff person in the claim department who can help policyholders handle these unusual problems can free claim representatives to settle other claims.

LOSS RESERVES

Claim representatives play a vital role in establishing an insurer's loss reserves. As stated previously, loss reserves are funds held by the insurer to pay claims for losses that have occurred but have not yet been settled. Loss reserves are the largest and most important obligation of property-casualty insurers.

Loss reserves are liabilities in the accounting sense because they are shown on an insurer's financial statements as sums that the insurer owes to others. They represent an estimate of the amount of claim payments the insurer will make in the future.

After the claim representative receives notice of a loss, obtains initial information, and verifies coverage, a loss reserve for that claim is established. (Loss reserves assigned to individual claims are often called **case reserves**.) Assume, for example, that an insured had a minor auto accident in which the insured's car hit a guardrail on a foggy night and that no injuries or other cars were involved. After obtaining initial information concerning the accident, verifying coverage, and receiving written estimates of the cost to repair the insured's car, the claim representative establishes a case reserve of $1,500. (Many insurers establish an initial case reserve as soon as a claim is reported, using an average amount for that type of claim and later adjusting the reserve based on the claim representative's findings.) This figure is probably a very accurate estimate because a single-car collision loss is relatively easy to evaluate. Two weeks later, the repairs are made to the insured's car, and the insurer issues a check for $1,500. Once the loss is paid, the reserve is reduced to zero because no future loss payment is expected. Therefore, the $1,500 claim paid by the insurer equals the initial case reserve.

Conversely, complex claims are often difficult to estimate, especially liability claims. Assume, for example, that an insured was involved in a serious auto accident and that two persons in the other car were hospitalized with severe injuries. The cause of the accident is not immediately clear because of conflicting testimony of witnesses, and it is difficult to determine whether the insured is responsible for the accident. What case reserve should be established? The amount eventually paid because of this accident could range from almost nothing (if the insured is not found to be legally responsible) to hundreds of thousands of dollars (if the insured is responsible and the injured victims die or are permanently disabled). The eventual payment on this particular claim, which may not be made for several years, can vary significantly from the original reserve.

Calculating case reserves is always an estimate—no one knows exactly how much the insurer will pay in the future for an individual claim or all claims for a particular period. Claim representatives generally estimate case reserves for individual claims based on their knowledge and experience. For inclusion on the insurer's financial statements, and for rate development, actuaries calculate an insurer's overall loss reserves. Actuaries use case reserve totals as a starting point in determining the overall loss reserves. No system of estimating overall loss reserves can be accurate unless the underlying reserves on individual claims are reasonably accurate. A claim representative who properly estimates a case reserve for a given claim provides a valuable service to the insurer, who in turn is better able to report appropriate loss reserves to regulators, investors, and others.

Case reserve

A loss reserve assigned to an individual claim.

The process of setting case reserves varies by insurer. Often, the claim representative's input, based on an analysis of the many factors associated with a particular claim, is combined with the knowledge and experience of a claim supervisor or manager. Reserving is not a one-time activity for any particular claim; the case reserve must be regularly evaluated as new information becomes available.

UNFAIR CLAIM PRACTICES LAWS

Throughout the claim handling process, the claim representative must remember that a loss often produces strong emotions. The claim representative is dealing with an insured or a claimant who has been through a trying, if not traumatic, experience. Good interpersonal and communication skills are vital. Although dealing with persons in such circumstances can be a challenge, the claim representative may find it rewarding to help people through a difficult time.

The claim representative must treat all parties fairly by promptly paying valid claims according to the policy provisions and by denying claims for which no coverage applies. Failure to pay a claim that is covered by an insurance policy hurts the person who is denied a fair settlement. On the other hand, paying a claim that is not covered penalizes the insurer and all of the insurer's policyholders. If an insurer pays claims that are not covered by a particular insurance policy, the ultimate cost will be shared by all of the insurer's policyholders, who will eventually pay higher premiums. It is important to policyholders that insurers neither overpay nor underpay claims.

Most claim representatives strive to treat insureds and claimants as fairly as possible while adhering to policy terms and state regulations. It is difficult to gain the expertise to understand complex policy conditions and to determine the value of the loss. Also, the claim handling process requires sound interpersonal skills to manage a situation that may involve stress and disagreements.

Because of problems that have occurred in the claim process, most states have enacted **unfair claim practices laws**, which specify claim practices that are illegal. The prohibited claim practices usually include the following:

Unfair claim practices law
A state law that specifies illegal claim practices.

- Misrepresentation of material facts or insurance policy provisions relating to coverage at issue in a claim
- Failure to acknowledge and promptly respond to communications about claims arising under insurance policies
- Actions that compel an insured to sue to recover amounts due under insurance policies by offering amounts that are substantially lower than the amounts ultimately recovered in legal actions brought by such insureds
- Refusal to pay claims without first conducting a reasonable investigation based on all available information

Insurance regulators usually learn of unfair claim practices when they receive complaints from insureds and claimants. Claim representatives must be able to justify their actions and provide proper documentation when asked to do so by state insurance regulators. Some complaints are frivolous, often occurring because the claimant is annoyed that the policy does not cover a loss. On the other hand, some complaints are valid, and regulators may take action when a serious complaint occurs or when several complaints, especially of a similar nature, are registered against a claim representative or insurer. The claim representative or insurer must justify the practices that are under scrutiny or face a reprimand, fine, license suspension, substantial legal judgment, or some other legal penalty.

SUMMARY

When an insurer sells a policy, it promises to pay claims covered by that policy. The purpose of the claim handling process is to fulfill that promise. A claim representative is the key person responsible for interacting with the claimant and handling claims.

Depending on the circumstances, the following different types of claim representatives may handle claims, including:

- Staff claim representatives, who are insurer employees and include inside claim representatives and outside (field) claim representatives
- Independent adjusters, who are claim representatives who offer claim handling services to insurers for a fee
- Producers, who often have claim settlement authority to settle certain small claims
- Public adjusters, who are hired by and represent the insured in the claim handling process

Self-insurance also requires claim handling services. The self-insuring organization may use its own personnel to settle claims, or it may use the services of a third-party administrator.

Regardless of who handles claims, the claim handling process involves the following same four activities:

1. Verifying coverage
2. Determining the cause of loss
3. Determining the amount of damages or extent of loss
4. Negotiating and settling (or denying) the claim

For property claims, investigation usually includes inspecting the damaged property to determine the cause of loss and to assess the damage. The investigation also involves verifying coverage to determine whether an insurable interest exists, whether the policy covers the damaged property, whether the policy covers the cause of loss involved, and whether any additional coverages, endorsements, or limitations apply. The procedure for valuing the loss depends on whether the policy specifies actual cash value, replacement cost, agreed value, or some other method for valuing losses.

In liability claims, the claim representative's investigation focuses on whether the activity leading to liability comes within the scope of the policy and whether the insured could be legally responsible for the loss. The valuation of a bodily injury loss involves examining medical records and physicians' reports. If the case goes to court, the total liability loss can result in compensatory damages (which include special damages and general damages) and, sometimes, punitive damages. Often, however, it is in the best interest of all parties to negotiate a settlement out of court rather than to incur the expense and delay of legal proceedings.

Claim representatives deal with many day-to-day claim situations, but occasionally face claims that result from a catastrophic event. Such catastrophe claims present a dramatic short-term increase in the number of claims which must be handled. The increased volume presents a new set of challenges to the claim representative and draws greater scrutiny on the claim handling process.

In addition to having a key role in fulfilling the promise contained in the insurance contract, claim representatives also play an important role in establishing an insurer's loss reserves. A case reserve for a particular claim is the best estimate of the amount the insurer will eventually have to pay for that claim.

Many states have passed laws prohibiting unfair claim practices. Regulators also monitor complaints from insureds and claimants. A number of valid complaints about a particular insurer or claim representative could lead to a reprimand, a fine, license suspension, substantial legal judgment, or some other legal penalty.

CHAPTER NOTE

1.   Insurance Information Institute, *The III Insurance Fact Book 2005* (New York: Insurance Information Institute, 2005), p. 23.

Segment C

Insurance Contracts, Loss Exposures, and Risk Management

Direct Your Learning

Insurance Contracts

After learning the content of this chapter and completing the corresponding course guide assignment, you should be able to:

- Explain the four elements of any valid contract.

- Describe the special characteristics of insurance contracts.

- Describe the principle of indemnity.

- Summarize the information usually found in the declarations page(s) of an insurance policy.

- Explain the purpose of the following categories of insurance policy provisions:

  - Definitions

  - Insuring agreements

  - Exclusions

  - Conditions

  - Miscellaneous provisions

- Distinguish between manuscript policies and standard forms.

- Describe the advantages and disadvantages of standard forms to insurers and insureds.

- Distinguish between a self-contained policy and a modular policy.

- Describe the conditions commonly found in property and liability insurance policies.

- Explain how subrogation works.

- Define or describe each of the Key Words and Phrases for this chapter.

Develop Your Perspective

What are the main topics covered in the chapter?

The insurance contract documents the promise of coverage made by an insurer to an insured. Because the contract is the essence of an insurer's future performance, there are rules that apply to forming and interpreting an insurance contract.

Compare the elements of all valid contracts to characteristics that are unique to insurance contracts.

- What elements of insurance contracts are not necessarily found in other contracts?
- Why are standard forms frequently used by insurers?

Why is it important to learn about these topics?

Insurance contracts are the essence of the agreement between the insurer and the insured. For this reason, the language and intent of the contract is scrutinized to determine whether a valid contract exists and whether a claim will be paid.

Consider how a missing element of a valid contract might eliminate or change coverage provided by an insurer.

- How does coverage change if an applicant misrepresents information on an insurance application, and the insurer issues a policy based on the incorrect information?

How can you use what you will learn?

Evaluate the protection that is provided to insureds under insurance contracts.

- How do the unique characteristics of insurance contracts protect the insureds' interests?
- Why should contract ambiguities be interpreted in the insureds' favor?

Chapter 7

Insurance Contracts

Purchasing insurance differs from buying groceries, clothes, or other tangible goods. A car buyer, for example, can examine and even test drive a car before buying it. Although warranties and promises of reliable service may influence the decision to buy, the primary consideration is the car itself. The car's physical characteristics are readily apparent at the time of the sale. The buyer cannot blame the dealer if the car is too small or the wrong color. Insurance, in contrast, is not something a person can test before buying. The essence of insurance is the insurer's promise that it will pay claims in the future for losses that are covered under the policy.

The evidence of this promise is the insurance contract, or policy. The policy defines in detail the rights and duties of both parties to the contract: the insured and the insurer. A particular insurance policy meets a buyer's needs only if the terms of the policy obligate the insurer to provide the protection desired. Although it is possible to evaluate a car with a test drive, evaluating an insurance policy requires an analysis of its terms.

This chapter provides a foundation for such an analysis. The chapter first discusses contracts in general and then describes the special characteristics of insurance contracts, their content, and their structure. It concludes with a description of several conditions that are common to most property and liability insurance policies.

ELEMENTS OF A CONTRACT

An insurance contract, called a **policy**, is an agreement between the insurer and the insured. An insurance policy must meet the same requirements as any other valid **contract**, which is a legally enforceable agreement between two or more parties.

If a dispute arises between the parties to a contract, a court will enforce only valid contracts. The validity of a contract depends on the following four essential elements:

1. Agreement (offer and acceptance)
2. Competent parties
3. Legal purpose
4. Consideration

Policy
A complete written contract of insurance.

Contract
A legally enforceable agreement between two or more parties.

If a court cannot confirm the presence of all four elements, it will not enforce the contract.

Agreement (Offer and Acceptance)

One essential element of a contract is that the parties to the contract must be in agreement. One party must make a legitimate *offer* and another party must *accept* the offer. In legal terms, there must be "mutual assent."

In the case of insurance, the process of achieving mutual assent generally begins when someone who wants to purchase insurance completes an insurance application—an offer to buy insurance. The details on the application describe the exposures to be insured and indicate the coverage the applicant requests.

In an uncomplicated case, an insurer underwriter (or an agent, acting on behalf of an insurer) accepts the application and agrees to provide the coverage requested at a premium acceptable to both the insurer and the applicant. The premium is the payment by an insured to an insurer in exchange for insurance coverage. At this point, agreement exists; the insurer has accepted the applicant's offer to buy insurance.

In a more complicated case, the underwriter may not be willing to meet all the requests of the applicant. One of the underwriter's options is to accept the application with modification. The underwriter may be willing to provide coverage, but only on somewhat different terms. For example, the underwriter may insist on a higher deductible than the applicant had requested. When the underwriter communicates the proposed modifications to the applicant, these modifications constitute a counteroffer. Several offers and counteroffers may be made before both parties agree to an exact set of terms. If the other essential elements of a contract exist, the mutual assent of the insurer and the applicant forms a contract.

To be enforceable, the agreement cannot be the result of duress, coercion, fraud, or a mistake. If either party to the contract can prove any of these circumstances, a court could declare the contract to be void.

Competent Parties

For the contract to be enforceable, all parties must be legally competent. In other words, each party must have the legal capacity to make the agreement binding. Individuals are generally considered to be competent and able to enter into legally enforceable contracts, unless they are one or more of the following:

- Insane or otherwise mentally incompetent
- Under the influence of drugs or alcohol
- Minors (persons not yet of legal age)

However, minors are sometimes considered competent to purchase auto insurance, especially when auto insurance qualifies as a necessity. State laws vary in regard to issues involving minors.

Another aspect of legal capacity is that, in most states, an insurer must be licensed to do business in the state. If an insurer mistakenly writes a policy in a state where that insurer is not licensed, the insured might later argue that the contract is not valid and demand the return of the premium. This demand would be based on the fact that the insurer did not have the legal capacity to make the agreement.

Legal Purpose

An enforceable contract must also have a legal purpose. The courts may consider a contract to be illegal if its purpose is against the law or against public policy (as defined by the courts). For example, an agreement to pay a bribe to a government official in exchange for receiving a government job would not be enforced by the courts because such activities are against public policy.

Although most insurance policies do not involve a question of legality, certain situations do exist that may invalidate an insurance policy. Courts will refuse to enforce any insurance policy that is illegal or that tends to injure the public welfare. Insurance contracts must involve a legal subject matter. Property insurance on illegally owned or possessed goods is invalid. For example, property insurance covering illegal drugs would be illegal and therefore unenforceable. If fireworks are illegal in a particular state, then an insurance policy covering fireworks would be illegal in that state. In addition, no insurance contract will remain valid if the wrongful conduct of the insured causes the operation of the contract to violate public policy. Thus, arson by an insured would render a property insurance policy unenforceable and would preclude recovery by the insured under the policy for a building the insured intentionally burned.

Consideration

Consideration is something of value given by each party to a contract. For example, when an auto is purchased, the buyer gives money (consideration) to the seller who, in turn, provides the car (which is also consideration).

Some contracts do not involve the exchange of one tangible item for another, but instead involve performance. For example, an author may sign a contract agreeing to write a book in exchange for payment by the publisher.

Performance can also involve a promise to perform some act in the future that is dependent on a certain event occurring. In the case of an insurance contract, the insurer's consideration is its promise to pay a claim in the

Consideration
Something of value given by each party to a contract.

future *if* a covered loss occurs. If no loss occurs, the insurer is still fulfilling its promise to provide financial protection even though it does not pay a claim. In insurance contracts, the following two types of consideration are involved:

- The *insured's* consideration is the payment of (or the promise to pay) the premium.
- The *insurer's* consideration is its promise to pay claims for covered losses.

SPECIAL CHARACTERISTICS OF INSURANCE CONTRACTS

In addition to having the four essential elements of all contracts, insurance contracts have certain special characteristics. An insurance policy is all of the following:

- A conditional contract
- A contract involving fortuitous events and the exchange of unequal amounts
- A contract of utmost good faith
- A contract of adhesion
- A contract of indemnity
- A nontransferable contract

Conditional Contract

Conditional contract
A contract in which one or more parties must perform only under certain conditions.

An insurance policy is a **conditional contract** because the parties have to perform only under certain conditions. Whether the insurer pays a claim depends on whether a covered loss has occurred. In addition, the insured must fulfill certain duties before a claim is paid, such as giving prompt notice to the insurer after a loss has occurred.

A covered loss might not occur during a particular policy period, but that fact does not mean the insurance policy for that period has been worthless. In buying an insurance policy, the insured acquires a valuable promise—the promise of the insurer to make payments if a covered loss occurs. The promise exists, even if the insurer's performance is not required during the policy period.

Contract Involving Fortuitous Events and the Exchange of Unequal Amounts

While noninsurance contracts involve an exchange of money for a certain event, such as the provision of goods or services, insurance contracts involve an exchange of money for protection upon the occurrence of uncertain, or fortuitous, events. Insurance contracts involve an exchange of unequal amounts. Often, there are few or no losses and the premium paid by the insured for a particular policy is more than the amount paid by the insurer to, or on behalf of, the insured. If a large loss occurs, however, the insurer's claim payment might be much more than the premium paid by the insured. It is the possibility that the insurer's obligation might be much greater than the insured's that makes the insurance transaction a fair trade.

For example, assume an insurer charges a $1,000 annual premium to provide auto physical damage coverage on a car valued at $20,000. The following three situations may occur:

1. If the car is not damaged while the policy is in force, the insurer pays nothing.
2. If the car is partially damaged, the insurer pays the cost of repairs, after subtracting a deductible.
3. If the car is a total loss, the insurer pays $20,000 (minus any deductible).

Unless, by chance, the insurer's obligations in a minor accident total exactly $1,000, unequal amounts are involved in all three of these cases. However, it does not follow that insureds who have no losses—or only very minor losses—do not get their money's worth or that insureds involved in major accidents profit from the insurance.

The premium for a particular policy should reflect the insured's share of estimated losses that the insurer must pay. Many insureds have no losses, but some have very large losses. The policy premium reflects the insured's proportionate share of the total amount the insurer expects to pay to honor its agreements with all insureds having similar policies.

Contract of Utmost Good Faith

Because insurance involves a promise, it requires complete honesty and disclosure of all relevant facts from both parties. For this reason, insurance contracts are considered contracts of **utmost good faith**. Both parties to an insurance contract—the insurer and the insured—are expected to be ethical in their dealings with each other.

Utmost good faith
An obligation to act in complete honesty and to disclose all relevant facts.

The insured has a right to rely on the insurer to fulfill its promises. Therefore, the insurer is expected to treat the insured with utmost good faith. An insurer that acts in bad faith, such as denying coverage for a claim that is clearly covered, could face serious penalties under the law.

The insurer also has a right to expect that the insured will act in good faith. An insurance buyer who intentionally conceals certain information or misrepresents certain facts does not act in good faith. Because an insurance contract requires utmost good faith from both parties, an insurer could be released from a contract because of concealment or misrepresentation by the insured.

Concealment

Concealment
An intentional failure to disclose a material fact.

Concealment is an intentional failure to disclose a material fact. Courts have held that the insurer must prove two things to establish that concealment has occurred. First, it must establish that the failure to disclose information was intentional, which is often difficult. The insurer must usually show that the insured knew that the information should have been given and then intentionally withheld it.

Material fact
In insurance, a fact that would affect the insurer's decision to provide or maintain insurance or to settle a claim.

Second, the insurer must establish that the information withheld was a **material fact**—information that would affect an insurer's underwriting or claim settlement decision. In the case of an auto insurance applicant, for example, material facts include how the applicant's autos are used, who drives them, and the ages and driving records of the drivers. If an insured intentionally conceals the material fact that a sixteen-year-old son lives in the household and is the principal driver of one of the cars, that concealment could void the policy.

Insurers carefully design applications for insurance to include questions regarding facts material to the underwriting process. The application includes questions on specific subjects to which the applicant must respond. These questions are designed to encourage the applicant to reveal all pertinent information.

Misrepresentation

In normal usage, a misrepresentation is a false statement. In the insurance context, a **misrepresentation** is a false statement of a material fact on which the insurer relies. The insurer does not have to prove that the misrepresentation is intentional.

Misrepresentation
A false statement of a material fact on which a party relies.

For example, an applicant for auto insurance is assumed to have had two speeding tickets during the eighteen months immediately before submitting the application for insurance. When asked if any driving violations have occurred within the past three years (a question found on most auto insurance application forms), an applicant giving either of the following answers would be making a misrepresentation:

- "I remember having one speeding ticket about two years ago."
- "I've never been cited for a moving violation—only a few parking tickets."

The first response provides incorrect information, and this false statement may or may not be intentional. The false statement made in the second response is probably intentional. The direct question posed in the application requires a full and honest response from the applicant because the insurer relies on the information. Anything less is a misrepresentation, whether intentional or not.

As with a concealment, if a material fact is misrepresented, the insurer could choose to void the policy because of the violation of utmost good faith.

Contract of Adhesion

The wording in insurance contracts is usually drafted by the insurer (or an insurance advisory organization), enabling the insurer to use preprinted forms for many different insureds. Because the insurer determines the exact wording of the policy, the insured has little choice but to "take it or leave it." That is, the insured must adhere to the contract drafted by the insurer. Therefore, insurance policies are considered to be **contracts of adhesion**, which means one party (the insured) must adhere to the agreement as written by the other party (the insurer). This characteristic significantly influences the enforcement of insurance policies.

Contract of adhesion
A contract to which one party (the insured) must adhere as written by the other party (the insurer).

If a dispute arises between the insurer and the insured about the meaning of certain words or phrases in the policy, the insured and the insurer are not on an equal basis. The insurer either drafted the policy or used standard forms of its own choice; in contrast, the insured did not have any say in the policy wording. For that reason, if the policy wording is ambiguous, a court will generally apply the interpretation that favors the insured.

Contract of Indemnity

The purpose of insurance is to indemnify an insured who suffers a loss. To indemnify is to restore a party who has had a loss to the same financial position that party held before the loss occurred. Most property and liability insurance policies are contracts of indemnity. With a **contract of indemnity**, the insurer agrees, in the event of a covered loss, to pay an amount directly related to the amount of the loss.

Contract of indemnity
A contract in which the insurer agrees, in the event of a covered loss, to pay an amount directly related to the amount of the loss.

Property insurance generally pays the amount necessary to repair covered property that has been damaged or to replace it with similar property. The policy specifies the method for determining the amount of the loss. For example, most auto policies, both personal and commercial, specify that vehicles are to be valued at their actual cash value (ACV) at the time of a loss. If a covered accident occurs that causes a covered vehicle to be a total loss, the insurer will normally pay the ACV of the vehicle, less any applicable deductible.

Liability insurance generally pays to a third-party claimant, on behalf of the insured, any amounts (up to the policy limit) that the insured becomes legally obligated to pay as damages because of a covered liability claim, as well as the legal costs associated with that claim. For example, if an insured with a liability limit of $300,000 is ordered by a court to pay $100,000 for bodily injury incurred by the claimant in a covered accident, the insurer will pay $100,000 to the claimant and will also pay the cost to defend the insured in court.

A contract of indemnity does not necessarily pay the full amount necessary to restore an insured who has suffered a covered loss to the same financial position. However, the amount the insurer pays is directly related to the amount of the insured's loss. Most policies contain a policy limit that specifies the maximum amount the insurer will pay for a single claim. Many policies also contain limitations and other provisions that could reduce the amount of recovery. For example, a homeowners policy is not designed to cover large amounts of cash. Therefore, most homeowners policies contain a special limit, such as $200, for any covered loss to money owned by the insured. If a covered fire destroys $1,000 in cash belonging to the insured, the homeowners insurer will pay only $200 for the money that was destroyed.

Principle of indemnity
The principle that insurance should provide a benefit no greater than the loss suffered by the insured.

According to the **principle of indemnity**, the insured should not profit from a covered loss. That is, insurance should provide a benefit no greater than the loss suffered by the insured. Insurance policies usually include certain provisions that reinforce the principle of indemnity. For example, policies generally contain an other insurance provision to prevent an insured from receiving full payment from two different insurance policies for the same claim. Insurance contracts usually protect the insurer's subrogation rights, as discussed earlier. Other insurance provisions and subrogation provisions clarify that the insured cannot collect more than the amount of the loss. For example, following an auto accident in which the insurer compensates its insured when the other driver is at fault, the subrogation provision stipulates that the insured's right to recover damages from the responsible party is transferred (subrogated) to the insurer. The insured cannot collect from both the insurer and the responsible party.

Another factor enforcing the principle of indemnity is that a person usually cannot buy insurance unless that person is in a position to suffer a financial loss. In other words, the insured must have an insurable interest in the subject of the insurance. For example, property insurance contracts cover losses only to the extent of the insured's insurable interest in the property. This restriction prevents an insured from collecting more from the insurance than the amount of the loss he or she suffered. A person cannot buy life insurance on the life of a stranger, hoping to gain if the stranger dies. Insurers normally sell life insurance when there is a reasonable expectation of a financial loss from the death of the insured person, such as the loss of an insured's future income that the insured's dependents would face. Insurable interest is not an issue in liability insurance because a liability claim against an insured results in a financial loss if the insured is legally responsible. Even if the insured is not responsible, the insured could incur defense costs.

Valued policy
A policy in which the insurer pays a stated amount in the event of a specified loss (usually a total loss), regardless of the actual value of the loss.

Some insurance contracts are not contracts of indemnity but valued policies. When a specified loss occurs, a **valued policy** pays a stated amount, regardless of the actual value of the loss. For example, a fine arts policy may specify that it will pay $250,000 for loss of a particular painting or sculpture. The actual market value of the painting or sculpture may be much smaller or much greater than $250,000, but the policy will pay $250,000 in either case. In most valued policies, the insurer and the insured agree on a limit that approximates the current market value of the insured property.

Nontransferable Contract

The identities of the persons or organizations insured are important to the insurer, which has the right to select those applicants with whom it is willing to enter into contractual agreements. After an insurance policy is in effect, an insured may not freely transfer the policy to some other party (a practice called "assignment"). If such a transfer were allowed to take place, the insurer would be legally bound to a contract with a party it may not wish to insure. Most insurance policies contain a provision that requires the insurer's written permission before an insured can transfer a policy to another party.

Traditionally, insurance textbooks used language stating that "insurance is a personal contract" to indicate its nontransferable nature, and cited clauses in property policies to illustrate the principle. The policy language does differ between typical property and liability policies, but in both types, the intention is to prohibit the insured from transferring the policy to another party without the insurer's consent.

CONTENT OF INSURANCE POLICIES

Insurance policies must be drafted carefully. The parties must agree on how to handle many situations that could arise even if these situations are not likely to occur. Familiarity with both the general content and structure of insurance policies helps in analyzing the terms of a particular policy.

An insurance policy specifically describes the coverage it provides. Because no insurance policy can cover every possibility, the policy must describe its limitations, restrictions, and exclusions as clearly as possible. For example, most insurance policies do not cover losses caused by acts of war or nuclear contamination. If the insurer does not intend to cover such losses, the policy must clearly state that fact. The only way to determine the coverage provided by a particular policy is to examine its provisions, which are generally included in the following categories:

- Declarations
- Definitions
- Insuring agreements
- Exclusions
- Conditions
- Miscellaneous provisions

Declarations

An insurance policy must first identify the parties to the contract. Information such as the name and location of the insurer and the name and address of the insured is usually shown on the first page of the policy. This information page is often called the **declarations page**, although it can be more than one page; it is also known simply as the **declarations** or the **dec**. As its name implies,

Declarations page, or **declarations**, or **dec.**
An insurance policy information page or pages providing specific details about the insured and the subject of the insurance.

a declarations page declares important information about the specific policy of which it is a part. The name of the insurer is almost always preprinted on the declarations page and the name and address of the insured are entered when the policy is issued. Exhibit 7-1 shows a sample declarations page of a personal auto policy.

Insurance policies usually provide coverage for a specified period. The inception date of the policy is stated in the declarations. The expiration date may also appear in the declarations, or the policy period may be clarified elsewhere in the policy, usually as part of the conditions.

The insurance policy must describe the consideration involved. As stated previously, the insured's consideration is the premium, and the insurer's consideration is its promise to pay if a covered loss occurs. The premium amount is usually shown in the policy declarations. Other statements regarding when the premium should be paid, to whom it should be paid, and the consequences if it is not paid may appear elsewhere in the policy.

The declarations also show the policy limit (or limits). A limit is the maximum amount of coverage the insurer will pay for a given type of loss. In some situations, however, the insurer may ultimately pay an amount greater than a policy limit. For example, under some liability policies, defense costs may be paid in addition to the amount of damages. Some property policies include additional coverages, such as debris removal, which may be paid in addition to a policy limit.

In addition, the declarations usually include any information that specifically describes the covered property or locations, specific coverages, deductibles, policy forms, endorsements, and other important details about the insured, the subject of the insurance, and the coverages provided by the policy.

Definitions

Because insurance policies often contain technical terms that are used in a precise way, most policies define words that have a specific meaning with regard to the coverage provided. The terms may be defined in a separate section of the policy or where they first appear in the policy. If a policy definition differs from normal usage for a term, the definition in the policy prevails. Unless the contract provides specific definitions, the words in insurance policies and other contracts are generally interpreted according to their ordinary meanings or dictionary definitions. If ambiguity exists, the words could be interpreted by the courts.

Insurance policies sometimes distinguish defined terms by placing quotation marks around the terms or by printing them in boldface type each time they appear in the policy. Exhibit 7-2 shows the definitions section of a typical homeowners policy.

EXHIBIT 7-1

Sample Declarations Page of a Personal Auto Policy

Granton Insurer, Malvern, PA
Personal Auto Policy Declarations

POLICYHOLDER: David M. and Joan G. Smith
(Named Insured)   216 Brookside Drive
                        Anytown, USA 40000

POLICY NUMBER: 296 S 468211

POLICY PERIOD: FROM: December 25, 2004

                       TO: June 25, 2005

But only if the required premium for this period has been paid, and for six-month renewal periods if renewal premiums are paid as required. Each period begins and ends after 12:01 AM standard time at the address of the policyholder.

INSURED VEHICLES AND SCHEDULE OF COVERAGES

VEHICLE	COVERAGES	LIMITS OF INSURANCE	PREMIUM
1. 1998 Toyota Camry ID #JT2AL21E0B3306553			
	Coverage A—Liability	$300,000 Each Occurrence	$202
	Coverage B—Medical Payments	$ 5,000 Each Person	$ 28
	Coverage C—Uninsured Motorists	$300,000 Each Occurrence	$ 51
		TOTAL	$281
2. 2003 Ford Taurus ID #1FABP3OU8GG212619			
	Coverage A—Liability	$300,000 Each Occurrence	$202
	Coverage B—Medical Payments	$ 5,000 Each Person	$ 28
	Coverage C—Uninsured Motorists	$300,000 Each Occurrence	$ 51
	Coverage D—Other Than Collision	Actual Cash Value Less $250	$ 81
	—Collision	Actual Cash Value Less $500	$196
		TOTAL	$558
		TOTAL PREMIUM	$839

POLICY FORM AND ENDORSEMENTS: PP 00 01 PP 03 06

COUNTERSIGNATURE DATE: December 1, 2004

AGENT: J. Jones

EXHIBIT 7-2

Definitions Section of a Homeowners Policy

DEFINITIONS

A. In this policy, "you" and "your" refer to the "named insured" shown in the Declarations and the spouse if a resident of the same household. "We", "us" and "our" refer to the Company providing this insurance.

B. In addition, certain words and phrases are defined as follows:

1. "Aircraft Liability", "Hovercraft Liability", "Motor Vehicle Liability" and "Watercraft Liability", subject to the provisions in **b.** below, mean the following:

   a. Liability for "bodily injury" or "property damage" arising out of the:

     (1) Ownership of such vehicle or craft by an "insured";

     (2) Maintenance, occupancy, operation, use, loading or unloading of such vehicle or craft by any person;

     (3) Entrustment of such vehicle or craft by an "insured" to any person;

     (4) Failure to supervise or negligent supervision of any person involving such vehicle or craft by an "insured"; or

     (5) Vicarious liability, whether or not imposed by law, for the actions of a child or minor involving such vehicle or craft.

   b. For the purpose of this definition:

     (1) Aircraft means any contrivance used or designed for flight except model or hobby aircraft not used or designed to carry people or cargo;

     (2) Hovercraft means a self-propelled motorized ground effect vehicle and includes, but is not limited to, flarecraft and air cushion vehicles;

     (3) Watercraft means a craft principally designed to be propelled on or in water by wind, engine power or electric motor; and

     (4) Motor vehicle means a "motor vehicle" as defined in **7.** below.

2. "Bodily injury" means bodily harm, sickness or disease, including required care, loss of services and death that results.

3. "Business" means:

   a. A trade, profession or occupation engaged in on a full-time, part-time or occasional basis; or

   b. Any other activity engaged in for money or other compensation, except the following:

     (1) One or more activities, not described in **(2)** through **(4)** below, for which no "insured" receives more than $2,000 in total compensation for the 12 months before the beginning of the policy period;

     (2) Volunteer activities for which no money is received other than payment for expenses incurred to perform the activity;

     (3) Providing home day care services for which no compensation is received, other than the mutual exchange of such services; or

     (4) The rendering of home day care services to a relative of an "insured".

4. "Employee" means an employee of an "insured", or an employee leased to an "insured" by a labor leasing firm under an agreement between an "insured" and the labor leasing firm, whose duties are other than those performed by a "residence employee".

5. "Insured" means:

   a. You and residents of your household who are:

     (1) Your relatives; or

     (2) Other persons under the age of 21 and in the care of any person named above;

   b. A student enrolled in school full time, as defined by the school, who was a resident of your household before moving out to attend school, provided the student is under the age of:

     (1) 24 and your relative; or

     (2) 21 and in your care or the care of a person described in **a.(1)** above; or

c. Under Section **II:**

   (1) With respect to animals or watercraft to which this policy applies, any person or organization legally responsible for these animals or watercraft which are owned by you or any person included in **a.** or **b.** above. "Insured" does not mean a person or organization using or having custody of these animals or watercraft in the course of any "business" or without consent of the owner; or

   (2) With respect to a "motor vehicle" to which this policy applies:

     (a) Persons while engaged in your employ or that of any person included in **a.** or **b.** above; or

     (b) Other persons using the vehicle on an "insured location" with your consent.

Under both Sections **I** and **II,** when the word an immediately precedes the word "insured", the words an "insured" together mean one or more "insureds".

6. "Insured location" means:

  a. The "residence premises";

  b. The part of other premises, other structures and grounds used by you as a residence; and

   (1) Which is shown in the Declarations; or

   (2) Which is acquired by you during the policy period for your use as a residence;

  c. Any premises used by you in connection with a premises described in **a.** and **b.** above;

  d. Any part of a premises:

   (1) Not owned by an "insured"; and

   (2) Where an "insured" is temporarily residing;

  e. Vacant land, other than farm land, owned by or rented to an "insured";

  f. Land owned by or rented to an "insured" on which a one, two, three or four family dwelling is being built as a residence for an "insured";

  g. Individual or family cemetery plots or burial vaults of an "insured"; or

  h. Any part of a premises occasionally rented to an "insured" for other than "business" use.

7. "Motor vehicle" means:

  a. A self-propelled land or amphibious vehicle; or

  b. Any trailer or semitrailer which is being carried on, towed by or hitched for towing by a vehicle described in **a.** above.

8. "Occurrence" means an accident, including continuous or repeated exposure to substantially the same general harmful conditions, which results, during the policy period, in:

  a. "Bodily injury"; or

  b. "Property damage".

9. "Property damage" means physical injury to, destruction of, or loss of use of tangible property.

10. "Residence employee" means:

  a. An employee of an "insured", or an employee leased to an "insured" by a labor leasing firm, under an agreement between an "insured" and the labor leasing firm, whose duties are related to the maintenance or use of the "residence premises", including household or domestic services; or

  b. One who performs similar duties elsewhere not related to the "business" of an "insured".

A "residence employee" does not include a temporary employee who is furnished to an "insured" to substitute for a permanent "residence employee" on leave or to meet seasonal or short-term workload conditions.

11. "Residence premises" means:

  a. The one family dwelling where you reside;

  b. The two, three or four family dwelling where you reside in at least one of the family units; or

  c. That part of any other building where you reside;

and which is shown as the "residence premises" in the Declarations.

"Residence premises" also includes other structures and grounds at that location.

Insuring Agreements

Insuring agreement
An insurance policy statement indicating that the insurer will, under certain circumstances, make a payment or provide a service.

An insurance policy contains at least one **insuring agreement**, which is a specific statement indicating that the insurer will, under certain circumstances, make a payment or provide a service. For example, the Personal Auto Policy developed by Insurance Services Office (ISO) contains a separate insuring agreement for each of the four coverages provided by the policy: liability, medical payments, uninsured motorists, and coverage for damage to the insured's auto.

A typical insuring agreement in the ISO Personal Auto Policy for Part D—Coverage for Damage to Your Auto would read, in part, as follows:

> We will pay for direct and accidental loss to "your covered auto" or any "non-owned auto," including their equipment, minus any applicable deductible shown in the Declarations.

The words enclosed in quotation marks in this insuring agreement are defined in the definitions section of the policy.

Exclusions

The exclusions in an insurance policy describe what the insurer does not cover. Although the insuring agreement makes a broad promise to provide coverage, the **exclusions** eliminate coverage for specified loss exposures. No insurance policy can reasonably cover all possible losses. Insurance policies contain exclusions for several reasons as follows:

Exclusion
A policy provision that eliminates coverage for specified exposures.

- *To eliminate duplicate coverage.* Some losses are best covered by one type of insurance and are thus excluded by other types of policies. For example, most motor vehicle exposures are excluded from homeowners policies because they should be covered under automobile insurance policies.

- *To assist in managing moral hazards.* Moral hazards are conditions that may lead some people to exaggerate losses or intentionally cause them to collect insurance proceeds. Most policies exclude losses expected or intended by the insured. For example, coverage is excluded when an insured commits arson for the purpose of collecting the insurance proceeds.

- *To avoid insuring other losses that are deliberate.* Some liability losses are within the control of the insured. Many policies exclude coverage for bodily injury or property damage intentionally caused by the insured. The motivation may be different than the profit incentive that is common with moral hazards. For example, a person may deliberately back his truck into his neighbor's car door out of anger or spite. As with moral hazards, most policies exclude losses that are deliberate.

- *To assist in managing attitudinal (morale) hazards.* Attitudinal hazards, also called morale hazards, exist when the frequency or severity of loss is increased because a person is not as careful as he or she could be. Some exclusions help manage morale hazards by making the insureds themselves bear the losses that might easily have been avoided. For instance, the

ISO homeowners policy excludes losses caused by the insured's neglect to use reasonable means to protect property at the time of loss or afterwards.

- *To avoid covering losses that are not economically feasible to insure.* Some losses cannot reasonably be insured by private insurers. For example, war and nuclear events involve a potential for catastrophic losses that are not economically feasible for one insurer to cover.

- *To eliminate coverage that most insureds do not need.* For example, the average homeowner does not own a private airplane or need coverage for destruction of aircraft. Accordingly, the homeowners policy excludes aircraft.

- *To eliminate coverage for exposures that require special handling by the insurer.* For example, most commercial property policies exclude coverage for steam boiler explosions because boilers require special inspections and coverage that many insurers do not have the expertise to handle. Also, such coverage may be obtained under a policy designed for that purpose.

- *To keep premiums reasonable.* For example, auto insurance policies exclude coverage for wear and tear of the auto. If auto insurers were to provide coverage for all regular maintenance of insured autos, premiums would probably become unreasonable because of the large number of expected losses.

Many exclusions, including the previous examples, fit into more than one of the preceding categories. Any exclusion can serve more than one purpose. To a certain extent, all exclusions fit the last purpose of keeping premiums reasonable. Logically, it would require a higher premium to pay for the additional losses that may be covered whenever a policy is broadened by eliminating an exclusion.

Although exclusions often appear in a separate section or sections labeled "Exclusions," they can also appear in various places throughout the policy. The term "exclusion" can accurately apply to any policy provision whose function is to eliminate coverage for specified loss exposures—whether or not the provision is labeled as an exclusion. For example, in the ISO homeowners policies, exclusions appear in various parts of the policy, labeled in different ways, including the following:

- "Property Not Covered," which lists specific types of uninsured property
- "Section I—Perils Insured Against," which lists both covered causes of loss and specific causes of loss that are not covered
- "Section I—Exclusions," which specially lists exclusions that apply to covered property

Conditions

Insurance policies contain several conditions relating to the coverage provided. A **policy condition** is any provision that qualifies an otherwise enforceable promise of the insurer. The insured must generally comply with

Policy condition
Any provision that qualifies an otherwise enforceable promise of the insurer.

these conditions if coverage is to apply to a loss. Some of the more common conditions included in insurance policies are discussed later in this chapter.

Miscellaneous Provisions

Insurance policies often contain provisions that do not qualify as one of the policy components described previously. These miscellaneous provisions sometimes deal with the relationship between the insured and the insurer, or they may help to establish procedures for carrying out the terms of the contract. However, actions by the insured that differ from the procedures in the miscellaneous provisions normally do not affect the insurer's duty to provide coverage.

Some miscellaneous provisions are unique to particular types of insurers. For example, a policy issued by a mutual insurer is likely to describe the right of each insured to vote in the election of the board of directors.

STANDARD FORMS AND MANUSCRIPT POLICIES

Although insurance contracts, like all other contracts, represent freely negotiated agreements between the parties, most insurance policies are made up of standard, preprinted forms. The parties do not normally negotiate all the terms of the contract each time someone purchases an insurance policy. Only in a special situation, usually involving a large amount of insurance, might such negotiation happen. When it does, the result is a **manuscript policy** or **manuscript endorsement**, specifically drafted according to terms negotiated between a specific insured (or group of insureds) and an insurer.

Manuscript policy or **manuscript endorsement**
An insurance policy that is specifically drafted according to terms negotiated between a specific insured (or group of insureds) and an insurer.

As mentioned earlier, insurance advisory organizations such as ISO and the American Association of Insurance Services (AAIS) develop industrywide standardized forms for different types of insurance, and many insurers use these standard forms for any insured accepted for a particular coverage. Similarly, an insurer may develop its own forms that meet the coverage needs of most insureds. A standard policy form has no specific reference to the insured's name, address, policy limits, premiums, and so forth. Instead, the standard form is attached to a declarations page that contains all of the specific information relating to the insured.

The use of standard forms has many advantages for insurers and is an efficient way to provide contracts to thousands of insureds. Not only do standard forms save considerable time and expense in issuing the policy, but they also promote consistency in the insurer's operations. When a prospective insured applies for a specific insurance policy, the underwriter knows the scope of the coverage provided by that policy, including the applicable restrictions and exclusions. If the underwriter had to develop a manuscript policy for each individual case, underwriting efficiency and consistency would be seriously hampered. With standard forms, the underwriter can choose from among applicants for the same coverage and can determine appropriate premiums on a consistent basis. Similarly, claim representatives know the extent of coverage provided by standard forms and can more quickly and easily decide whether the policy covers a particular loss.

Standard policies benefit insureds and insurers. For informed buyers, often in commercial insurance, selecting an insurer requires comparing differences in policy provisions and language if the various insurers do not use the same standard form. In addition, if a loss is covered by two or more insurers, the likelihood of claim disputes is reduced if all insurers involved have provided coverage under the same standard form.

Standardized wording also leads to a more consistent interpretation of insurance policies. When disagreements arise between the insured and the insurer concerning the interpretation of a particular insurance contract, a court ruling may be necessary to determine the appropriate legal interpretation of the contested policy language. If the identical language appears in many other policies of the same type, the insurer knows how the court is likely to interpret this language in the future and can properly underwrite and price the policy based on that interpretation. If the language were constantly changing or were different for each insured, more disputes would occur, and there would be no standard legal interpretation on which the insurer and the insured could rely.

After the policy wording has been drafted by the insurer or advisory organization and approved by state regulators, the insurer prints thousands of copies of each standardized form, or stores the forms electronically. When insurance is purchased, the appropriate documents are combined with the declarations to create the policy for that particular insured. The documents can be combined in many different ways to create policies that meet the needs of many different insureds.

STRUCTURE OF INSURANCE POLICIES

Insurers use two approaches when structuring an insurance policy, whether manuscript or standardized. A policy's structure can be either self-contained or modular, as discussed next.

Self-Contained Policies

A **self-contained policy** is a single document that contains all the agreements between the insurer and the insured; it forms a complete policy by itself. One example of a self-contained policy is the ISO Personal Auto Policy. A widely used auto insurance policy, the ISO Personal Auto Policy includes both property and liability insurance coverage in a single document.

The cover of a Personal Auto Policy may be a multicolor "wrapper" or "jacket" containing the name and logo of the insurer. Like the wrappers on most products, the purpose of the cover is to enhance the appearance of the product, to highlight the provider's name, and to protect the contents.

Self-contained policy
A single document that contains all the agreements between the insurer and the insured; forms a complete policy by itself.

Inside the cover of a Personal Auto Policy is the declarations page. Although the preprinted Personal Auto Policy form is the same for all insureds, the declarations page and any attached endorsements personalize it for a particular insured. As described earlier, the policy contains a broad insuring agreement and separate insuring agreements that relate specifically to the four coverages provided. Exclusions and conditions that relate to each coverage are also presented. The Personal Auto Policy contains a definitions section that defines certain terms as they are used in the policy. The policy also includes a section that states the duties of the insured after a loss occurs. A separate General Provisions section provides conditions that apply to the policy as a whole.

Endorsement
A document that amends an insurance policy.

The Personal Auto Policy, with the declarations page added to the standard form, is a complete contract of insurance. However, it is often modified by the addition of one or more endorsements. An **endorsement** is a document that amends an insurance policy. It may add coverage—such as coverage for towing and labor on a car that breaks down. Or, an endorsement may modify the policy in some way to conform to the requirements of the state where the insured lives. For example, an endorsement may change the termination provision in the policy by placing some state-specific restrictions on cancellation of the policy by the insurer. An endorsement may also deal with a change in the insured's loss exposures, such as the purchase of an additional car.

Modular Policies

Modular policy
A policy consisting of several different documents, none of which by itself forms a complete contract.

Modular policies combine coverage forms and other documents to tailor a policy to the insured's needs. Commercial package policies (CPPs), for example, are modular policies.

CPPs can provide many different coverages to businesses and other organizations. Unlike the Personal Auto Policy, which contains four coverages in one form, a CPP combines different forms, depending on the coverages a particular insured purchases. Modular policies offer a combination of coverages, some of which may not be purchased by a given insured. An insured elects coverages by having a limit and premium shown in the declarations, and declines other coverages by leaving the limit and premium blank.

The components that can be used to compile a CPP are illustrated in Exhibit 7-3.

Under ISO's program, all CPPs must contain common policy declarations and Common Policy Conditions. The common policy declarations contain information that applies to the entire policy, such as the name and address of the insured, the policy period, and the coverage(s) for which a premium has been or will be paid. The Common Policy Conditions form contains standard provisions that apply to all CPPs, regardless of the coverages included.

EXHIBIT 7-3

Components of the ISO Commercial Package Policy (CPP)

Commercial Package Policy CPP	=	Common Policy Conditions	+	Common Declarations	+	Commercial Property Declarations Page	Commercial Property Coverage Form(s)	Commercial Property Causes of Loss Form(s)	Commercial Property Conditions Form
						CGL Declarations Page	CGL Coverage Form		
						Crime Declarations Page	Crime Coverage Form		
						Equipment Breakdown Protection Declarations Page	Equipment Breakdown Protection Coverage Form		
						Inland Marine Declarations Page	Inland Marine Coverage Form(s)	Inland Marine Conditions Form	
						Auto Declarations Page	Auto Coverage Form		
						Farm Declarations Page	Farm Coverage Form(s)	Other Farm Provisions Form	

The remaining components of a CPP vary depending on the insured's desired coverages. In most cases, a separate declarations page is included for each coverage provided in the CPP. As illustrated in Exhibit 7-3, a CPP can be used to provide many types of coverage that a business may need. Unlike a self-contained policy such as the Personal Auto Policy, however, a CPP includes several different documents. For example, if a businessowner wanted to purchase property and general liability insurance, the CPP would include the following documents:

- Common policy declarations
- Common policy conditions
- Commercial property declarations
- One or more commercial property coverage forms
- Commercial property conditions
- One or more causes of loss forms
- Commercial general liability declarations
- Commercial general liability coverage form

If the businessowner wanted other coverages, such as coverage for autos used in the business, additional documents would be added to the CPP.

CONDITIONS COMMONLY FOUND IN PROPERTY AND LIABILITY INSURANCE POLICIES

An insurance policy describes the coverage the insurer provides and also stipulates the conditions under which the coverage is provided. These conditions provide the rules for the relationship between the insurer and the insured. Without such rules, insurers would find it difficult to operate efficiently. Some conditions relate to a specific coverage and appear only in policies providing that coverage. Other conditions typically appear in most property and liability insurance policies. Similarly, some conditions appear in both personal and commercial insurance policies, while others are in only one or the other type of policy. Conditions common to most property and liability insurance policies, both personal and commercial, address the following matters:

- Cancellation
- Policy changes
- Duties of the insured after a loss
- Assignment
- Subrogation

The descriptions of policy conditions in this section are based on policies developed by ISO. Policies developed by other advisory organizations, such as AAIS, and by individual insurers may have different names for these conditions, or the provisions themselves may differ from those presented here.

Cancellation

Cancellation occurs when either the insurer or the insured terminates a policy during the policy term. The cancellation provision states the procedures that must be followed when cancellation is initiated by the insured or by the insurer. This provision also states any limitations on the rights of either party to cancel the policy midterm and explains how any premium refunds will be computed.

Cancellation by the Insured

The insured may usually cancel the policy at any time. To do this, the insured may either return the policy to the insurer or provide the insurer with advance written notice of the date the policy is to be canceled.

Written notice eliminates the possibility of a dispute over a verbal cancellation request. Suppose, for example, an insured were permitted to request that an insurer cancel insurance on a given building as of six months earlier and return the premium for those six months. The insurer would have been obligated to pay a claim if the building had been damaged during that six-month period because there was a policy in force. Now that the time has passed and no loss has occurred, the insurer has a right to keep the premium for that period during which claims would have been paid if they had occurred.

Cancellation by the Insurer

The insurer may also cancel most insurance policies. However, the procedures described in the policy provide the insured with some safeguards, such as a given number of days' written notice before the cancellation takes effect. Many policies also prohibit the insurer from canceling, except for certain stated reasons. State law may require a longer notification period or limit the reasons for which an insurer may cancel. If the law is more favorable to the insured than are the policy provisions, the law prevails.

When a policy is canceled, the insured may be entitled to a refund. If the insurer cancels the policy, the return premium is calculated on a pro rata basis and is called a **pro rata refund**. For example, if the insurer cancels a one-year policy and the cancellation is effective exactly six months after the policy's inception date, the insurer will return to the insured a pro rata refund of exactly half the premium.

Some policies state that if the insured requests the cancellation, the premium refund will be less than pro rata and is called a **short rate refund**. For example, the insurer may return only 45 percent of the premium on a policy that is canceled at exactly the halfway point of the policy term. This cancellation penalty (also known as a short rate charge) reflects the fact that the insurer incurred some expense in issuing the policy and will not be able to keep the full premium. The short rate refund also discourages insurance buyers from canceling their insurance before the end of the policy period.

Cancellation
Termination of a policy, by either the insurer or the insured, during the policy term.

Pro rata refund
The unused premium (based on the pro rata portion of the premium for the number of days remaining in the policy) returned to the insured when a policy is canceled.

Short rate refund
A refund of premium that is less than what the pro rata refund would be; sometimes used when the insured cancels a policy midterm.

Policy Changes

Many policies contain a Policy Changes condition stating that the written insurance policy contains all the agreements between the insurer and the insured and that the terms of the policy can be changed only by a written endorsement issued by the insurer. Other policies state that changes to the policy are valid if the insurer agrees to the change in writing.

Liberalization clause
A policy condition providing that if a policy form is broadened at no additional premium, the broadened coverage automatically applies to all existing policies of the same type.

Some insurers revise their policies fairly frequently, perhaps to clarify policy language or to broaden or restrict coverage. If a revision broadens coverage with no additional premium charge to insureds, the **liberalization clause** makes it clear that the revision automatically applies to all similar policies in force at the time of the revision. The liberalization clause is a benefit to insurers as well as insureds because it precludes the need for such a change to be endorsed on every similar policy already in force.

Duties of the Insured After a Loss

If a covered loss is to be paid, the insurer must be informed that the loss occurred. Therefore, under property and liability insurance policies, the insured must immediately notify the insurer of the loss; most policies state that notice be given "promptly" or "as soon as is practical." Insureds also are required to cooperate with the insurer and to perform certain other duties in settling a loss. The type of cooperation and the duties required depend on the type of coverage. For example, property insurance policies generally require that the insured prepare an inventory of damaged and undamaged property and protect the property from further damage. Liability insurance policies usually require that the insured promptly forward all papers regarding a claim or suit to the insurer. Other specific duties of the insured are determined by the type of coverage provided and by the wording of the policy.

Exhibit 7-4 shows Part E of the ISO Personal Auto Policy, which lists the duties of the insured after an accident or loss.

Assignment

As discussed, an insurance policy is a personal contract between the insurer and the insured. Insurers select their insureds carefully. The selection process would be bypassed if an insured were permitted to transfer the insurance coverage to some other person. The other person might be someone with whom the insurer would prefer not to do business.

Assignment
The transfer of rights or interest in a policy to another party by the insured.

The assignment provision, which is sometimes labeled "Transfer of Your Rights and Duties Under This Policy," makes it clear that **assignment** of the policy to another party is not permitted without the written consent of the insurer. For example, a homeowner cannot transfer his or her homeowners policy to a new owner when the house is sold unless the insurer agrees, in writing, to the transfer, which is seldom the case. Insurers rarely agree to such policy transfers because they want the right to underwrite the policy again based on the loss exposures presented by the new owner.

EXHIBIT 7-4

Part E of the ISO Personal Auto Policy

PART E – DUTIES AFTER AN ACCIDENT OR LOSS

We have no duty to provide coverage under this policy if the failure to comply with the following duties is prejudicial to us:

A. We must be notified promptly of how, when and where the accident or loss happened. Notice should also include the names and addresses of any injured persons and of any witnesses.

B. A person seeking any coverage must:

1. Cooperate with us in the investigation, settlement or defense of any claim or suit.

2. Promptly send us copies of any notices or legal papers received in connection with the accident or loss.

3. Submit, as often as we reasonably require:

   a. To physical exams by physicians we select. We will pay for these exams.

   b. To examination under oath and subscribe the same.

4. Authorize us to obtain:

   a. Medical reports; and

   b. Other pertinent records.

5. Submit a proof of loss when required by us.

C. A person seeking Uninsured Motorists Coverage must also:

1. Promptly notify the police if a hit-and-run driver is involved.

2. Promptly send us copies of the legal papers if a suit is brought.

D. A person seeking Coverage For Damage To Your Auto must also:

1. Take reasonable steps after loss to protect "your covered auto" or any "non-owned auto" and their equipment from further loss. We will pay reasonable expenses incurred to do this.

2. Promptly notify the police if "your covered auto" or any "non-owned auto" is stolen.

3. Permit us to inspect and appraise the damaged property before its repair or disposal.

Based on policy language from Form PP 00 01 01 05. Includes copyrighted material of Insurance Services Office, Inc. with its permission. Copyright ISO Properties, 2003.

The assignment provision could present a problem when an insured dies, because coverage would cease at the time of death. Property that is now part of the insured's estate could be damaged or destroyed, or liability claims could be brought against the estate. Because of this problem, insurance policies usually state that the rights and responsibilities of an insured who has died pass to the insured's legal representative (such as the executor of an insured's estate).

Subrogation

Most property and liability insurance policies contain a subrogation provision. This provision is sometimes labeled "Our Right to Recover Payment" or "Transfer of Rights of Recovery Against Others to Us." Insurance practitioners, however, often use the term subrogation even when that word is not used in the policy.

When the insurer pays an insured for a loss, the insurer assumes the insured's right to collect damages from any other person responsible for the loss. As discussed in an earlier chapter, the insurer is subrogated to the insured's rights of recovery, and the insurer's process of recovering is called subrogation. In short, subrogation shifts the ultimate cost of a loss to the party responsible for causing the loss.

For example, if Michael drives his car too fast for the existing road conditions and slides off the road into Joanne's building. Joanne would have a right to recover damages from Michael. However, Joanne may also file a claim with the insurer providing her property coverage, and her insurer would pay for the damage to her building. After paying the property insurance claim, Joanne's insurer has the right of subrogation against Michael. In this example, Joanne has no further rights of recovery if she has been fully indemnified for her loss. If she could also recover from Michael, the principle of indemnity would be violated. Joanne's insurer now has any rights of recovery Joanne had before the insurer paid for the loss, including the right to file a claim against Michael. If Michael has liability insurance, his insurer is obligated to defend him and to pay damages on his behalf.

However, if Joanne has not been fully indemnified, she could recover the portion of her loss that her insurer did not cover. For example, if Joanne had a deductible of $1,000 on her property insurance policy, she could recover the $1,000 from Michael that her insurer deducted from its payment to her. Usually, insurers will help insureds recover deductibles as part of the subrogation process.

Most subrogation provisions require that the insured do nothing after a loss to impair the insurer's subrogation rights. Therefore, in the previous example, Joanne may not tell Michael, "Don't worry about the damage—you won't have to pay anything because my property insurance will cover it." If Joanne were to make such a statement, her property insurer could refuse to pay for the loss because Joanne has no authority to waive the insurer's rights.

Some insurance policies, however, permit an insured to waive rights of recovery before a loss. For example, in a property lease that states the tenant will not be held responsible for accidental damage to property owned by the insured, the insurer will have no right to recover from the tenant if the tenant accidentally causes a fire that damages the insured's property.

SUMMARY

When someone buys an insurance policy, the value he or she receives is the insurer's binding promise to pay for specified kinds of losses. The promise is binding because the policy is a contract that can be enforced in a court of law. To be legally valid, a contract must have certain essential elements as follows:

- It must represent an agreement between the parties.
- Each party must be legally competent to make the agreement.
- The purpose of the agreement must be legal.
- Each party must give some form of consideration to the other party.

Although all of the rules of contract law apply to insurance policies, certain special characteristics distinguish insurance policies from other contracts. An insurance policy is all of the following:

- A conditional contract
- A contract involving fortuitous events and the exchange of unequal amounts
- A contract of utmost good faith
- A contract of adhesion
- A contract of indemnity
- A nontransferable contract

All insurance policies contain certain components, and the insured should review the provisions in each of these components to determine the coverage provided. Most policies include the following:

- Declarations page
- Definitions
- One or more insuring agreements
- Exclusions
- Conditions
- Miscellaneous provisions

In general, insurance policies consist of standard forms to which only the specific details regarding a particular insured must be added. Occasionally, a manuscript policy is drafted according to terms specially negotiated between the insured and the insurer.

An insurance policy can be either self-contained or modular. A self-contained policy (such as a Personal Auto Policy) is a single document that, when combined with a declarations page, forms a complete policy. A modular policy (such as a Commercial Package Policy) comprises several different documents, none of which forms a complete contract by itself.

Insurance policies stipulate certain conditions under which the policy is issued. The insured accepts those conditions as part of the transaction. Typical conditions address the following:

- Cancellation
- Policy changes
- Duties of the insured after a loss
- Assignment
- Subrogation

This chapter provides a basis for studying the material in the next two chapters, which cover property and liability loss exposures and specific provisions in policies that insure many of these exposures.

Chapter 8

Direct Your Learning

Property Loss Exposures and Policy Provisions

After learning the content of this chapter and completing the corresponding course guide assignment, you should be able to:

- Describe the types of property that may be exposed to loss and that are typically covered by property insurance.

- Explain how causes of loss (perils) are treated in named perils policies and in special form policies, and their effect on burden of proof.

- Describe the financial consequences of property losses.

- Explain how parties with an insurable interest would be affected by property losses.

- Describe the types of property and their locations commonly covered in property insurance policies.

- Explain how property insurance policies typically describe covered causes of loss.

- Explain why property insurance policies usually exclude some causes of loss.

- Describe the financial consequences of loss that may be covered by property insurance policies.

- Identify the parties that can be covered by property insurance policies.

- Explain how property insurance policies provide coverage for the named insured and other parties.

- Explain how policy limits and other provisions affect the amount of recovery under a property insurance policy.

- Define or describe each of the Key Words and Phrases for this chapter.

Develop Your Perspective

What are the main topics covered in the chapter?

This chapter provides an overview of property loss exposures, potential causes of loss, and potential financial consequences that can result from such losses. Exposures for different types of property are discussed as well as methods for valuing the property. The chapter concludes with a discussion of common property insurance policy provisions.

List the types of property exposed to loss and the types of losses that can occur to the property.

- What are the categories of property and loss exposures to which the various properties are exposed?

- How do the loss exposures for buildings and contents differ from the loss exposures for property in transit?

Why is it important to learn about these topics?

By understanding the loss exposures to which various types of property are subject, insurance professionals can help clients ensure that those exposures are appropriately addressed for an adequate amount and type of insurance.

Consider how named perils policies and special form policies differ in their treatment of loss exposures.

- How do the covered loss exposures change between the different policy forms?

- How does the burden of proof change between the different policy forms?

How can you use what you will learn?

Evaluate the need for policy exclusions in the insurance property contracts with which you work.

- What would the consequences be for an insurer that failed to exclude catastrophe perils from its property policies?

- How would the premiums charged for automobile policies change if an insurer failed to exclude maintenance coverage from its policies?

Chapter 8

Property Loss Exposures and Policy Provisions

Everything seemed normal when Mr. Brown closed the supermarket for the night. Therefore, he was shocked when he was later awakened by a telephone call from someone exclaiming, "Get down to the shopping center. Your store is on fire!"

The fire apparently started in the store's storage area. A problem in an electrical fixture may have caused some sparks that ignited trash in a nearby bin. Paper goods, bags of charcoal, and other combustible materials in the storage area were apparently ablaze long before the fire was visible from outside the building. The fire spread rapidly through the store's sprawling open spaces.

A few months after the fire, Mr. Brown cut the ribbon for the store's grand reopening sale, and it was soon business as usual. Thanks to his property insurance, Mr. Brown was in almost the same financial condition as he was before the fire. The building had been rebuilt, and the food, freezers, and other contents had been replaced. Business income insurance also reimbursed Mr. Brown for the income lost while the store was closed, as well as for the extra expenses he incurred because of the fire.

It was not by chance that Mr. Brown's insurance enabled him to reopen quickly because he had planned ahead. With the help of his insurance agent, he had identified his property loss exposures and made sure that he was insured against the financial consequences of damage from fire and other causes. Mr. Brown had to identify the various items of property that could be lost or damaged, and he had to determine what could occur to cause loss or damage. In addition, he had to estimate the amount that he could potentially lose. Having done these things well, he was aware of his property loss exposures and had taken steps to properly insure the property.

This chapter illustrates how Mr. Brown was able to successfully handle the consequences of the fire by exploring the various aspects of property loss exposures and then describing important property insurance policy provisions that cover those loss exposures.

PROPERTY LOSS EXPOSURES

Three important aspects of property loss exposures are as follows:

1. *Types of property.* The types of property that may be exposed to loss, damage, or destruction
2. *Causes of loss.* The causes of loss that may result in property being lost, damaged, or destroyed
3. *Financial consequences.* The financial consequences that may result from a property loss

These aspects are important because they create the framework for the contract. They describe (1) what is covered, (2) what causes of loss are covered, and (3) how much will be paid to cover the losses.

In addition to describing these aspects of property loss exposures, this section discusses the parties that may be affected when property is lost, damaged, or destroyed.

Types of Property

Property is any item with value. Individuals, families, and businesses own and use property, depend on it as a source of income or services, and rely on its value. Property can decline in value—or even become worthless—if it is lost, damaged, or destroyed. Different kinds of property have different qualities that affect the owner's or user's exposure to loss.

Two basic types of property are real property and personal property. Insurance practitioners further divide these types of property into the following categories:

- Buildings
- Personal property (contents) contained in buildings
- Money and securities
- Motor vehicles and trailers
- Property in transit
- Ships and their cargoes
- Boilers and machinery

These categories overlap to some extent. For example, motor vehicles, when carried on trucks, can be property in transit. When motor vehicles are on ships for long distance trips, they are waterborne cargo. These categories are listed separately here because they represent types of property for which specific forms of insurance have been developed.

Buildings

Buildings are more than bricks and mortar. Most buildings also include plumbing, wiring, and heating and air conditioning equipment, which can lead to leaks, electrical fires, and explosions. Most buildings also contain basic portable equipment—fire extinguishers, snow shovels, lawn mowers, and so forth—required to service the building and surrounding land. Under most insurance policies, such equipment is considered part of the building. A high-rise building usually has elevators and may have specially designed portable platforms, hoists, and tracks for use by window washers. This equipment is also considered to be part of the building. Property that is permanently attached to the structure, such as wall-to-wall carpeting, built-in appliances, or paneling, is generally considered part of the building as well.

Personal Property (Contents) Contained in Buildings

The contents of a typical home include personal property such as furniture, clothing, electronic equipment, jewelry, paintings, and other personal possessions. The contents of a commercial building may include the following:

- Furniture, such as the desks in an office or file cabinets in Mr. Brown's store
- Machinery and equipment, such as the cash registers in Mr. Brown's supermarket
- Stock, such as the groceries in Mr. Brown's store or the raw materials and completed products in the inventory of a shoe factory. A shoe factory's stock includes leather (raw materials), partly finished shoes (goods in process), and shoes (finished goods)

Although most policies use the term "personal property" to refer to the contents of a building, many insurance practitioners and policyholders use the term "contents" as a matter of convenience and common practice. Property insurance policies refer to personal property, rather than contents, because the property is often covered even when it is not literally contained in the building. When the contents of a commercial building are involved, policies generally use the term "business personal property."

Money and Securities

For insurance purposes, money and securities are separate from other types of contents because their characteristics present special problems. **Money** is currency, coins, bank notes, and sometimes traveler's checks, credit card slips, and money orders held for sale to the public. **Securities** are written instruments representing either money or other property, such as stocks and bonds. Money and securities are highly susceptible to loss by theft. Cash is particularly difficult to trace, because it can be readily spent. In contrast, other types of property must be sold for cash before the thief can make a profit. Money and securities are also lightweight, easily concealed, and easy to transport.

Besides being susceptible to theft, money and securities can be quickly destroyed by fire. Unless Mr. Brown made a bank deposit every night when the store closed, he probably lost a considerable amount of currency and checks during the fire in his store.

Money
Currency, coins, bank notes, and sometimes traveler's checks, credit card slips, and money orders held for sale to the public.

Securities
Written instruments representing either money or other property, such as stocks and bonds.

Motor Vehicles and Trailers

The primary purpose of most vehicles is to move people or property, and this movement exposes vehicles to several causes of loss. Vehicles may be grouped by vehicle type, by operator type, by typical usage, or by a combination of these types. No matter what types are used, some vehicles (such as snowmobiles or utility vehicles) fit into more than one category, depending on the purpose for which they are owned and used. However, the following categories are useful in identifying property loss exposures:

- Autos and other highway vehicles
- Mobile equipment
- Recreational vehicles

Auto
In insurance, a broad term that includes cars, trucks, trailers, buses, and other motorized vehicles designed for road use.

In insurance terminology, the term **auto** has a broad meaning. It includes motorized vehicles, such as cars, trucks, trailers, and buses, designed for road use but can also include such diverse vehicles as fire engines, ambulances, motorcycles, and camping trailers. **Mobile equipment** includes tractors, bulldozers, road graders, front-end loaders, forklifts, backhoes, and power shovels, and the equipment attached to them. Mobile equipment may be damaged in a highway collision, but the most frequent exposures to loss involve off-road situations. **Recreational vehicles** include a wide range of vehicles used for sports and recreational activities, such as dune buggies, all-terrain vehicles, and dirt bikes. Most snowmobiles also fall into this category. In some cases, the owners of recreational vehicles face exposures to loss both on and off the road.

Mobile equipment
Various types of land vehicles and the equipment attached to them, such as tractors, bulldozers, forklifts, and backhoes, designed primarily for off-road use.

Recreational vehicle
A vehicle used for sports and recreational activities, such as a dune buggy, all-terrain vehicle, or dirt bike.

Property in Transit

A great deal of property is transported by truck, but property is also moved in cars, buses, trains, airplanes, and ships. When a conveyance containing cargo overturns or is involved in a collision, the cargo can also be damaged. In addition, cargo can be destroyed without damage to the transporting vehicle. Liquids can leak out of a truck, fragile articles can be jostled during transit, and perishables can melt or spoil in a conveyance with a defective refrigeration system.

When property is damaged or lost in transit, it must be replaced. Delays often result, because replacement property may have to be shipped from the place of the original shipment. The property owner may also incur expense to move the damaged property.

Ships and Their Cargoes

Ships and their cargoes are exposed to special perils not encountered in other means of transit. For example, a ship can sink for a variety of reasons, resulting in a total loss of its cargo. Even more than other property, ocean cargoes fluctuate in value according to their location. If the ship cannot reach its intended destination and the cargo must be sold in a different port, the price received for the cargo might be less than the price expected at the original destination.

Boilers and Machinery

Boilers and machinery include any of the following:

- Steam boilers (large water tanks heated by burning gas, oil, or coal to produce steam for heating or to produce power)
- Unfired pressure vessels, such as air tanks
- Refrigerating and air conditioning systems
- Mechanical equipment, such as compressors and turbines
- Production equipment
- Electrical equipment

Boilers and machinery share the following two characteristics:

1. They are susceptible to explosion or breakdown that can result in serious losses to the unit and to persons and property nearby.
2. They are less likely to have explosions or breakdowns if they are periodically inspected and properly maintained.

Many buildings use steam boilers to provide heat. Refineries and steel mills often use boilers to provide power for factory processes. Machinery, such as transformers and other electrical apparatus, is found in most factories and power stations.

Causes of Loss to Property

A **cause of loss** (or **peril**) is the actual means by which property is damaged or destroyed and includes fire, lightning, windstorm, hail, and theft. Most causes of loss adversely affect property and leave it in an altered state. A fire can change a building to a heap of rubble. A collision can change a car to twisted scrap. Some causes of loss do not alter the property itself, but they do affect a person's ability to possess or use the property. For example, property lost or stolen can still be usable, but not by its rightful owner.

Many property insurance policies list the covered causes of loss. Such policies are commonly known as **named perils** policies because they "name" or list the covered perils. Usually, these policies also list the causes of loss that are excluded from coverage. Other policies cover all causes of loss except losses caused by a peril specifically excluded. These policies are known by several different terms, including **special form** or **open perils** policies. This text uses the term special form policies.

Perils and Hazards

The terms "peril" and "hazard" are often confused.

As stated earlier, a peril is a cause of loss. Fire, theft, collision, and flood are examples of perils that cause property losses. (Many property insurance policies use the term cause of loss instead of peril. This text uses these terms interchangeably.)

Cause of loss, or **peril**
The actual means by which property is damaged or destroyed.

Named peril
A specific cause of loss listed and described in an insurance policy. Also used to describe policies containing named perils.

Special form, or **open perils policy**
A policy that provides coverage for any direct loss to property unless the loss is caused by a peril specifically excluded.

A hazard is anything that increases the frequency of a loss or the severity of a loss. Examples include the following:

- Careless smoking practices are a fire hazard because they increase the frequency of fires.
- Paint cans and oily rags are fire hazards because they enable a fire to spread and cause severe damage.
- Keeping large amounts of money in a cash register overnight is a theft hazard affecting both the frequency of loss and the severity of loss. This practice would attract thieves if they became aware of it. The amount that would be stolen—the severity of the loss—is also affected by the amount of cash in the register.

Burden of Proof

An important difference between named perils and special form coverage involves the burden of proof, as follows:

- With a named perils policy, for coverage to apply, the insured must prove that the loss was caused by a covered cause of loss.
- With a special form policy, if a loss to covered property occurs, it is initially assumed that coverage applies. However, coverage may be denied if the insurer can prove that the loss was caused by an excluded cause of loss.

In the first case, the burden of proof is on the insured; in the second, it is on the insurer.

By shifting the burden of proof, a special form policy can provide an important advantage to the insured who suffers a property loss by an unknown cause. For example, suppose that after a flood strikes the community, the insured's wrought iron patio furniture is missing. Assume also that the patio furniture is clearly covered property. It is possible that the furniture was swept away in the flood, but it is also possible that the furniture was stolen following the flood. If a named perils policy covered theft but not flood, the insured would have to prove that the property had been stolen. Under a special form policy, the insurer would have to pay the claim (even if the policy excluded flood losses) unless the insurer could prove that the property was swept away in the flood.

Financial Consequences of Property Losses

The loss of or damage to property can have adverse financial consequences such as reduced property value, lost income, or extra expenses.

Reduced Property Value

When a property loss occurs, the property is reduced in value. The reduction in value can be measured in different ways, sometimes with differing results. If the property can be repaired or restored, the reduction in value can be measured by the cost of the repair or the restoration. Property that must be replaced has no remaining worth, unless some salvageable items can be sold. Consider the following examples:

- A fence worth $7,000 was damaged by a car, and the fence owner has to pay $2,000 to have the damage repaired. The fence owner has incurred a partial loss that reduced the fence's value by $2,000.
- A camera worth $400 is run over by a truck. The camera owner has incurred a total loss that reduced the camera's value by $400.

If property is lost, is stolen, or otherwise disappears, its value to the owner is reduced just as though it had been destroyed and retained no salvage value. A further reduction in value might occur if repaired property is worth less than it would be if it had never been damaged. This is true for items such as fine paintings and other art objects. Many collectibles are valuable largely because they are in mint or original condition. An object that has been repaired after damage from a tear, scratch, or fire is no longer in that unspoiled condition, and its value will decline. The owner faces loss in the form of the cost to repair the object, as well as a reduction in value because of the altered condition.

Property may have different values, depending on the method by which the value is determined. The most common valuation measures used in insurance policies, as discussed earlier in this text, are replacement cost and actual cash value (ACV). In certain situations, however, other valuation measures, such as agreed value, are used.

Lost Income

When property is damaged, income may be lost because the property cannot be used until it is repaired, restored, or replaced. In the supermarket fire example earlier in this chapter, Mr. Brown temporarily lost the income from his store because the building and its contents were damaged by fire.

Determining the amount of business income that may be lost following a property loss requires estimating the future level of activity of an organization and doing a "what if" analysis. The "what if" analysis would include such questions as: "What if the business could not operate for six months because it would take six months to rebuild after a fire? How much net income would be lost?" This analysis involves projecting the organization's net income (revenue minus expenses, including taxes) in normal circumstances. Those projected amounts are compared to expected post-loss net income for the same period to determine the income lost. This analysis requires comparing what the business might have expected its revenue and expenses to have been compared to what they actually were after the loss.

The following example shows expected revenue and expenses compared to those experienced after the fire. The post-loss amounts might be a "what if" in order to determine the amount of business income insurance needed, or the actual amounts following a loss. In either case, the lost income for the time period is simply the expected net income less the post-loss net income: $90,000 minus ($30,000) = $120,000.

	Expected (Normal Operations)	Post-Loss
Revenue	$ 150,000	$ 0
Expenses	$ 60,000	$30,000
Net Income	$ 90,000	($30,000)

The owner of rental property would face a similar situation because rental income would be lost if the property were damaged and temporarily could not be rented. The owner would probably continue to incur some expenses, such as mortgage payments and taxes, but would not receive the rent that helped to pay those expenses.

Extra Expenses

Determining the extent of a property loss exposure involves considering the extra expenses required in the event of the loss of property. When property is damaged, the property itself declines in value, and the owner or other affected party suffers a corresponding loss. In addition, the owner or other user of that property may incur extra expenses to acquire a temporary substitute or to temporarily maintain the property in usable condition. Consider the following examples:

- When a family's house is damaged, the family may have to live in a hotel temporarily at considerably greater expense than living at home.
- When a newspaper's printing presses are damaged, the newspaper may spend extra money to have the newspaper printed on another company's presses.
- When a car is damaged in a collision, the owner may rent an auto until the car's damage has been repaired.
- When a bank building is damaged, the bank may hire additional security guards until the building can be made secure.

Because so many variables are involved, it is difficult to estimate the extra expenses that might be required to stay in business following damage to business property or to keep a family together and maintain its standard of living after a home is damaged.

Parties Affected by Property Losses

Parties that may be affected by a property loss include the following:

- Property owners
- Secured lenders of money to the property owner
- Property users
- Property holders

Property Owners

The party most affected when property is lost, damaged, or destroyed is usually the owner of the property. If the property has some value, the owner of the property incurs a financial loss to repair or replace the property. In the supermarket fire example, Mr. Brown incurred a considerable financial loss because he had to rebuild his store and restock the shelves.

Secured Lenders

When money is borrowed to finance the purchase of a car, the lender usually acquires some conditional rights to the car, such as the right to repossess the car if the car's owner (the borrower) fails to make loan payments. This right gives the lender security. Such a lender is therefore called a secured lender or a secured creditor. When a person or business borrows money to buy a home or a building and the property serves as security for the loan, the secured lender is called a **mortgagee** (or **mortgageholder**), and the borrower is called a **mortgagor**.

When property is used to secure a loan, both the property owner and the lender are exposed to loss. If, for example, Mr. Brown had a mortgage on his supermarket building, the mortgagee would lose the security for the mortgage loan when the building burned. Similarly, if a financed car is destroyed in an accident and the owner has no money to repay the loan, there would be no car for the lender to repossess. Property insurance policies generally protect the secured lender's interest in the financed property by naming the lender on the insurance policy and by giving the lender certain rights under the policy.

Mortgagee, or mortgageholder
A lender that loans money on a home, building, or other real property.

Mortgagor
The person or organization that borrows money from a mortgagee to finance the purchase of real property.

Property Users

Some events result in losses to end users (such as consumers or resellers) of the damaged property, even though they do not own the property. Consider the following example: a fish store buys fresh shellfish from the only supplier within 200 miles. About one-third of the fish store's retail sales are shellfish. If fire or another peril were to destroy the supplier's processing facility, the fish store would not be able to sell fresh shellfish, and would incur a financial loss.

Property Holders

Some parties are responsible for safekeeping property they do not own. Dry cleaners, TV repair shops, common carriers, and many other businesses temporarily hold property belonging to others. A person or business that holds property entrusted to them by others is called a **bailee**. To estimate their property loss exposures, such businesses have to consider not only their owned property, but also the property held for others.

Bailee
A person or business that holds property entrusted to them by others.

PROPERTY INSURANCE POLICY PROVISIONS

A **property insurance** policy indemnifies an insured who suffers a financial loss because property has been lost, stolen, damaged, or destroyed. The policy

Property insurance
Any type of insurance that indemnifies an insured who suffers a financial loss because property has been lost, stolen, damaged, or destroyed.

must specify exactly which property loss exposures are covered—that is, the types and locations of property, causes of loss, and financial consequences that are covered. Policies must also identify the parties that are covered and how the value of insured property will be determined.

This section examines common characteristics of policies that provide property insurance and focuses on explaining general features rather than describing the content of specific policies. The following aspects of property insurance policies are discussed next:

- Covered property and locations
- Covered causes of loss
- Causes of loss often excluded
- Covered financial consequences
- Covered parties
- Amounts of recovery

Covered Property and Locations

An insurance policy specifies what property is covered and where it is covered. Covered property is often described broadly and then refined through a series of limitations and exclusions. Locations of property are often defined by geographical boundaries. For example, a typical personal auto insurance policy covers collision damage to an auto described in the declarations, provided the collision occurs in the United States, its territories and possessions, Puerto Rico, or Canada. When coverage is provided worldwide, such as personal property covered by a homeowners policy, some limitations are placed on the value of the property that will be covered when it is permanently kept at another location, such as at a secondary residence.

Many types of property insurance are designed primarily to cover buildings and personal property. The identification of a covered building is generally clear because its location is fixed. However, stating the location of covered property might not be as straightforward. One challenge lies in describing precisely what is and what is not covered under the insurance policy. Another challenge lies in the fact that personal property and, in some instances, buildings do not necessarily remain at a fixed location. Portions of a building may be removed from the premises for repair or storage. For example, screen windows may be removed from the building and placed in storage during the winter while storm windows are being used. Furniture may be located inside buildings as well as on outdoor patios and decks. Items usually kept in a building may be temporarily located in a car or truck.

Floater
A policy designed to cover property that floats, or moves, from location to location.

A property insurance policy for covering personal property that moves from place to place is often called a **floater** because it provides coverage that floats, or moves, with the property as it changes location. Examples of items that could be covered by a floater include jewelry, furs, cameras, and other types of property owned by individuals and families; property transported on trucks or other conveyances covered by a transportation policy; and earthmovers and other construction equipment owned by contractors. Policies covering movable property may have territorial limits, or they may provide coverage anywhere in the world.

Commercial package policies now typically include coverage for moveable property and homeowners policies usually provide worldwide coverage for many types of moveable property. The homeowners policy may, however, be endorsed with one or more floaters that add covered perils and increase coverage limits for items like jewelry and furs.

The following types of covered property are discussed next:

- Dwellings, buildings, and other structures
- Personal property
- Property other than the insured's buildings and contents

Dwellings, Buildings, and Other Structures

Some property insurance policies stipulate that they cover only the building(s) at the specific location(s) listed in the declarations. These policies also define exactly what property qualifies as part of the building and is therefore covered by insurance.

In personal insurance, a residential structure is generally called a dwelling and is usually covered under a homeowners policy. A typical policy on a dwelling covers the residence premises, which is defined as the location shown in the policy declarations. Usually, the policy definition of residence premises also includes other structures attached to the dwelling, and materials and supplies located on or next to the dwelling used to construct, alter, or repair the residence premises. The coverage for the residence premises does not apply to land.

Structures attached to the dwelling include an attached garage or carport. A free standing, detached garage is not part of the dwelling. A separate insuring agreement for other structures covers such detached items. Whether the garage is part of the dwelling or qualifies as an other structure is important to know because different policy limits (dollar amounts of insurance) apply for the dwelling and for other structures. When determining how much insurance the insured should purchase to adequately insure real property, it is necessary to know whether the garage is considered part of the dwelling or a separate structure.

In commercial insurance, a permanent structure with walls and a roof is usually called a building. Other outdoor structures such as carports, antenna towers, and swimming pools may not be buildings, but they also can be insured.

A typical commercial property policy covers the building or structure described in the declarations. The policy definition of building may include additions that are either completed or under construction as well as materials and supplies used for constructing the additions. Permanently installed fixtures, machinery, and equipment are also included as part of the building. Thus, items such as a pipe organ in a church or equipment installed in a manufacturing plant would be considered part of the insured building. The building coverage of a commercial property policy also includes other items, such as fire extinguishing equipment, outdoor furniture, wall-to-wall carpeting, and refrigerators.

Personal Property

The second type of covered property found in property insurance policies is personal property. Although buildings and personal property can be insured by the same policy, they are usually treated as separate coverage items. For example, when a building sustains damage by fire or some other peril, the personal property in that building is often damaged. Likewise, a fire that starts in a wastebasket, for example, may spread and damage the building.

Because personal property can be moved more easily than buildings, it is exposed to additional perils. In addition, property such as valuable papers, computer programs, accounts receivable records, fine arts, stamp collections, money, and securities are loss exposures that require special handling.

The personal property coverage of a homeowners policy typically covers personal property owned or used by an insured while the property is anywhere in the world. The homeowners insuring agreement for personal property is a very broad statement of coverage, but such broad coverage is restricted by a number of exclusions and limitations.

It is important to note that exclusions and limitations are not the same thing. While exclusions eliminate all coverage for excluded property or causes of loss, limitations place a specific dollar limit on specific property that is covered.

As stated earlier, commercial property insurance policies usually refer to the contents of buildings as business personal property, which includes personal property of the insured located in or on the building described in the declarations. Business personal property also includes personal property located outside (or in a vehicle) within 100 feet of the described premises.

The usual 100-foot limitation in commercial policies is far more restrictive than the worldwide coverage of most homeowners policies. Commercial property policies often include an additional coverage (known as a coverage extension) that provides a certain limit, such as $10,000, of coverage for property off-premises; this extension, however, applies only to losses that occur in the specified policy territory, which is typically the U.S. and Canada.

The definition of "your business personal property" in commercial property policies makes it clear that coverage for business personal property applies to such items as furniture, machinery, equipment, and stock that are not part of the building.

Property Other Than the Insured's Buildings and Contents

Property insurance policies usually clarify coverage by listing property not covered. Policies that cover buildings and personal property typically show autos in such a listing because autos are more appropriately covered under auto insurance policies. Some policies exclude money and securities because these items should be insured under crime insurance policies.

The declarations page of an auto insurance policy, either personal or commercial, describes the specific autos that are covered, including the vehicle identification number (VIN) unique to each vehicle. The declarations also state where each vehicle is normally kept (or garaged) because this information is necessary to establish the appropriate premium. However, the location where coverage applies is not limited to the garage but includes any location in the specified coverage territory.

Most auto insurance policies do not cover personal property while transported in autos, but some provide a minimal amount of coverage for personal effects. Such personal property owned by individuals or families can be covered by homeowners policies. When businesses need coverage, business personal property in transit can be covered by a transportation policy.

As noted previously, property insurance policies often provide coverage for property that is owned by someone other than the insured. Homeowners policies provide coverage for the personal property of others, such as guests or employees, while the property is in the insured's home. Commercial property policies generally include limited coverage for the personal effects of officers, partners, and employees as well as to the personal property of others while it is in the care, custody, or control of the insured. The personal auto policy provides coverage for damage to a borrowed auto if the owner of the borrowed auto does not have physical damage coverage.

As discussed earlier, some property insurance policies cover personal property that does not remain at a fixed location. For example, homeowners policies cover personal property of the insured while it is anywhere in the world. Auto insurance policies provide coverage while the insured's auto is in the U.S., its territories and possessions, Puerto Rico, or Canada. Commercial property insurance policies are more restrictive; they provide coverage for the insured's business personal property while it is in the insured building or within 100 feet of the building. Commercial policies also provide limited coverage for property away from the insured premises under certain circumstances. Many floaters provide coverage for movable property anywhere in the world.

Covered Causes of Loss

Most property insurance policies cover many causes of loss, including fire and crime. Losses from earthquake and flood can be covered by special types of policies or endorsements. Most property insurance policies group several causes of loss and offer coverage for them in one policy form. Insureds can obtain the coverage they need by selecting among the forms covering various causes of loss.

Personal and commercial property insurance policies on buildings and personal property are available with three different levels of coverage as follows:

1. *Basic form coverage.* The lowest-cost version that provides coverage for approximately a dozen named perils.
2. *Broad form coverage.* A higher-cost version of coverage that adds several perils to those covered by basic coverage.
3. *Special form (open perils) coverage.* The highest-cost version that covers all causes of loss that are not specifically excluded. Special form coverage covers all the perils of broad form coverage, as well as other perils.

Most homeowners policies provide either broad or special form coverage. Homeowners policies providing basic form coverage are not available in most states.

Basic Form Coverage

Property insurance policies define many causes of loss in detail, however, precise definitions vary by policy. The following causes of loss are discussed in this section:

- Fire and lightning
- Hail
- Vehicle damage
- Explosion
- Vandalism
- Sinkhole collapse

- Windstorm
- Aircraft
- Riot and civil commotion
- Smoke
- Sprinkler leakage
- Volcanic action

These causes of loss are generally included in both personal and commercial policies that provide basic form coverage.

Fire is one of the most serious causes of loss, but not every fire causes a loss. A gas fire in a kitchen oven, an oil fire in a furnace, and a wood fire in a fireplace serve a specific purpose and cause no loss—unless they blaze out of control.

Friendly fire
A fire that stays in its intended place, such as a fire in a fireplace.

The term **friendly fire** refers to a fire that remains in its intended place. Such a fire is generally not intended to be covered by a named peril property insurance policy but is covered under a special form policy.

Hostile fire
A fire that leaves its intended place, such as a spark that escapes a fireplace and sets the carpet on fire.

A fire that leaves its intended place is called a **hostile fire** and is generally covered by both named peril and special form property insurance. If a person's wig accidentally fell into a fireplace and was burned, many property insurance policies would not cover the loss because the fire did not leave its intended place. However, if sparks flying from the fireplace set the house on fire, a hostile fire would have occurred and the damage would be covered. Some fires originate from another peril, such as lightning, which might strike a house and set it on fire. It is standard practice that policies covering fire also cover loss caused by lightning.

In property policies, damage caused by fire includes damage resulting from conditions accompanying the fire (such as heat and smoke) and events that can be linked to the fire in an unbroken chain of causation (such as collapse resulting from the fire or water damage caused by firefighters). When these conditions occur because of a fire, the fire is considered the **proximate cause** of the entire loss because it was the event that set in motion the chain of events contributing to the loss. It does not matter that the fire itself was caused by some other peril, such as an earthquake. If property insurance covers loss from fire but not from earthquake, damage from fire would be covered even if the fire resulted directly from the earthquake. The insurance policy would cover the portion of the loss caused by the fire but not the portion caused exclusively by the earthquake.

Proximate cause
The event that sets in motion an uninterrupted chain of events contributing to a loss.

Like fire, a windstorm can cause serious damage to buildings and their contents, as well as to other property. Windstorms include hurricanes and tornadoes but are not confined to those disturbances. Less severe storms are also considered windstorms.

Water damage due to flood, waves, or spray sometimes accompanies a windstorm. Many insurance policies cover windstorm damage but not water damage, unless wind causes an opening in the structure through which water enters. When a loss occurs, it is not always easy to distinguish the damage done by wind from the damage done by water. Exhibit 8-1 shows coastal property destroyed by a hurricane. Consider the difficulty in determining what peril created the devastation to the buildings and property.

EXHIBIT 8-1

Coastal Property Destroyed by Hurricane

Hail consists of ice particles created by freezing atmospheric conditions. Hailstones the size of marbles, golf balls, or baseballs can cause substantial damage to autos, buildings, and other property. Aluminum siding and metal roofs are susceptible to dimpling caused by hail. Small hail that is not capable of damaging most property can cause serious crop damage by knocking kernels out of standing grain or by destroying blossoms on fruit trees, for example.

Aircraft damage occurs when all or part of an airplane or satellite strikes property on the ground. Although such incidents are rare, the damage can be severe. For example, if debris from an airplane crash damages a home, the homeowner could collect from his or her homeowners insurer for the damage to the house. (The insurer could then subrogate against the airline and thus attempt to recover its payment to the homeowner.)

Vehicle damage
Damage caused by a motor vehicle to some other kind of property.

Damage caused by a motor vehicle to some other kind of property is called **vehicle damage**. When a car runs into a house, the house suffers vehicle damage and the car suffers collision damage. The homeowner could submit a claim for the vehicle damage to his or her homeowners insurer, and the insurer could in turn subrogate against the driver and try to recover an amount equal to its payment to the homeowner.

While legal distinctions may exist between riot and civil commotion, both terms refer to similar kinds of unruly mob behavior, and insurance covering riot invariably covers civil commotion. Although losses from these perils do not occur very often, they can be quite large. For example, insured losses from the 1992 riots in Los Angeles totaled almost $800 million.

An explosion is a violent expansion or bursting accompanied by noise. An explosion may result from the ignition of gases, dust, or other explosive materials. Such explosions are often followed by fire. Explosions can also occur when a pressurized object bursts, such as a tank containing compressed air. An explosion can destroy an entire building, as illustrated in Exhibit 8-2.

The sudden or accidental release of large amounts of smoke can cause considerable damage to walls and other objects. When damaging smoke comes from a fire, the fire is generally considered to be the proximate cause of the loss. However, the sudden malfunction of an oil-burning furnace may result in the discharge of grimy, sooty smoke. In that case, the resulting damage is not caused by fire but by a peril independent of fire. Property insurance policies that cover loss from fire typically include smoke as a covered cause of loss as well. However, coverage for smoke damage does not include smoke produced by many industrial operations.

Certain kinds of property are particularly susceptible to smoke damage. In a clothing or grocery store, a relatively small amount of smoke can cause considerable damage. Clothes must be cleaned to remove the smell and may be permanently stained. Foods such as fresh vegetables may be a total loss. Other property—such as a stack of plumbing pipes—may be essentially undamaged by a large volume of smoke.

EXHIBIT 8-2

Building Destroyed by Explosion

Willful and malicious damage to or destruction of property is called **vandalism**. Vandalism losses are not accidental; they are intentionally caused, usually by an unknown person or persons. However, because they are not intentionally caused by the insured, they can be covered in insurance policies. Examples of vandalism include graffiti spray painted onto building walls and defacement of statues or other objects of art. Some insurance policies refer to vandalism and malicious mischief; others simply use the term vandalism. The meaning is largely the same in either case.

Vandalism
Willful and malicious damage to or destruction of property.

Many commercial and institutional buildings, as well as some private residences, are equipped with automatic sprinkler systems. An automatic sprinkler system is designed to discharge water (or a chemical or gas) when a fire occurs, thus extinguishing or containing the fire. When a fire sets off a sprinkler, the fire is considered the proximate cause of any water damage from the operation of the sprinkler. However, an automatic sprinkler system may discharge accidentally. The system's pipes can freeze and burst, or a buildup of heat from some cause other than fire can cause the system to discharge. Maintenance workers may accidentally bang a ladder against a sprinkler head and cause it to discharge. The peril of **sprinkler leakage** includes such accidental discharges. Compared to fire, sprinkler leakage is not usually a serious threat to a building. The vulnerability of a building's contents could

Sprinkler leakage
Accidental leakage or discharge of water or other substance from an automatic sprinkler system.

be another matter, however. With some occupancies, such as dealers in paper products, sprinkler leakage losses can be devastating.

The action of underground water on limestone or similar rock formations can create empty spaces underground. A **sinkhole collapse** occurs when land suddenly sinks or collapses into one of these empty spaces, as illustrated in Exhibit 8-3. This problem occurs most often in Florida, but other states are also susceptible to sinkhole losses. Sinkhole collapse is a covered cause of loss under the basic form of commercial property policies. For personal property policies such as homeowners, the coverage is not automatic and must be added by endorsement.

Sinkhole collapse
A cause of loss involving the sudden sinking or collapse of land into underground empty spaces created by the action of water on limestone or similar rock formations.

EXHIBIT 8-3

Sinkhole Collapse

Sinkhole problems also exist in states such as Pennsylvania and West Virginia because of underground mining. The **mine subsidence** peril is present when the ground surface sinks as underground open spaces, caused by mining operations, are gradually filled in by rock and earth from above. Typically, mine subsidence is not a covered cause of loss under the basic form for either commercial or personal property policies but can be added by endorsement.

Mine subsidence
A cause of loss involving the sinking of ground surface when underground open spaces, resulting from the extraction of coal or other minerals, are gradually filled in by rock and earth from above.

Volcanic action
A cause of loss involving lava flow, ash, dust, particulate matter, airborne volcanic blast, or airborne shock waves resulting from a volcanic eruption.

In the U.S., losses caused by volcanic action occur primarily in the Pacific coastal states, Alaska, and Hawaii. **Volcanic action** encompasses loss involving lava flow, ash, dust, particulate matter, airborne volcanic blast, or airborne shock waves resulting from the eruption of a volcano.

When Mount St. Helens erupted in 1980, many policies did not specifically provide or exclude coverage for volcanic action but did cover the peril of explosion. There was considerable debate over whether a volcanic eruption constitutes an explosion. Insureds, seeing explosion as a covered cause of loss and noting no policy definition of the term, requested coverage for damage from the eruption. The outcome was that many losses were treated as explosion losses, and claims were paid. Now, most property insurance policies specifically include coverage for volcanic action, but some specifically exclude such coverage.

Broad Form Coverage

While property insurance policies that cover basic form causes of loss cover the perils discussed previously, other property insurance policies add coverage against the following additional causes of loss that are commonly referred to as broad form coverage or broad form perils:

- *Falling objects.* Trees or other objects may fall onto a building.
- *Weight of snow, ice, or sleet.* The weight of accumulations of any of these may damage or destroy buildings and their contents.
- *Sudden and accidental water damage.* Sudden leaks may, for example, damage carpets, floors, or ceilings.

Special Form (Open Perils) Coverage

As noted, property insurance polices that cover all causes of loss that are not specifically excluded are called special form coverage or open perils. Special form coverage policies were once described as "all-risks" but this term is now less commonly used, because it may be misinterpreted to mean that no causes of loss are excluded.

Collapse

Although collapse is usually not listed as either a basic or a broad form peril, many property insurance policies provide an additional coverage for loss or damage involving collapse of all or part of a building, but only if the collapse is caused by one or more of the basic or broad causes of loss described previously. Other covered causes of collapse are hidden decay; hidden damage by insects or vermin; weight of people or contents; weight of rain that collects on a roof; and use of defective material or methods in construction, remodeling, or renovation if the collapse occurs during the construction, remodeling, or renovation.

Crime Perils

Coverage for various crime perils can be included in insurance policies. The definitions of these causes of loss for insurance purposes may differ somewhat from the usual definitions of these terms. For example, **burglary** is the taking of property from inside a building by someone who unlawfully enters or exits

Burglary
The taking of property from inside a building by someone who unlawfully enters or exits the building.

Robbery
The taking of property from a person by someone who has caused or threatened to cause the person harm.

Theft
Any act of stealing; includes burglary and robbery.

Collision
Damage to a motor vehicle caused by its impact with another vehicle or object, or by the vehicle's overturn.

Other than collision, or **comprehensive**
Losses to a covered auto by fire, theft, vandalism, falling objects, flood, and various other perils.

Specified causes of loss
For other than collision coverage in commercial auto policies, a named perils alternative that is less expensive than comprehensive because fewer causes of loss are covered.

the building. The definition of burglary in insurance policies includes breaking out of a building because thieves may hide inside a building before it is closed for the night and make a forcible exit after stealing some of the contents. **Robbery** is the taking of property from a person by someone who has caused or threatened to cause the person harm through use of intimidation or force. **Theft** is a general term meaning any act of stealing. It includes robbery, burglary, and other forms of stealing. Some insurance policies cover the peril of theft, but others cover only a specific type of theft, such as burglary or robbery.

Auto Physical Damage

Insurance policies that provide auto physical damage coverage offer the following types of coverage:

- **Collision**. Covers damage to a motor vehicle caused by its impact with another vehicle or object or by the vehicle's overturn.
- **Other than collision** (also called **comprehensive**). Covers losses caused by fire, theft, vandalism, falling objects, flood, and various other perils.
- **Specified causes of loss**. Used primarily in commercial auto policies, this is a named perils alternative that is less expensive than comprehensive because fewer causes of loss are covered.

Like other property, cars and trucks are subject to fire, theft, vandalism, and other perils. However, the most serious cause of loss to autos is collision. Insurance against collision costs considerably more than insurance against all other perils combined. Collision coverage is not included with either of the other coverages and must be purchased as a separate coverage.

Causes of Loss Often Excluded

Discussion to this point has focused on causes of loss covered by most property insurance policies. Numerous other perils can also cause loss to property but are usually excluded from insurance policies. In most instances, broad categories of exclusions can be matched to those concepts of ideally insurable loss exposures, as described earlier. An ideally insurable exposure has these characteristics: loss exposure involves pure, not speculative risk; loss exposure is subject to accidental loss; loss exposure is subject to losses that are definite in time and measurable; loss exposure is one of a large number of similar, but independent, exposures; loss exposure such that losses are not catastrophic; and loss exposure is economically feasible to insure.

Catastrophe Perils

Insurance functions best when many insureds pay relatively small premiums to provide a fund for paying large losses incurred by relatively few insureds. Some perils that affect a great many people at the same time are generally considered to be uninsurable by insurers because the resulting losses would be so widespread that the funds of the entire insurance business might be inadequate to pay all of the claims.

For this reason, almost all property insurance policies exclude coverage for losses from catastrophes such as war and nuclear hazard. However, there are policies that provide so-called war risks coverage on oceangoing vessels and cargo. Insurance against losses to property from nuclear hazard is available for nuclear power plants and transporters of nuclear materials. Most property insurance policies also exclude property losses resulting from governmental action, such as governmental seizure of property.

Most policies providing coverage on buildings and personal property at fixed locations exclude coverage for earthquake and flood losses. An earthquake can be a catastrophe affecting many different properties in the same geographic area at the same time. Also, the extent of earthquake damage depends in part on the type of construction of the property. A building that is susceptible to fire damage may be less susceptible to earthquake damage, and vice versa. For these and other reasons, insurers prefer to handle earthquake coverage separately, making a specific decision on each application for insurance.

Flood damage can also be catastrophic. However, floods can sometimes be predicted. For property in low-lying areas near rivers, creeks, or streams, the question is not whether floods will occur, but when. Insurers are generally not willing to provide coverage for a loss that is certain to occur. However, flood insurance on buildings and personal property is available through the National Flood Insurance Program sponsored by the federal government. Auto insurance policies and other policies covering movable personal property generally include coverage against flood losses.

Maintenance Perils

Property insurance policies also typically exclude loss from inherent vice and latent defect, as well as wear and tear and other maintenance perils. Such losses are generally uninsurable either because they are certain to occur, over time, or are avoidable through regular maintenance and care. Maintenance perils that are excluded from most policies include the following:

- Wear and tear
- Marring and scratching
- Rust
- Gradual seepage of water
- Damage by insects, birds, rodents, or other animals

These maintenance perils are usually not covered even in the broadest property insurance policies. As stated earlier, insurance works well only for definite and accidental losses. Some of these excluded perils (wear and tear, marring and scratching, or rust) involve the results of ordinary use and aging rather than unexpected damage. Damage from the other perils (water seepage, insects, or rodents) is preventable through proper care and maintenance.

Covered Financial Consequences

As discussed earlier in the chapter, property losses can lead to any or all of the following financial consequences: reduction in property value, lost income, and extra expenses. Property insurance policies must specify which financial consequences of a property loss are covered and which are not.

Reduction in Property Value (Direct Loss)

Direct loss
A reduction in the value of property that results directly and often immediately from damage to that property.

A reduction in the value of property that results directly and often immediately from damage to that property is often referred to as **direct loss**. If the property is not restored, it is not worth as much after the loss as before. For example, the insuring agreement of the Insurance Services Office, Inc. (ISO) commercial building and personal property coverage form states that the insurer will pay for "any direct physical loss of or damage to Covered Property at the premises described in the Declarations caused by or resulting from any Covered Cause of Loss."

Time Element (Indirect) Loss

Time element loss, or **indirect loss**
Loss of income or extra expenses resulting from direct loss to property.

Lost income and extra expenses resulting from direct loss to property can also be insured. Such losses are called **time element losses** or **indirect losses**. For example, the longer the property is unusable, the greater the time element loss. If a building cannot be occupied for six months, the financial loss for the insured is much more severe than if the building cannot be occupied for only a few days.

Business income insurance protects a business from income lost because of a covered direct loss to its building or personal property. Coverage is provided for the reduction in the organization's net income (business revenue less expenses and taxes) resulting from damage by a covered cause of loss to the property at the insured's location. By covering the insured's reduction in net income, business income insurance can put the business in the same financial position it would have been in if no direct loss had occurred.

Coverage for loss of income is also provided by homeowners policies. When a covered cause of loss damages the part of the residence that the insured rents, or holds for rental, to others, "fair rental value" coverage in the homeowners policy indemnifies the insured for the loss of rental income until the rented portion of the residence is restored to livable condition.

Extra expenses
Expenses that reduce the length of a business interruption or enable a business to continue some operations when the property has been damaged by a covered cause of loss.

In the case of a business income loss, **extra expenses** would include additional expenses that reduce the length of the business interruption or enable a business to continue some operations despite damage to its property. For example, Iris, an insurance agent, may rent office space to conduct her business at a temporary location during the repairs to her office building following a fire. Iris's rental expense would be covered as an extra expense, as would any extra expenses (over and above her normal expenses) such as installing telephone service and notifying her customers of the temporary location.

The additional living expense coverage in homeowners and other policies covering dwellings is another example of extra expense coverage. If a direct loss to the dwelling makes the dwelling uninhabitable, **additional living expense** coverage indemnifies the insured for the additional expenses that are incurred so that the household can maintain its normal standard of living while the dwelling is being restored. Such expenses may include moving expenses and the cost of renting an apartment or a hotel room.

Another example of coverage for extra expenses is the optional rental reimbursement coverage available by endorsement to personal auto policies. This coverage pays up to a certain amount per day toward the cost of renting a vehicle because the covered auto has been damaged by collision or some other covered cause of loss.

Additional living expense
A coverage in homeowners policies that indemnifies the insured for the additional expenses that are incurred following a covered property loss so that the household can maintain its normal standard of living while the dwelling is being restored.

Covered Parties

Although a property insurance policy is a contract between the insurer and the named insured, the named insured is not always the only party that can recover in the event of an insured loss. Depending on the policy terms and conditions, property insurance can protect the insured and sometimes other parties that have an insurable interest in the property and that suffer a financial loss because covered property is lost, damaged, or destroyed.

Persons or organizations with an insurable interest in property can include property owners, secured lenders, users of property, and other holders of property. Insurance policies are written to cover these persons or organizations as follows:

* The owner of a building is the named insured on a property insurance policy covering the building.
* A party that owns and occupies a building is the named insured on a policy covering both building and personal property.
* The tenant of a building is the named insured on a property insurance policy covering the tenant's personal property in that building.
* A secured lender, although usually not a named insured, is listed by name in the declarations (or in an endorsement) as a mortgagee or a loss payee.
* A bailee is the named insured on a bailee policy. The bailee policy covers property of others that is in the bailee's custody.

Named Insured(s)

The declarations page of a policy has a space labeled named insured(s). Only parties whose names appear in the **named insured** space (or on an attached endorsement listing "additional named insureds") are, in fact, named insureds. In personal insurance, the named insured's spouse usually receives the same coverage as the named insured, even if the spouse is not named on the declarations page. Coverage for the spouse of a named insured depends on the policy definition of named insured and generally requires that the spouse live

Named insured
The policyholder whose name(s) appears on the declarations page of an insurance policy.

in the same household as the named insured. For example, a homeowners policy states:

> In this policy, "you" and "your" refer to the "named insured" shown in the Declarations and the spouse if a resident of the same household.

Therefore, if Larry Maple's name is the only name that appears on the declarations page of his homeowners policy as a named insured, the policy also provides coverage for his wife, Susan, who lives in the house with Larry. The wording in the preprinted portion of the policy, following the declarations page, does not refer to them as "Larry" and "Susan" but uses the word "you" (or "your") to include both Larry and Susan.

The situation is somewhat different with commercial insurance because several different individuals and businesses may be listed as named insureds. Thus, commercial insurance policies often state that the first named insured is, in effect, the contact person. The **first named insured** is responsible for paying premiums and has the right to receive any return premiums and to cancel the policy. If the insurer decides to cancel or to not renew a policy, the first named insured receives the notice of cancellation or nonrenewal.

First named insured

The person or organization whose name appears first as the named insured on a commercial insurance policy; this person or organization is usually responsible for paying premiums and has the right to receive any return premiums, to cancel the policy, and to receive the notice of cancellation or nonrenewal.

Secured Lenders

Although secured lenders are generally not named insureds on insurance policies covering property for which they have loaned money, the insurable interests of such lenders are protected when they are listed in the policy. Secured lenders include mortgagees (or mortgageholders) and loss payees, as discussed next.

Until the loan is paid in full, the lender has an insurable interest in the property because destruction of the property could cause a financial loss to the lender. To protect its interest in real property, a lender usually requires the borrower to purchase property insurance covering the building and to have the lender listed by name as mortgagee on the policy's declarations page.

Mortgage clause, or **mortgageholders clause**

A clause in a property insurance policy that protects the insurable interest of the mortgagee by giving it certain rights, such as the right to be named on claim drafts for losses to insured property and the right to be notified of policy cancellation.

The mortgagee has certain rights under the **mortgage clause** (or **mortgageholders clause**), which protects the insurable interest of the mortgagee, including the following:

- The insurer promises to pay covered claims to both the named insured and the mortgagee as their interests appear (that is, to the extent of each party's insurable interest).
- The insurer promises to notify the mortgagee before any policy cancellation or nonrenewal. This notice enables the mortgagee to replace the policy with other insurance.
- If the insurer cancels the policy and neglects to inform the mortgagee, the mortgagee's interest is still protected, even if the named insured no longer has coverage.

- The mortgagee has the right to pay the premium to the insurer if the insured fails to pay the premium so that the policy will remain in effect.

- In case of loss, the mortgagee may file a claim if the insured does not.

- If a claim is denied because the insured did not comply with the terms of the policy, the mortgagee may still collect under the policy. For example, a policyholder who commits arson may be barred from compensation. However, the mortgagee may still be able to receive payment for the claim up to its financial interest in the property (the value of the outstanding loan).

While a mortgage clause is used in a policy covering real property, a loss payable clause is used when a secured lender has an insurable interest in personal property. The secured lender is listed as a **loss payee**. A **loss payable clause** provides that a loss will be paid to both the insured and the loss payee as their interests appear. In addition, a loss payee is entitled to the same advance notice of cancellation or nonrenewal as is the named insured. Therefore, to the extent of its insurable interest, a loss payee has the right to participate in the recovery whenever any covered claim entitles the insured to payment. However, a loss payee does not have any right to recover in cases in which the insured cannot recover. In this regard, a loss payee does not have the same level of protection that a mortgagee has.

Loss payee
A lender, named on an insurance policy, who has loaned money on personal property, such as a car.

Loss payable clause
A clause that provides that a loss will be paid to both the insured and the loss payee as their interests appear and gives the loss payee certain rights.

Other Parties Whose Property Is Covered

Many property insurance policies provide coverage to parties who are neither named insureds nor secured lenders. The following examples illustrate this point:

- A homeowners policy can provide coverage for property owned by others who reside in the named insured's household—relatives of any age, and other persons (such as a foster child) under the age of twenty-one.

- A homeowners policy can provide coverage for property belonging to guests, residence employees, and others while it is in the named insured's home.

- A commercial property policy providing coverage on the named insured's personal property can also provide limited coverage for (1) the personal effects of officers, partners, or employees and (2) the personal property of others in the care, custody, or control of the insured.

- A personal auto policy can provide coverage for collision damage if the named insured borrows a car belonging to somebody else, the car sustains collision damage, and the owner of the borrowed car has no insurance.

The typical property policy provides that property of others is covered only if the named insured submits a claim. In the previous examples, the other parties do not enter into the insurance contract with the insurer, and they have no specific rights to collect under someone else's policy. However, the named insured can request that the insurer pay claims of this type.

Amounts of Recovery

When covered property is damaged by a covered cause of loss, how much will an insurer pay to a covered party with an insurable interest? That question must be clearly addressed in any insurance policy providing property coverage. The answer depends on policy provisions in the following categories:

- Policy limits
- Valuation provisions
- Settlement options
- Deductibles
- Insurance-to-value provisions
- "Other insurance" provisions

Policy Limits

When buying property insurance, the applicant usually requests a certain dollar amount of coverage. If the insurer agrees to provide that amount of coverage, the policy limit is established and the applicable policy limit is entered in the policy declarations. If a policy provides more than one coverage, a separate limit may be shown for each coverage.

A policy limit has several roles. It tells the insured the maximum amount of money that can be recovered from the insurer after a loss. By comparing the policy limit to the value that may be lost, the insured can determine whether the amount of insurance is adequate.

The policy limit tells the insurer the maximum amount it may have to pay for a covered loss. This limit is important, because insurers must keep track of their overall obligations in any one geographic area. For example, a fire or windstorm that affected several insured properties on one city block could have an unexpected effect on an insurer that relied on a spread of risk.

The policy limit is also important to both the insurer and the insured because the premium charged is directly related to the policy limit for most property insurance coverages. For example, a building might be insured for a rate of $0.50 per $100 of coverage. If the policy limit were $1 million, the corresponding premium for a one-year term would be $5,000. If the policy limit were $1.5 million, the premium would be $7,500.

Valuation Provisions

Several approaches may be used to set a value on a single item. As previously discussed, the two most common valuation approaches in property insurance policies are replacement cost and actual cash value. A third approach, used for certain types of property, involves agreed value.

Valuation provisions may create the impression that all insured losses are paid in money. Actually, property insurance policies usually give the insurer a choice of different settlement options.

Settlement Options

An insurer generally has the following three options to settle a loss:

1. Paying the value (as determined by the valuation provision) of the lost or damaged property

2. Paying the cost to repair or replace the property (if repair or replacement is possible)

3. Repairing, rebuilding, or replacing the property with other property of like kind and quality

These options for settling property losses can often reduce the insurer's costs of settling claims without diminishing the insured's actual indemnification. For example, the insurer may choose the second option and pay the cost to repair a partially burned garage if the cost of repair is less than an appraiser's estimate of the garage's decrease in value as a result of the fire. The third option would allow an insurer to replace a stolen watch, for example, with one of the same kind. An insurer may exercise that option because it can obtain the watch at a price that is less than the retail value of the watch.

Deductibles

Property insurance policies usually contain a **deductible** provision, which states that a portion of a covered loss will be subtracted (deducted) from the amount the insurer would otherwise be obligated to pay. Property insurance deductibles serve several functions. They encourage the insured to try to prevent losses because the insured will bear a part of any loss. Shifting the cost of small claims to the insured also enables the insurer to reduce premiums. Handling claims for small amounts often costs more than the dollar amount of the claim. Thus, deductibles enable people to purchase coverage for serious losses at a reasonable price without unnecessarily involving the insurer in small losses.

Deductible
A portion of a covered loss that is subtracted from the amount the insurer would otherwise be obligated to pay the insured.

Insurance-to-Value Provisions

Many property insurance policies include **insurance-to-value provisions**, which encourage insureds to purchase an amount of insurance that is equal to, or close to, the value of the covered property. Few losses are total. Unless all insureds purchase an amount of insurance close to the full value of their property, some insureds will pay considerably less for what usually provides the same recovery for a loss.

Insurance-to-value provision
A provision in property insurance policies that encourages insureds to purchase an amount of insurance that is equal to, or close to, the value of the covered property.

Assume, for example, that the grocer in the opening example, Mr. Brown, owns the supermarket building, which is worth $2 million. He insures the building for $2 million. Across town, Ms. Rodriguez owns a competing supermarket, and her building is worth $4 million. Ms. Rodriguez believes that the largest amount of loss she will suffer is $2 million so she insures her building for that amount. If their policies do not contain insurance-to-value provisions and each building suffers losses totaling $2 million, Mr. Brown and Ms. Rodriguez will each receive $2 million from their insurers to pay for the damage.

Ms. Rodriguez took a chance that her loss would be no more than $2 million (a fairly safe assumption in most cases) and paid much less for her coverage. This result is not only unfair to other policyholders, but it could also result in the insurer receiving inadequate premiums to cover losses. It is inequitable because Ms. Rodriguez pays the same premium as the owner of a $2 million building who insures it for $2 million, yet she is much more likely to sustain a $2 million dollar loss. (Two million dollars constitutes a partial loss on a $4 million building, but would be a total loss on the $2 million building. Most building property losses are partial losses.)

Insurers could solve this problem by charging a higher rate for those insureds who insure to less than the property's value. Because such a solution is complicated, however, it can be used only in some rare cases. Consequently, insurers have encouraged their insureds to buy insurance to value or to insure to a high percentage of the property's value. The traditional approach to encouraging insurance to value is to include a **coinsurance** provision in the policy. A coinsurance provision states that if the property is underinsured, the amount that an insurer will pay for a covered loss is reduced. The insurer's goal is to have property insured to its full value.

Coinsurance

An insurance-to-value provision in many property insurance policies providing that if the property is underinsured, the amount that an insurer will pay for a covered loss is reduced.

"Other Insurance" Provisions

In some cases, more than one insurance policy provides coverage for the same item of property. If two or more insurers paid in full for the same loss, the insured could profit from the loss, violating the principle of indemnity. Most policies contain an "other insurance" provision to deal with this problem. When more than one policy covers a loss, the amount paid by each policy depends on the allocation procedure specified in the "other insurance" provisions of the policies.

SUMMARY

Three important aspects of property loss exposures are (1) the types of property exposed to loss, (2) potential causes of loss, and (3) financial consequences that may result from a property loss.

Types of property include the following:

- Buildings
- Personal property (contents) contained in buildings
- Money and securities
- Motor vehicles and trailers
- Property in transit
- Ships and their cargoes
- Boilers and machinery

These categories are useful for insurance purposes because they emphasize the characteristics that affect property loss exposures.

Causes of loss, or perils, that can damage or destroy property are sometimes listed in insurance policies, called named perils policies. Other policies, called special form coverage or open perils policies, provide coverage for any direct loss to property unless the loss is covered by a peril that is specifically excluded by the policy.

The financial consequences of a property loss can include the following:

- Reduced property value
- Lost income because the property cannot be used
- Extra expenses

Parties other than the property owner who may be affected by a property loss include secured lenders, users of property, and other holders of property.

Property insurance policy provisions specify exactly which property loss exposures are covered. These provisions specify covered property and locations, covered causes of loss, excluded causes of loss, covered financial consequences, and the covered parties.

Policy limits stipulate the maximum amount the insurer will pay in the event of a loss. Policy valuation provisions explain how the amount of a loss payment will be determined, that is, according to replacement cost, actual cash value, or some other valuation method. Settlement options provide insurers with several ways to settle a loss. Property insurance policies often specify a deductible to be subtracted from the amount of the loss payment. Some policies also include an insurance-to-value provision that encourages insureds to purchase insurance equal or close to the value of the property. When more than one policy covers a loss, the amount paid by each policy depends on the allocation procedure specified in the "other insurance" provisions of the policies.

Chapter 9

Direct Your Learning

Liability Loss Exposures and Policy Provisions

After learning the content of this chapter and completing the corresponding course guide assignment, you should be able to:

■ Distinguish among the following:
  - Constitutional law
  - Statutory law
  - Common law

■ Distinguish between criminal law and civil law.

■ Explain how each of the following can be the basis for legal liability:
  - Torts
  - Contracts
  - Statutes

■ Describe the four elements of negligence.

■ Describe the potential financial consequences of liability loss exposures.

■ Describe circumstances that create liability loss exposures.

■ Identify the parties that may be insured by a liability insurance policy.

■ Describe the various types of injury or damage that are typically covered in liability insurance policies.

■ Describe loss exposures typically excluded in liability insurance policies.

■ Describe the costs typically covered in liability insurance policies and how these costs are determined.

■ Explain the difference between occurrence basis and claims-made coverage.

■ Explain how claim payments are affected by policy limits and defense cost provisions.

■ Define or describe each of the Key Words and Phrases for this chapter.

Develop Your Perspective

What are the main topics covered in the chapter?

This chapter describes the sources of law that underlie legal liability in the United States. From this foundation, liability loss exposures for negligence and other torts are determined. Liability insurance policies cover damages that the policyholder may be required to pay, and they defend the policyholder in related legal actions.

Describe the sources of law in the U.S.

- How have the laws evolved?
- How can a single act be subject to both criminal and civil law?

Why is it important to learn about these topics?

The elements of negligence are universal principles that can be used to examine any liability loss exposure or determine liability for any claim.

Examine the elements of negligence.

- How are they used to resolve questions of responsibility and compensation in a liability claim?
- How are they used to examine loss exposures to determine the potential for liability losses?

How can you use what you will learn?

Evaluate a liability insurance claim that you have witnessed or experienced.

- What was the duty owed to another?
- How was the duty breached?
- What injury or damage resulted?
- How was the unbroken chain of events from the breach of duty to the injury or damage determined?

Chapter 9

Liability Loss Exposures and Policy Provisions

The day seemed like any other at the Atwell Insulation Company (AIC). Trucks entered and left the plant, and the chemical processing operations ran at full capacity to keep up with demand. The only unusual event in the day's schedule was a tour by chemical engineering students who were impressed by the plant's efficiency.

However, disaster struck at 11:08 AM when the No. 2 storage tank exploded. Minor explosions had occurred before but had done little damage. Things turned out differently this time.

Apparently the No. 2 storage tank had been filled beyond its listed capacity, leaving inadequate space for expansion as the temperature of the contents increased. A pressure relief device failed to function, and the tank wall popped at a seam, causing the contents of the tank to spread into the plant yard. A large amount of the contents also went into a drain leading to a nearby river. Some of the fluid flowed into one of AIC's buildings, where a furnace ignited it. The fire spread quickly and burned for two days. Fumes from the fire injured thirty-five of AIC's employees, killed two other employees, and injured seven of the visiting engineering students. Five more employees were injured in an auto accident as they attempted to escape from the fire and fumes. The accident injured three occupants in another vehicle and caused major damage to both cars.

The neighborhoods around the plant had to be evacuated, and some nearby businesses were closed for two weeks. Over the next twelve months, a series of customer complaints and claims led AIC to conclude that the spillage and fire had caused impurities in its products from several production runs.

In addition to the losses that AIC suffered to its own property because of the explosion and ensuing fire, AIC could suffer devastating financial consequences because of the harm suffered by others. AIC could be legally liable to a number of persons and businesses, suffering large liability losses as a result of the explosion and fire.

This accident will inevitably result in claims for monetary damages. These claims arise from AIC's legal obligations to the people and the organizations that suffered bodily injury or property damage caused by the explosion and its aftermath. The explosion could lead to at least one court case, which might last for many months or even years. If the court rules against AIC and the ruling is upheld despite any appeals made by AIC's attorneys, the company will have no choice but to pay the amount awarded by the court. AIC's liability losses may not be as obvious on the day after the explosion as its property losses, but the financial consequences of AIC's legal liability could be much greater than the financial consequences of its property losses. This chapter explores liability loss exposures, based on the concept of legal liability, and the insurance policy provisions that deal with those exposures.

LEGAL LIABILITY

Legal liability
A person or an organization's status as legally responsible for injury or damage suffered by another person or organization.

The term **legal liability** refers to a person or an organization's status as legally responsible for injury or damage suffered by another person or organization. An understanding of legal liability is essential to recognizing liability loss exposures. Although complex legal questions require the professional expertise of an attorney, knowledge of some fundamental legal terms and concepts is essential for anyone dealing with liability loss exposures or liability insurance.

Laws exist in a civilized society to enforce certain standards of conduct. Although laws generally make the world safer and more secure, they also impose certain duties. Where there are rights, there are also responsibilities. People must accept the constraints of the law in order to enjoy its benefits. The law accomplishes its objectives by holding people responsible for their actions.

Sources of Law

The legal system in the United States derives essentially from the following:

- The Constitution, which is the source of constitutional law
- Legislative bodies, which are the source of statutory law
- Court decisions, which are the source of common law

Constitutional Law

The supreme law in the U.S. is the Constitution, which specifies the structure of the federal government and outlines the respective powers of its legislative, executive, and judicial branches. The Constitution provides for a federal system of government in which powers not specifically granted to the federal government are reserved for the individual states. With its amendments, the Constitution also guarantees to all citizens certain fundamental rights, such as freedom of speech, freedom of religion, freedom from unreasonable searches and seizures, the right to a trial by jury, and the right to due process of law.

Constitutional law
The Constitution itself and all the decisions of the Supreme Court that involve the Constitution.

All other laws must conform to **constitutional law,** which is the Constitution itself and all the decisions of the Supreme Court that involve the Constitution. The courts interpret the Constitution to decide constitutional issues. If the U.S. Supreme Court decides that a particular law conflicts with the

Constitution, that law is invalidated. The Supreme Court is the highest court of appeal, and lower courts must follow the Supreme Court's decision in judging future cases involving the same issue.

Each state also has a constitution establishing the powers of the state government. Further, each state has some type of supreme court to resolve legal conflicts in the state government and to hear appeals on matters of state law. States must ultimately follow the U.S. Constitution.

Statutory Law

National, state, and local legislatures enact laws, or statutes, to deal with perceived problems. At the national level, Congress considers many newly proposed laws each year. Any member of the U.S. Senate or House of Representatives may introduce a bill. After its introduction, a bill may be referred to a committee for study or perhaps for hearings before it is debated on the floor of the Senate or the House. If the bill receives a majority vote in both the Senate and the House and the President signs it, the bill becomes law. State legislatures also make new laws in similar fashion. Laws made by local governments are often called ordinances. Collectively, these formal enactments of federal, state, or local legislative bodies are referred to as **statutory law**.

Statutory law
The formal laws, or statutes, enacted by federal, state, or local legislative bodies.

Numerous federal, state, and local government agencies have regulatory powers derived from authority granted by legislative bodies. Examples of such agencies include the Federal Trade Commission, the Environmental Protection Agency, state public utility commissions, and local zoning boards. These regulatory bodies issue detailed rules and regulations covering a particular public concern or relating to a particular industry. They also render decisions on the application of these rules and regulations in certain cases.

Common Law

In contrast to statutory law, common law has evolved in the courts. When the king's judges began hearing disputes in medieval England, they had little basis for their decisions except common sense and the prevailing notions of justice. Each decision, however, became a precedent for similar cases in the future. Gradually, certain principles evolved over time that the judges applied consistently to all the cases they heard. These principles became known as **common law**, or **case law**.

Common law, or **case law**
A body of principles and rules established over time by courts on a case-by-case basis.

These common-law principles guided judges not only in England but also in the English colonies in America. Thus, the English common law heavily influenced the U.S. legal system. When neither constitutional nor statutory law applies, judges still rely on precedents of previous cases in reaching their decisions. In many areas, laws have been passed that modify or replace common-law principles, but common law is still important in matters of legal liability.

Criminal Law Versus Civil Law

The U.S. legal system makes an important distinction between criminal law and civil law. While criminal law cases generally receive more headlines, legal cases related to insurance usually involve civil law.

Criminal Law

Criminal law

The category of law that applies to wrongful acts that society deems so harmful to the public welfare that government takes the responsibility for prosecuting and punishing the wrongdoers.

Criminal law applies to wrongful acts that society deems so harmful to the public welfare that the government takes the responsibility for prosecuting and punishing the wrongdoers. To cite only a few examples, criminal laws prohibit murder, rape, robbery, arson, fraud, theft, and driving while intoxicated. Such offenses are crimes (wrongs against society).

Crimes are punishable by fines, imprisonment, or, in some states, death. The government uses its power to punish in order to enforce criminal laws. When a crime occurs, the police investigate and, if sufficient evidence is found, criminal charges are brought on behalf of the state against the accused wrongdoer. For example, if Jesse James were arrested for robbing a bank, the case would go to court as "The State versus Jesse James." The district attorney presenting the evidence against Jesse James would represent society as a whole, not just the bank. If the jury were to find Jesse James guilty of the bank robbery, he would probably go to jail. Such a punishment is intended to protect the public, to punish Jesse, and to deter other people from committing the same crime.

Civil Law

Civil law

The category of law that deals with the rights and responsibilities of citizens with respect to one another; applies to legal matters not governed by criminal law.

Civil law deals with the rights and responsibilities of citizens with respect to one another, and applies to legal matters not governed by criminal law. Actions that are not necessarily crimes can still cause considerable harm to other people. In the absence of laws, a dispute between neighbors can turn into an endless feud. Civil law proceedings provide a forum for hearing disputes between private parties and rendering a decision binding on all parties. This procedure enables individuals to protect themselves against infringement of their rights by others.

Civil law protects personal and property rights. If someone invades the privacy or property of another person or harms another's reputation, the injured person may seek amends in court. By protecting such personal and property rights, civil law contributes to the welfare and safety of society.

Contract law

The branch of civil law that deals with contracts and settles contract disputes.

Civil law also protects contract rights. People and businesses are more willing to make agreements or contracts with one another when they know that those contracts are enforceable. If two parties make a contract that one party does not honor, the other party can ask the court to enforce compliance to the contract or to assess damages. **Contract law** is the branch of civil law that deals with contracts and settles contract disputes. Such laws promote commerce by making contracts more reliable.

Criminal and Civil Consequences of the Same Act

Criminal and civil law do not necessarily deal with entirely different matters. A particular act can often have both criminal and civil law consequences. Consider, for example, the following two incidents in the life of Karen Smith.

Because she is an entrepreneur who travels frequently, Karen usually has large amounts of cash in her purse. Once when she was walking down the street, a stranger grabbed her purse and ran off. The police later found the stranger. He still had some of the contents of Karen's purse, but the purse and money were gone. The stranger was arrested, tried, and convicted of the crime of robbery. Karen might also have started civil law proceedings against the robber to recover her money, but that would have accomplished little because the robber had no money and was going to jail.

Another time Karen was returning from a business trip when her car was broadsided by another vehicle. Beyond the damage to her car, Karen's injuries required medical care costing thousands of dollars; she missed two weeks of work, losing existing customers and opportunities to secure new customers. Following the accident investigation, the other driver was charged and convicted of driving while intoxicated. Karen's auto insurer paid most of her medical and auto physical damage bills. However, Karen did bring a civil suit against the other driver for her lost business opportunities, and the court ordered the other driver to pay an amount equal to the income Karen had lost.

In each incident, both criminal and civil law proceedings were possible results. The differing circumstances influenced the practical effectiveness of each type of legal action.

ELEMENTS OF A LIABILITY LOSS EXPOSURE

A liability loss exposure involves the possibility of one party becoming legally responsible for injury or harm to another party. This section examines the following elements of a liability loss exposure:

- The legal basis of a claim by one party against another for damages
- The potential financial consequences of liability loss exposures

The Basis for Legal Liability

The most common bases for legal liability are torts, contracts, and statutes. Exhibit 9-1 illustrates the different aspects of civil law that can give an injured party the legal basis for recovering damages from another party.

EXHIBIT 9-1

Legal Basis of a Liability Claim

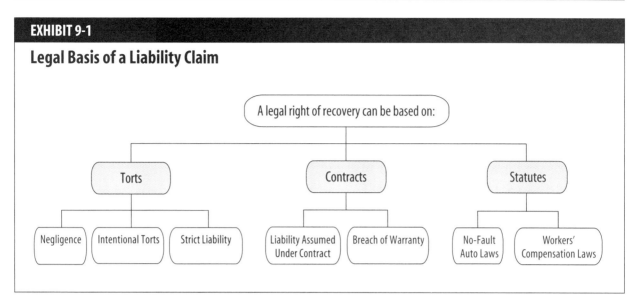

Torts

Tort
A wrongful act, other than a crime or breach of contract, committed by one party against another.

Tort law
The branch of civil law that deals with civil wrongs other than breaches of contract.

A **tort** is any wrongful act, other than a crime or breach of contract, committed by one party against another. Crimes differ from torts, because criminal law allows the state to prosecute and civil law does not. The central concern of **tort law**, which deals with civil wrongs other than breaches of contract, is determining responsibility for injury or damage. Although largely modified or restated in statutes, tort law is still based mainly on common law.

A person who is legally responsible for an injury may be compelled to compensate the victim only if there is some standard for assigning that responsibility. Under tort law, an individual or organization can face a claim for legal liability on the basis of any of the following:

- Negligence
- Intentional torts
- Strict liability

Exhibit 9-2 presents a summary of the types of torts that may give rise to a liability loss.

Negligence
A person or an organization's failure to exercise the level of care that a reasonably prudent person would have exercised under similar circumstances.

Negligence occurs when a person or an organization fails to exercise the level of care that a reasonably prudent person would have exercised under similar circumstances. The greatest number of liability cases arise from negligence. Tort law gives injured parties the right to seek compensation if they can demonstrate that someone else's negligence led to their injuries.

A liability judgment based on negligence requires proof of all four of the following elements:

1. *A duty owed to another.* The first element of negligence is that a person or an organization must have a duty to act (or not to act) that constitutes a responsibility to another party. For example, the driver of an automobile

has a duty to operate the car safely. In the AIC example, AIC had a duty to provide safe conditions at its plant.

2. *A breach of that duty.* In order for a person or an organization to be held negligent, a breach of the duty owed to another party must occur. A breach of duty is the failure to exercise a reasonable degree of care expected in a particular situation. In the tank explosion example earlier in this chapter, the fact that a storage tank had been filled beyond its listed capacity could indicate that AIC had failed to act reasonably and had breached its duty to provide safe conditions. However, if no breach of duty can be proved, no negligence can be found.

3. *Injury or damage.* The third element of negligence requires that the claimant must suffer definite injury or harm. Although a legal duty to act and a breach of that duty may exist, no recovery can be made based on negligence unless someone suffers injury or damage to property. For example, AIC could be accused of causing injury to the visiting students by breaching its duty to provide safe conditions.

4. *Unbroken chain of events between the breach of duty and the injury or damage.* A finding of negligence also requires that the breach of duty initiate an unbroken chain of events leading to the injury. The breach of the duty must be the proximate cause of the injury. In the AIC example, the injured students would have to prove that AIC's breach of its duty to provide safe conditions was the proximate cause of their injuries.

EXHIBIT 9-2

Types of Torts

	Description	Element(s)	Examples
Negligence	Failure to act in a prudent manner	• Duty owed to another • Breach of that duty • Injury or damage • Unbroken chain of events from breach of duty to injury or damage	• Driving while intoxicated and causing an accident • Allowing a pet dog to run loose and bite a child
Intentional Torts	Deliberate acts that cause harm	Deliberate act (other than a breach of contract) that causes harm to another person	• Assault • Battery • Libel • Slander • False arrest • Invasion of privacy
Strict Liability	Inherently dangerous activities	Inherently dangerous activities or dangerously defective products that result in injury or harm	• Owning a wild animal • Blasting operations

Tortfeasor
A person, a business, or another party who has committed a tort.

Vicarious liability
Legal responsibility that occurs when one party is held liable for the actions of another party.

Intentional tort
A deliberate act (other than a breach of contract) that causes harm to another person.

Assault
The intentional threat of bodily harm.

Battery
The unlawful physical contact with another person.

Defamation
An intentional false communication, either written or spoken, that damages another's reputation or good name.

Slander
A spoken untrue statement that damages a person's reputation.

Libel
A written or printed untrue statement that damages a person's reputation.

False arrest
Any unlawful physical restraint of another's freedom.

Invasion of privacy
An encroachment on another person's right to be left alone.

A person or an organization whose conduct is proved to be negligent is generally responsible for the consequences. This party is called the **tortfeasor**, the wrongdoer, or the negligent party. All of these terms refer to a party who does something that a reasonable person would not do (or fails to do something that a reasonable person would do) under similar circumstances.

In addition to the person who actually commits the act, other persons or organizations may be held responsible for the tortfeasor's action. This responsibility is called **vicarious liability**. Vicarious liability often arises in business situations from the relationship between employer and employee. An employee performing work-related activities is generally acting on behalf of the employer. Therefore, the employer can be vicariously liable for the actions of the employee. If, for example, an employee drives a customer to a meeting and negligently causes an accident in which the customer is injured, both the employee and the employer could be held liable for the customer's injuries. Responsibility would not shift from the employee to the employer but rather could extend to include the employer.

An **intentional tort** is a deliberate act (other than a breach of contract) that causes harm to another person, regardless of whether the harm is intended. Assault and battery are common examples of intentional torts. **Assault** is an intentional threat of bodily harm under circumstances that create a fear of imminent harm. **Battery** is any unlawful and unprivileged touching of another person. Assault and battery often happen together at approximately the same time, but either can happen without the other.

Another common example of an intentional tort is defamation. **Defamation** is an intentional false communication, either written or spoken, that damages another's reputation. Defamation includes both slander and libel. **Slander** is a spoken, untrue statement about another person. **Libel** most often occurs when someone prints and distributes an untrue statement about another person that damages the person's reputation. However, libel can take place through any medium, such as radio, television, film, or the Internet. As a rule, the law affords public figures less protection against libel and slander than ordinary persons except when a false statement is also malicious. For defamation to occur, someone other than the defamed person must read or hear the false statement. Moreover, true statements, no matter how offensive they may be, are not defamation according to the law.

False arrest or detainment is any unlawful physical restraint of another's freedom. This intentional tort presents a potential problem for retail stores. False arrest can occur when a store employee detains a customer suspected of shoplifting. If it is later determined that the customer had not stolen any merchandise, the detainment is a false arrest that inconveniences and embarrasses the customer.

Still another intentional tort is **invasion of privacy**, which is an encroachment on another person's right to be left alone. Liability for invasion of privacy can arise from the unauthorized release of confidential information, the illegal use of hidden microphones or other surveillance equipment, an unauthorized search, or the public disclosure of private facts.

Strict liability (or **absolute liability**) is the legal liability arising from inherently dangerous activities or dangerously defective products that result in injury or harm to another, regardless of how much care was used in the activity.

Although most liability cases arise from negligence and some arise from intentional torts, liability under tort law is not entirely limited to cases of injury caused by negligent or deliberate conduct. In situations involving inherently dangerous activities, tort law can give an injured person a right of recovery without having to prove negligence or intent. Such inherently dangerous activities can give rise to strict liability for any injury regardless of the intent or the carefulness of the person held liable. The situation itself, rather than the person's conduct, becomes the standard for determining liability.

For example, the owner of a wild animal is liable for any injury the animal inflicts, regardless of the precautions the owner may have taken. Blasting operations present an exposure to strict liability for businesses. The mere fact that the business conducts blasting operations is enough to make the owners of the business liable for any injuries or damage that results.

Contracts

Contract law enables an injured party to seek recovery because another party has breached a duty voluntarily accepted in a contract. As discussed, a contract is a legally enforceable agreement between two or more parties. If one party fails to honor the contract, the other may sue to enforce it. In such a case, it is the specific contract, rather than the law in general, that the court interprets. Two areas of contract law important to insurance are liability assumed under contract and breach of warranty, discussed next.

Parties to a contract sometimes find it convenient for one party to assume the financial consequences of certain types of liability faced by the other. The party assuming the liability may be closer to the scene, exercise more control over operations, or have the ability to respond to claims more efficiently. For example, James Smith, the owner of a building, and Jane Jones, a contractor, make a contract in which Jones accepts responsibility for certain actions of Bob White, a subcontractor. If one of the specified actions of White injures a customer, Bonita Brown, and Brown sues Smith, then Jones will pay any damages owed to Brown because of White's specified action. Such arrangements, called **hold-harmless agreements**, are common in construction and service businesses and obligate one party to assume the financial consequences of legal liability for another party. They are called hold-harmless agreements because they require one party to "hold harmless and indemnify" the other party against liability arising from the activity (or product) that is specified in the contract.

Businesses can transfer the financial consequences of certain types of liability to other persons and organizations through contracts, but, as a matter of

Strict liability, or **absolute liability**

Legal liability that arises from inherently dangerous activities or dangerously defective products that result in injury or harm to another, regardless of how much care was used in the activity. Also used to describe the liability imposed by certain statutes, such as workers' compensation laws.

Hold-harmless agreement

A contractual provision that obligates one party to assume the financial consequences of legal liability for another party.

public policy, not all types of liability can be transferred. Normally, one party cannot transfer its liability for gross negligence, willful or wanton misconduct, or criminal actions to another party.

Warranty
A promise, either written or implied, such as a promise by a seller to a buyer that a product is fit for a particular purpose.

The law of contracts also governs claims arising from breach of warranty. Contracts for sales of goods include **warranties**, or promises made by the seller. The law also implies certain warranties. A seller warrants, for example, that an item is fit for a particular purpose. If Juanita buys the hair conditioner recommended and sold by her beautician, she relies on the warranty that the conditioner will be good for her hair. If the conditioner damages her hair instead, the beautician (as well as the manufacturer) could be held liable for a breach of warranty. The buyer does not have to prove negligence on the part of the seller. The fact that the product did not work shows that the contract was not fulfilled.

Statutes

Statutory liability
Legal liability imposed by a specific statute or law.

Statutory liability is legal liability imposed by a specific statute or law. Although common law may cover a particular situation, statutory law may extend, restrict, or clarify the rights of injured parties in that situation or similar ones. One reason for such legislation is to ensure adequate compensation for injuries without lengthy disputes over who is at fault. Examples of this kind of statutory liability involve no-fault auto laws and workers' compensation laws. In these legal areas, a specific statute (rather than the common-law principles of torts) gives one party the right of recovery from another or restricts that right of recovery.

Automobile accidents are among the leading causes of injury in the U.S. Because of this fact, state legislatures seek ways to improve the system for distributing the generally high costs of these accidents. Specific statutes now modify many of the common-law principles of negligence that apply to automobile accidents. Because these laws are enacted by state legislatures, the provisions vary considerably by state.

In an effort to reduce the number of lawsuits resulting from auto accidents, some states have enacted "no-fault" laws. These laws recognize the inevitability of auto accidents and restrict or eliminate the right to sue the other party in an accident, except in the more serious cases defined by the law. Victims with less serious injuries collect their out-of-pocket expenses from their own insurers without the need for expensive legal proceedings.

A similar concept of liability without regard to fault applies to workplace injuries. Each of the fifty states has a workers' compensation statute. Such a statute eliminates an employee's right to sue the employer for most work-related injuries and also imposes on the employer automatic (strict) liability to pay specified benefits. In place of the right to sue for negligence, workers' compensation laws create a system in which injured employees receive benefits specified in these laws. As long as the injury is work-related, the employer pays the specified benefits regardless of who is at fault. In the AIC case, the workers' compensation law in AIC's state would require that

AIC provide benefits (such as medical, disability, and rehabilitation benefits) to the injured employees as well as death benefits to the survivors of the employees who were killed.

Potential Financial Consequences of Liability Loss Exposures

A person must sustain definite harm for a liability loss to result in a valid claim. Returning to the loss example involving AIC, the visiting engineering students can collect damages from AIC only if they can prove that they actually suffered some harm as a result of the explosion. Perhaps they had to be treated in the hospital emergency room, their clothing was ruined, or they could not go to their jobs and thus lost a day's pay. To those who can show that actual harm or injury was suffered because of AIC's negligence, the court may award damages that AIC will have to pay. In addition, AIC may incur defense costs to defend itself in court. In addition to damages and defense costs, AIC can suffer other financial consequences, such as loss of reputation. Exhibit 9-3 shows the various types of damages and defense costs that may have to be paid as the result of a liability claim.

EXHIBIT 9-3

Potential Financial Consequences of Liability Loss Exposures

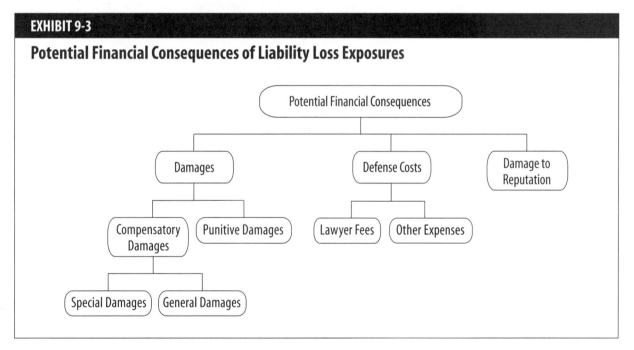

Damages

As explained earlier in the chapter, compensatory damages are intended to compensate the victim for the harm actually suffered. An award of compensatory damages is the amount of money that has been judged to equal the victim's loss, and it is the amount the party responsible for the loss will have to pay. Compensatory damages include both special damages and general damages. In addition, the court could award punitive damages.

Defense Costs

In addition to the damages that may have to be paid because of liability for bodily injury or property damage, the financial consequences of a liability loss may also include costs to defend the alleged wrongdoer in court. These defense costs include not only the fees paid to lawyers but also all the other expenses associated with defending a liability claim. Such expenses can include investigation expenses, expert witness fees, premiums for necessary bonds, and other expenses incurred to prepare for and conduct a trial. Even in the unlikely event that all the possible lawsuits against AIC are ultimately found groundless, AIC and its liability insurer will probably incur substantial defense costs.

Damage to Reputation

A third financial consequence of liability loss may be the loss of reputation—the overall adverse effects of liability losses on the business. Such consequences are often difficult to quantify, but they do exist. For example, in 2000 a tire manufacturer recalled over six million tires after they were alleged to be a factor in rollover crashes. In addition to damages paid and defense costs for the lawsuits that followed, the manufacturer suffered a damaged reputation and resultant loss of sales.

CATEGORIES OF LIABILITY LOSS EXPOSURES

Liability loss exposures exist whenever some activity or relationship can create liability to others. Although the following list is far from exhaustive, liability can arise from any of the following:

- Automobiles and other conveyances
- Premises
- Business operations
- Completed operations
- Products
- Advertising
- Pollution
- Liquor
- Professional activities

Automobiles and Other Conveyances

A significant liability loss exposure for almost all persons and businesses comes from the ownership, maintenance, and use of automobiles. In the U.S., auto accidents produce the greatest number of liability claims. Even people or businesses that do not own an auto can be held vicariously liable for the operation of an auto by others. As shown in the AIC case, AIC could be held liable for the auto accident caused by its employee fleeing the fire, whether the employee was driving his own vehicle or one owned by AIC.

Liability loss exposures are also created by owning and operating other conveyances such as watercraft, aircraft, or recreational vehicles.

Premises

Anyone who owns or occupies property has a premises liability loss exposure. If a visitor slips on an icy front porch, the homeowner may be held liable for the injury. A business has a similar loss exposure arising from its premises. As seen in the AIC case, the engineering students were injured while on AIC's premises, and AIC will probably be held liable for their injuries.

Business Operations

Businesses must be concerned not only about the condition of the premises but also about their business operations. As AIC discovered, whatever activity the business performs has the potential to go wrong and cause harm to someone else. Many business operations occur away from the organization's premises. A plumbing contractor, for example, may start a fire in a customer's house while soldering a copper pipe. Similarly, a roofing contractor may drop debris from a ladder, injuring the customer's family members. In both cases, the customer will probably make a liability claim against the contractor.

Completed Operations

Even after a plumber, an electrician, a painter, or another contractor completes a job and leaves the work site, a liability loss exposure remains. If faulty wiring or toxic paint leads to an injury, the person or business who performed the work may be liable. Considerable time could pass in the interim, but the person or business may still be held liable if faulty workmanship created the condition that eventually caused the injury. If, for example, AIC could prove that the explosion was caused by the negligence of the contractor who installed the pressure relief device on the storage tank, the contractor may be liable for some or all of the resulting damage and injury.

Products

Liability resulting from products that cause bodily injury or property damage is a significant exposure for manufacturers. This exposure begins with the design of the product and might not cease until the product is properly disposed of by the ultimate consumer. Millions of customers use or consume mass-produced products, foods, and pharmaceuticals. A prescription drug may be dangerous, but the danger might not be known for several years, when it is too late to help those who have taken the drug. AIC's customers complained of impurities in its products; if these impurities caused injury to one or more of its customers, AIC could be held liable for damages. If the manufacturer of the pressure relief device was found to be negligent, the manufacturer might also incur some liability.

Advertising

Businesses often include pictures of people using their products in their advertisements. If a local retailer cannot afford professional models, it might use pictures of people using its products or shopping in its store. Unless the retailer obtains proper permission, publishing the pictures could lead to a law-suit alleging invasion of privacy. Using another company's trademarked slogan or advertisement can also give rise to a liability claim.

Pollution

Many types of products pollute the environment when they are discarded. In addition, the manufacture of some products creates contaminants that, if not disposed of properly, can cause environmental impairment, or pollution. If the explosion at AIC's plant polluted the nearby river, AIC might have yet another liability loss. The Love Canal case in New York State remains a good example of how industrial products or wastes can have serious detrimental effects on the environment. Toxic wastes in the Love Canal area polluted the ground water and made the surrounding community a dangerous place in which to live. Cleanup costs and expenses to relocate persons living in the contaminated area can be enormous in such cases.

Liquor

Serious dangers exist when people consume too much alcohol. Intoxicated persons can pose a threat to themselves as well as to others. Providers of alcohol can be held responsible for customers or guests who become intoxicated and injure someone while driving drunk. Both the drunk driver and the person who served the alcohol can be held legally liable. A business that sells or serves alcoholic beverages, therefore, has a significant liability loss exposure.

Professional Activities

As explained earlier, negligence involves a failure to exercise the degree of care that is reasonable under given circumstances. It is reasonable to expect that professionals with special competence in a particular field or occupation will exercise great care in performing their duties. Attorneys, physicians, architects, engineers, and other professionals are considered experts in their field and are expected to perform accordingly. Professional liability arises if injury or damage can be attributed to a professional's failure to exercise the appropriate standard of care. For insurance professionals and others, this failure is sometimes called errors and omissions (E&O). For medical professionals, it is often called malpractice. For example, a physician who prescribes a drug but ignores the possible side effects may be held liable for any resulting harm to the patient, because accepted medical practice requires the doctor to consider possible side effects. When professionals make errors, the injured party usually expects to be compensated.

LIABILITY INSURANCE POLICY PROVISIONS

Liability insurance covers losses resulting from bodily injury to others or damage to the property of others for which the insured is legally liable and to which the coverage applies. Because of differences between liability loss exposures and property loss exposures, liability insurance differs from property insurance in several ways as follows:

- Property insurance claims usually involve only two parties—the insurer and the insured. Liability insurance claims involve three parties—the insurer, the insured, and a third party, who is the claimant who makes a claim against the insured for injury or damage allegedly caused by the insured. Although the claimant is not a party to the insurance contract, he or she is a party to the claim settlement.

- In property insurance, insurers typically pay claims to an insured when covered property is damaged by a covered cause of loss during the policy period. In liability insurance, insurers pay a third party on behalf of the insured against whom a claim has been made, provided the claim is covered by the policy.

- Property insurance policies must clarify which property and causes of loss the policy covers. In contrast, liability insurance policies must indicate the activities and types of injury or damage that are covered.

The insuring agreements of most liability insurance policies make essentially the same broad promise: to pay damages (usually for bodily injury or property damage) for which an insured becomes legally liable and to which the coverage applies. The insurer also promises to pay related defense costs. In order to clarify the intent of the insuring agreement, which is usually a relatively brief statement, the provisions of a liability insurance policy must answer several questions, including the following:

- What parties are insured?
- What activities are covered?
- What types of injury or damage are covered?
- What loss exposures are excluded?
- What costs are covered in addition to damages and defense costs?
- What time period is covered?
- What factors affect the amount of claim payments?

Liability insurance
Insurance that covers losses resulting from bodily injury to others or damage to the property of others for which the insured is legally liable and to which the coverage applies.

Covered Parties

Liability insurance policies provide coverage for the named insured as well as others. A liability policy generally gives the broadest protection to the named insured. Coverage for others is generally based on their family or business relationship with the named insured. Therefore, liability insurance policy provisions must define the relationships that determine coverage. For example, many policies provide the spouse of a named insured with the same coverage that is provided to the named insured if they live in the same household. If several named insureds are listed in the declarations of a commercial liability policy, a policy provision usually stipulates that the first named insured is the insured with whom the insurer has contact for payment of premiums, claim reporting and claim payment, notices of cancellation or nonrenewal, or interim policy changes.

The extent of liability coverage provided to parties other than the named insured is determined by their relationship to the named insured as well as by the circumstances. For example, the liability coverage of a typical homeowners policy applies to the following:

- The named insured and the named insured's spouse, if the spouse is a resident in the household

- Relatives of the named insured or spouse, if the relatives reside in the household

- Full-time students who were residents before moving out to attend school, if under twenty-four and a relative or under twenty-one and in the care of an insured

- Any person or organization legally responsible for animals or watercraft owned by an insured (except in business situations)

- Employees using a covered vehicle, such as a lawn tractor, and other people using a covered vehicle on an insured location with the named insured's consent

Commercial liability policies also cover the named insured and certain others, depending on their relationship to the named insured. For example, a commercial general liability policy (CGL policy) usually contains provisions that specify the relationships and circumstances that determine who is insured under the policy. One provision clarifies who is insured when the named insured is an individual, a partnership, or some other type of organization, such as a corporation. Another provision defines others who may be covered because of their business relationship to the named insured and the circumstances under which they are covered. The parties who are insureds under this provision include the following:

- The named insured's employees and volunteer workers

- Real estate managers for the named insured

- Persons responsible for the property of a named insured who has died

- Any organization that is newly acquired or formed by the named insured for up to a certain number of days after it is acquired or formed

As these examples illustrate, both personal and commercial liability insurance policies generally cover many individuals and organizations—including some that are not named in the policy declarations.

Covered Activities

Under a liability policy, the insurer will pay damages only to those who suffer injury or damage for which the insured is legally liable if the harm arose from a covered activity.

Just as property insurance policies use either a named perils or a special form coverage approach to define covered causes of loss, liability insurance policies use two approaches to define covered activities. Certain policies state the specific activity or source of liability covered. For example, an auto insurance liability policy states that it applies to claims that result from covered auto accidents. In contrast, general liability insurance covers all activities or sources of liability that are not specifically excluded.

A CGL policy is an example of general liability insurance. A general liability insurer agrees to pay damages "to which this insurance applies." However, the extent of coverage depends on the exclusions. That is, general liability policies essentially cover those claims that are not excluded and specifically exclude coverage for claims that are better handled by other liability insurance policies, such as automobile liability, workers' compensation, aircraft liability, watercraft liability, and professional liability.

In addition to excluding losses covered by other types of liability policies, general liability insurance policies contain exclusions dealing with difficult to insure exposures, losses expected or intended by the insured, and loss exposures that would be too costly to insure. For example, as with property insurance policies, nearly all liability policies exclude coverage for losses arising from war and nuclear hazard.

Covered Types of Injury or Damage

Liability policies typically cover claims for bodily injury and property damage for which the insured is legally liable. Other types of injury may also be covered; for example, the CGL policy also covers personal and advertising injury.

Bodily Injury

The standard CGL policy defines **bodily injury** as follows:

> "Bodily injury" means bodily injury, sickness or disease sustained by a person, including death resulting from any of these at any time.[1]

This definition indicates that, as used in the CGL policy, the term bodily injury also includes some things that may not be included in the everyday use

Bodily injury
As defined in many liability policies, any physical injury to a person, including sickness, disease, and death.

of that term. Sickness and disease are often considered forms of illness that do not involve injury. Death could be considered the severest form of injury, but unless it is specified in the policy, there might be reason to question whether coverage for claims for bodily injury liability includes coverage for death claims. Through the bodily injury definition, the CGL policy clarifies that it covers claims for injury, sickness, disease, and resulting death.

Property Damage

Property damage
Insurance term referring to physical injury to, destruction of, or loss of use of tangible property.

The definition of **property damage** in a typical CGL policy reads in part as follows:

> "Property damage" means:
>
> a. Physical injury to tangible property, including all resulting loss of use of that property; or
>
> b. Loss of use of tangible property that is not physically injured.

The definition of property damage also specifies that data are not tangible property.

The definition of property damage in a typical homeowners policy is considerably briefer and reads as follows:

> "Property damage" means physical injury to, destruction of, or loss of use of tangible property.[2]

Thus, according to both of these definitions, property damage includes both direct losses and time element (or indirect) losses. For example, the fire at AIC's plant caused indirect damage to the owners of surrounding businesses because they had to cease operations temporarily. Although there was no actual direct physical damage to these surrounding businesses, the business owners still lost the use of their property because of the explosion at AIC. As for the auto accident, if the owner(s) of the other car temporarily lost the use of their car because of the accident, AIC might be liable not only for direct damage to the car but also for a time element loss, such as the cost of a rental car until the car was repaired or replaced.

Personal and Advertising Injury

Personal injury
Injury, other than bodily injury, arising from intentional torts such as libel, slander, or invasion of privacy.

In addition to bodily injury, harm can be inflicted in other ways, such as damage to one's reputation. One may expect bodily injury and personal injury to mean the same thing. In fact, attorneys tend to use the term personal injury when referring to bodily injuries. However, when used in liability insurance policies, **personal injury** usually refers to a specific group of intentional torts, including defamation (which includes libel and slander), false arrest, and invasion of privacy. Any of these acts may cause harm to another person for which the tortfeasor may be held liable. For insurance purposes, intentional torts are usually considered personal injury offenses and are either excluded from coverage or are covered separately.

Some liability policies define personal injury in a way that includes not only the types of offenses listed previously but also bodily injury. When that definition is used, personal injury coverage is broader than bodily injury coverage. However, the more common approach allows for separate coverage for bodily injury and personal injury, in which case personal injury coverage supplements bodily injury coverage. For example, the CGL policy includes personal injury coverage (combined with advertising injury) under a separate insuring agreement.

Advertising injury, which is covered by most CGL policies, typically includes the following types of offenses:

- Libel and slander
- Publication of material that constitutes an invasion of privacy
- Misappropriation of advertising ideas or business style
- Infringement of copyright, trade dress, or slogan

The definitions of personal injury offenses and advertising injury offenses overlap somewhat. Therefore, current versions of the CGL policy include both personal and advertising injury in the same insuring agreement, so no coverage duplication results from repeating that a certain type of claim is covered.

Coverage for personal injury liability (but not advertising injury) also can be added by endorsement to a homeowners policy.

Excluded Loss Exposures

No insurance policy can reasonably cover all loss exposures. Just as some types of injuries or damages are typically excluded by liability insurance policies, some loss exposures are also excluded. The exclusions in liability insurance policies generally fall into the following broad categories:

- *To avoid covering uninsurable losses.* For example, war is an exclusion that appears under many policies for both property and liability exposures. Losses from such catastrophic events are not economically feasible to insure.
- *To avoid insuring losses that could be prevented.* Expected or intended injury exclusions can be found under most broad liability coverages. In addition, losses resulting from the possession of controlled substances, such as illegal drugs, are excluded by the liability section of the homeowners policy. Such losses can be prevented by avoiding activity that is prohibited by criminal and civil law.
- *To eliminate duplicate coverage.* For example, watercraft liability and aircraft liability are excluded under CGL policies and the liability section of homeowners policies. Such exclusions eliminate duplicate coverage provided by the liability portion of the policies specifically designed to address these exposures.

- *To eliminate coverage that most insureds do not need.* For example, racing exclusions appear under personal and commercial automobile policies. Most individuals and organizations are not involved in racing vehicles. Therefore, the coverage is generally excluded.

- *To eliminate coverage for exposures that require special handling by the insurer.* The homeowners policy excludes coverage for professional services, such as coverages required by physicians, architects, and lawyers. Providing appropriate liability coverage to these professionals for their unique loss exposures would require specialized coverages and underwriting.

- *To keep premiums reasonable.* For example, commercial liability policies generally exclude all but limited exposures from pollution. Businesses with this type of exposure must purchase specialty policies to cover cata-strophic pollution exposures. If broad pollution coverage were provided under all liability policies, the coverage would not be affordable.

Covered Costs

Liability insurance policies typically cover the following two types of costs:

1.   The damages that the insured is legally liable to pay
2.   The cost of defending the insured against the claim

In addition, liability policies commonly cover incidental expenses (such as the cost of certain required bonds or the insured's loss of earnings while attending trials) under the policy's supplementary payments provision. Finally, many liability policies cover medical payments for injured persons, regardless of whether the insured is legally liable.

Damages

The CGL policy contains a typical agreement to pay damages on behalf of the insured:

> We agree to pay those sums that the insured becomes legally obligated to pay as damages because of "bodily injury" or "property damage" to which this insurance applies.

A person who has suffered bodily injury, property damage, or personal injury for which the insured is allegedly responsible may make a claim for damages. The claim is often settled out of court, and the insurer pays the claimant on behalf of the insured. If a case goes to court, the claimant may be awarded two types of damages—compensatory damages and punitive damages. These damages may or may not be covered by insurance.

Compensatory damages, intended to compensate the claimant for the injury or damage suffered, are covered by liability insurance if the insured is liable for a covered loss. As stated earlier, compensatory damages include both special damages and general damages. A party who is held to be liable for another's injury may have to compensate the injured party for special damages, such as hospital bills, physicians' fees, lost income, and rehabilitation expenses. In addition to these actual expenses, the liable party may be required to pay general damages, such as pain and suffering, to compensate the victim for the physical and mental suffering experienced because of the bodily injury. In the opening example in this chapter, AIC's liability insurer may have to pay both special damages and general damages if AIC is found liable for both types of compensatory damages because of the explosion and fire.

Most liability insurance policies do not specifically state whether punitive damages, which are intended to punish the insured for some outrageous conduct, are covered. Some states do not permit insurers to pay punitive damages for their insureds because the punishment is viewed as less effective if the responsible party does not personally pay the required damages. On the other hand, insurers pay punitive damages if allowed by the state and not excluded by the policy. Some people argue that punitive damages are as much a source of unexpected financial loss as compensatory damages, and that the insured should be entitled to insure against a judgment for punitive damages.

The damages that the insured is legally liable to pay can be determined in court, or can be agreed on in an out-of-court settlement. In practice, few liability claims are decided by the courts. Most liability claims are settled before the claimant even files a lawsuit. Most are settled privately between the claimant (or the claimant's lawyer) and the liability insurer (or the insurer's lawyer) on behalf of its insured.

The claimant can decline to voluntarily settle a claim, in which case a lawsuit usually occurs, and a court eventually decides the claim. Parties agree to settle claims when they believe a proposed voluntary settlement is more attractive than a lawsuit and court verdict.

Generally, out-of-court settlements are attractive to both sides for the following two reasons:

1. *Out-of-court settlements resolve cases quickly.* Out-of-court settlements spare the parties from significant financial and emotional costs.
2. *Out-of-court settlements eliminate uncertainty about the outcome of a claim.* Court verdicts are unpredictable, and either party may do worse than expected. A claimant or a defendant may bear substantial lawsuit costs and receive a court verdict less favorable than an out-of-court settlement that was available months or years earlier.

An out-of-court settlement is a voluntary agreement to drop a claim in exchange for an agreed amount of money. Such settlements occur only after negotiation, by which one party suggests a settlement amount and the other party either accepts the amount, rejects it, or suggests another amount. Settlement negotiations can conclude quickly or go on for months, depending on the personalities and experience of the negotiators and on the underlying facts of the claim. Proposed settlement amounts should be based on each party's perception of what a likely court verdict would be. Therefore, anything that would be relevant in court should be relevant in settlement negotiations, including the nature of the injuries or damage, the respective legal liability of the parties, and the quality of the witnesses or evidence for each side.

Once negotiations have concluded with a settlement, the parties sign a release, which is a written agreement in which the claimant agrees to drop his or her claim. The insured, through the insurer, promises to pay the agreed settlement to the claimant.

Insurers depend on out-of-court settlements. Claim costs would soar if insurers had to resolve all liability claims through the courts. An ordinary automobile accident claim can cost thousands of dollars in legal fees to prepare for trial and thousands more to put on trial.

The court system and society in general favor out-of-court settlements. The courts would be overwhelmed with cases and expenses if every legal issue had to go to court. Society benefits when injured parties receive prompt compensation and when all parties put their legal disputes behind them as quickly as possible.

Defense Costs

It is sometimes said that an insurer's duty to defend insureds against liability claims is even more important than its duty to pay damages. If the defense is successful, the court delivers a judgment in favor of the defendant (that is, the insured), and no damages are awarded. In other cases, damages may be awarded, but an effective defense results in a lower award than the award sought by the plaintiff (the claimant).

Most liability insurance policies obligate the insurer to pay the costs of defending the insured against any claim or lawsuit in which a claimant seeks damages that would be covered by the policy. For example, the CGL insuring agreement specifies:

> We will have the right and duty to defend the insured against any "suit" seeking (BI or PD) damages.

Even if the claim seems to have no legitimate basis, as in the case of a fraudulent claim, the insurer must defend the insured whenever the claimant's allegations (if proven) would be covered under the policy. Often, the defense can prove that the insured was not responsible for the injury or damage alleged.

Defense costs are the insurer's responsibility. Some of these defense costs may be specifically described in the policy; others are implicit. The duty to defend, for example, implies that the insurer will retain the attorneys and pay their fees and expenses. Defense costs may also include investigation, legal research, expert witness fees, and similar costs incurred in preparing and presenting the case.

Supplementary Payments

Liability insurance policies typically include a **supplementary payments** section describing various expenses that the insurer agrees to pay in addition to liability limits. The expenses covered as supplementary payments usually include the following:

- All expenses incurred by the insurer such as investigating accidents, hiring external claim adjusters, and paying fees for police reports
- The cost, up to a specified limit, of bail bonds or other required bonds (persons involved in auto accidents, for example, are sometimes required to post bail bonds)
- Expenses incurred by the insured at the insurer's request such as travel to attend a trial or deposition
- The insured's loss of earnings (up to a specified amount per day) because of attendance at hearings or trials at the insurer's request

Other costs that relate to the claim, such as prejudgment or postjudgment interest, may also be included in the list of supplementary payments.

Liability claims that go to trial often involve long delays between the time of the injury or damage and the time when a court awards a judgment to the claimant. The court award to the plaintiff may include damages as well as **prejudgment interest**, which represents the interest that may accrue on damages before a judgment has been rendered.

When an award for damages is successfully appealed to a higher court, the plaintiff receives no payment. If the higher court upholds the initial judgment, the plaintiff may also be entitled to receive **postjudgment interest** as compensation for the money that would have been earned if the insurer had paid the claim at the time of the first judgment. Postjudgment interest forces the insurer to bear the expense of the delay in payment caused by the appeal.

Medical Payments

Some liability policies also provide medical payments coverage, which is sometimes offered as an optional coverage the insured can purchase. **Medical payments coverage** pays necessary medical expenses incurred within a specified period by a claimant for a covered injury, regardless of whether the insured was at fault. Medical payments can help avoid larger liability claims. If a homeowners policy includes $1,000 of medical payments coverage, for example, a neighbor injured on the insured's property can receive emergency medical treatment up to that amount without having to sue the insured to recover the cost. Payment of this relatively modest amount reduces the possibility of a much more expensive claim for damages. In some cases, such as in homeowners policies, this coverage is called "medical payments to others" and does not cover injuries sustained by an insured or regular residents of his or her household. In other cases, such as in personal auto policies, medical payments coverage does cover an insured's injuries up to a specified limit.

Supplementary payments
Various expenses the insurer agrees to pay under a liability insurance policy (in addition to the liability limits) for items such as premiums on bail bonds and appeal bonds, loss of the insured's earnings because of attendance at trials, and other reasonable expenses incurred by the insured at the insurer's request.

Prejudgment interest
Interest that may accrue on damages before a judgment has been rendered.

Postjudgment interest
Interest that may accrue on damages after a judgment has been entered in a court and before the money is paid.

Medical payments coverage
Coverage that pays necessary medical expenses incurred within a specified period by a claimant (and in certain policies, by an insured) for a covered injury, regardless of whether the insured was at fault.

Covered Time Period

Personal auto insurance is usually written for a six-month term. Other types of liability insurance are usually written for a one-year period, although other policy terms are also possible.

A liability insurance policy states what must happen during the policy period to "trigger" coverage. Depending on the type of policy, coverage is usually triggered by either of the following:

- Events that occur during the policy period (in an occurrence basis policy)
- Claims made (submitted) during the policy period (in a claims-made policy)

Occurrence Basis Coverage

Occurrence basis coverage
Coverage for liability claims that occur during the policy period, regardless of when the claim is submitted to the insurer.

Bodily injury or property damage that occurs during the policy period triggers coverage under a liability policy that provides **occurrence basis coverage**. In most situations, bodily injury or property damage is apparent at the time of the accident or shortly thereafter. Under a liability policy that provides occurrence basis coverage, if a covered accident occurs during the policy period, the claim will be covered, regardless of when the claim is submitted. For example, if the claimant was injured in an automobile accident caused by the insured only a few hours before the policy period expired, the resulting claim would be covered, despite the fact that it might be submitted after the policy expired.

From the insured's standpoint, this coverage offers valuable protection for unknown and unforeseen claims. For the insurer, however, occurrence basis coverage means that liability claims may surface long after a policy has expired. This particular problem contributed to the development of claims-made coverage.

Claims-Made Coverage

Claims-made coverage
Coverage for liability claims that are first made against the insured during the policy period for covered events that occur on or after the retroactive date and before the end of the policy period.

Although personal liability insurance policies and most commercial general liability insurance policies are written on an occurrence basis, claims-made coverage is sometimes used to insure businesses that face certain types of liability loss exposures, such as medical malpractice, professional liability, and some especially hazardous products liability. Under a liability policy that provides **claims-made coverage**, the insurer agrees to pay all claims that are first made against the insured during the policy period (or before the end of an extended period specified in the policy) if the covered event occurs on or after a specified date (called a retroactive date) and before the end of the policy period.

In theory, the claims-made approach is ideal. An insured buys a series of claims-made policies, and each succeeding policy becomes effective when the preceding one expires. Unless coverage lapses, the insured will never be without coverage, because there is always a current policy to provide coverage when a claim is presented.

In practice, the situation becomes more complicated. Most claims-made policies contain a **retroactive date**, which is the date in a claims-made policy on or after which injury or damage must occur in order to be covered. Claims due to injuries occuring before that retroactive date are not covered even if the claim is made during the policy period. Occurrence policies also do not cover claims arising from occurrences before the policy's inception date. Therefore, an insured who replaces a claims-made policy either with an occurrence policy or with a claims-made policy with a new retroactive date may face a gap in coverage.

Because of periodic renewals and the possibility that the insured will shift coverage from one insurer to another, maintaining continuous coverage without gaps is perhaps the greatest difficulty with claims-made coverage. Thus, insurers, producers, and insureds must pay careful attention to the details of claims-made policies.

Retroactive date
The date in a claims-made policy on or after which injury or damage must occur in order to be covered.

Factors Affecting the Amount of Claim Payments

Even when a liability claim is covered, an insurer does not necessarily pay the full amount of the judgment awarded to a claimant. The extent of the insurer's payment depends on the following types of policy provisions:

- Policy limits
- Defense cost provisions
- "Other insurance" provisions

Policy Limits

It is difficult to predict the dollar amount of liability insurance needed to cover an insured's future claims. Legal obligations depend on uncertain future events in a changing legal environment. Still, it is necessary for the insured and the insurer to agree on some dollar amount of coverage. As with property insurance, policy limits help an insurer measure the extent of its obligation. Limits also provide options to the insured, who must decide not only how much coverage is desirable but also how much is affordable. Liability insurance limits are generally round numbers such as $100,000, $500,000, or $1 million.

Limits are expressed in different ways, such as the following:

- An **each person limit** is the maximum amount an insurer will pay for injury to any one person for a covered loss. If several persons are injured in a given occurrence, this limit applies separately to each one.
- An **each occurrence limit** is the maximum amount an insurer will pay for all covered losses from a single occurrence, regardless of the number of persons injured or the number of parties claiming property damage. There may be several different covered occurrences during one policy period.
- An **aggregate limit** is the maximum amount an insurer will pay for all covered losses during the policy period.

Each person limit
The maximum amount an insurer will pay for injury to any one person for a covered loss.

Each occurrence limit
The maximum amount an insurer will pay for all covered losses from a single occurrence, regardless of the number of persons injured or the number of parties claiming property damage.

Aggregate limit
The maximum amount an insurer will pay for all covered losses during the covered policy period.

Split limits
Separate limits for bodily injury and property damage liability coverage.

Single limit
The maximum amount an insurer will pay for the insured's liability for both bodily injury and property damage that arise from a single occurrence.

Separate limits for bodily injury and property damage liability coverage are known as **split limits**. For example, a personal auto policy may provide bodily injury liability coverage with a $100,000 limit for each person and a $300,000 limit for each occurrence with a separate limit of $50,000 for each occurrence for property damage liability coverage. A **single limit** applies to any combination of bodily injury and property damage liability claims arising from the same occurrence. For example, a $300,000 single limit covers a bodily injury loss up to $300,000, a property damage liability loss up to $300,000, or any combination of bodily injury and property damage arising from a single occurrence up to $300,000.

Examples of Split Limits and Single Limit

Split Limits

Jessica has a personal auto policy with the following split limits:

Bodily Injury:

- $100,000 each person
- $300,000 each occurrence

Property Damage:

- $50,000 each occurrence

Jessica is liable for a covered auto accident resulting in injuries to Richard, the driver of the other car, and Marcy, his passenger. When the case went to trial, the court awarded $200,000 in bodily injury damages to Richard and $150,000 to Marcy. In addition, the damage to Richard's car amounted to $10,000, which Jessica was also ordered to pay. Jessica's insurer would pay $110,000 to Richard ($100,000 each person limit for bodily injury plus $10,000 for property damage) and $100,000 to Marcy (the each person limit). Thus, the insurer would pay a total of $210,000 for this accident (plus Jessica's defense costs, which are paid in addition to the policy limits in a personal auto policy). Jessica would have to pay the remaining bodily injury damages of $150,000.

Single Limit

If Jessica's personal auto policy instead had a single limit of $300,000 in lieu of the split limits, her insurer would pay a total of $300,000 to Richard and Marcy for both bodily injury and property damage (plus defense costs) in the accident. (A determination of exactly how much each party receives would depend on the circumstances of this particular claim.)

In this situation, Jessica's insurer would pay more under the single limit policy than the split limits policy, but such is not always the case. For example, if three people had had bodily injury of $150,000 each plus the $10,000 property damage, the insurer would have paid a total of $310,000 under the split limits policy ($100,000 bodily injury for each person plus $10,000 property damage); under the single limit policy, the insurer would pay only $300,000, the maximum payable for any one occurrence.

Defense Cost Provisions

Most liability policies place no dollar limit on the defense costs payable by the insurer. The only limitation is that the insurer is not obligated to provide further defense once the entire policy limit has been paid in settlement or judgment for damages.

Stated differently, defense costs are usually payable in addition to the policy limits, and policy limits include only payment for damages. Practical limitations, however, tend to restrict defense costs. For example, an insurer is not likely to spend $100,000 defending a claim for $10,000 in damages. The insurer has a duty to defend, but also the right to settle the claim. In this instance, the insurer is likely to choose settlement.

Some liability policies place defense costs within the overall policy limit. In such policies, for example, if the policy limit is $100,000 and the insured has a covered claim involving damages of $90,000 and defense costs of $30,000, the insurer would pay a total of $100,000 for both the damages and the defense. The insured would be responsible for paying the additional $20,000.

"Other Insurance" Provisions

In some cases, two or more policies may cover the same claim. Like property insurance policies, liability insurance policies contain "other insurance" provisions to resolve this problem and preserve the principle of indemnity. Several approaches can be used, and the applicable approach depends on the wording of the particular policy and on the situation.

SUMMARY

This chapter discusses liability loss exposures and the liability policy provisions that deal with those exposures. Liability loss exposures are based on the concept of legal liability. By holding individuals and businesses responsible for their conduct, the legal system protects the rights of individuals and businesses. The legal system in the U.S. derives essentially from the following:

- The Constitution, which is the source of constitutional law
- Legislative bodies, which are the source of statutory law
- Court decisions, which are the source of common law

The U.S. legal system makes an important distinction between criminal law and civil law. Criminal law imposes penalties on those who commit wrongs against society. Civil law provides a means to settle disputes among individuals and to determine responsibility for injuries or damage.

Liability loss exposures involve the following elements:

- The legal basis of a claim by one party against another for damages
- The potential financial consequences of liability loss exposures

Any of several legal principles can serve as the basis for holding one party responsible for another's injury. Most liability cases rely on tort law, which allows an injured party to sue for damages if the other party's negligence, intentional tort, or strict liability (from an inherently dangerous activity) caused the injury or damage. Liability can also arise from a breach of contract, which allows one party to seek relief in court from the other party to a contract. Statutes, such as workers' compensation laws, also impose liability on certain parties when a legislative body has determined that it is in the interest of society to hold those persons liable.

A liability loss occurs only if an insured causes another person to suffer definite harm. A liability claim can lead to compensatory damages, consisting of special damages (for medical expenses, lost income, and rehabilitation expenses) as well as general damages (for pain and suffering). Many liability claims also lead to defense costs, including legal fees, investigation expenses, and other expenses to defend the claim.

Many activities and situations can create liability to someone else. These include owning or operating an automobile, owning or occupying property, conducting business operations, manufacturing or selling products, advertising, polluting the environment, selling or otherwise providing alcoholic beverages, and practicing a profession.

Liability insurance policies cover damages that the insured becomes legally obligated to pay and that arise out of the activities covered by the policy. The following must be specified in the provisions of liability insurance policies:

- *Covered parties.* Liability policies provide coverage to the named insured and to others. The extent of liability coverage provided to parties other than the named insured is determined by their relationship to the named insured as well as by circumstances surrounding the claim.
- *Covered activities.* A liability policy must clearly express the insurer's intent to cover claims against the insured for which the insurer is legally obligated to pay damages. An auto liability insurance policy states the specific activity or source of liability covered: claims resulting from covered auto accidents. In contrast, general liability insurance covers all activities or sources of liability that are not specifically excluded.
- *Covered types of injury or damage.* Liability policies must specify what types of injury or damage are covered, such as bodily injury, property damage, personal injury, and advertising injury. Liability policies must also specify what kinds of loss exposures are excluded.

- *Covered costs.* Typical policies cover damages that the insured is legally liable to pay and the cost of defending the insured against the claim.

- *Covered time period.* Depending on the type of policy, coverage is usually triggered by events that occur during the policy period (in an occurrence basis policy) or by claims made during the policy period (in a claims-made policy).

- *Factors affecting the amount of claim payments.* The extent of the insurer's payment depends on the policy provisions regarding policy limits, defense costs, and other insurance.

CHAPTER NOTES

1. This quotation and, unless stated otherwise, all other quotations of policy language in this chapter are from the Commercial General Liability Coverage Form, CG 00 01 12 04. Includes copyrighted material of Insurance Services Office, Inc., with its permission. Copyright, ISO Properties, Inc., 2003.

2. Homeowners 3 Special Form, HO 00 03 05 01. Includes copyrighted material of Insurance Services Office, Inc. with its permission. Copyright ISO Properties, 2000.

Chapter 10

Direct Your Learning

Managing Loss Exposures: Risk Management

After learning the content of this chapter and completing the corresponding course guide assignment, you should be able to:

■ Describe the six steps in the risk management process.

■ Describe three primary methods of identifying loss exposures.

■ Explain why measuring loss frequency and loss severity is important in analyzing loss exposures.

■ Describe the risk management techniques of risk control and risk financing.

■ Describe the financial criteria and guidelines for selecting risk management techniques.

■ Describe procedures for implementing risk management techniques.

■ Describe procedures for monitoring and revising a risk management program.

■ Explain the benefits of sound risk management.

■ Given a case, recommend risk management techniques appropriate for an individual, a family, or a business.

■ Define or describe each of the Key Words and Phrases for this chapter.

Develop Your Perspective

What are the main topics covered in the chapter?

This chapter introduces risk management as a comprehensive process for identifying and addressing loss exposures. It then discusses several of the more widely used risk management techniques, including insurance, which works best as a component in a risk management program designed specifically to address the unique loss exposures of each insured.

Identify the steps in the risk management process.

- How do these steps create an ongoing cycle of identifying and addressing loss exposures?
- How might this process be considered more comprehensive than simply purchasing insurance to address every loss exposure?

Why is it important to learn about these topics?

Insurance professionals are often asked to help customers examine loss exposures and determine the best method for addressing those exposures. By viewing insurance as only one technique for addressing loss exposures, the insurance professional can provide a more complete set of alternatives for the customer to consider.

Consider all of the risk management techniques that might be appropriate in addressing the loss exposure to a house from the peril of fire.

- How might loss prevention and loss reduction be applied?
- How might retention be applied with insurance?

How can you use what you will learn?

Evaluate the loss exposures you face as an individual.

Which of these loss exposures:

- Could reasonably be addressed by insurance?
- Could only be addressed through other risk management techniques?
- Might be best addressed through a combination of insurance and other risk management techniques?

Chapter 10

Managing Loss Exposures: Risk Management

Individuals and organizations face risk on a daily basis. Risk can have many meanings, but for the purposes of this text, it simply means uncertainty concerning loss. For those risks having the potential for substantial financial consequences, prudent persons and groups practice risk management, often without realizing it. For example, a person who decides not to take up skiing from fear of being injured is practicing the risk management technique of avoidance. A person who decides to ski, but chooses to wear a helmet while skiing, is practicing the risk management technique of loss control. On the back of the lift ticket from the ski resort is evidence of a form of noninsurance transfer, by which the skier agrees to not hold the resort responsible for any injury incurred. A skier who does not have health insurance against accidental injury is practicing the risk management technique of retention. Someone who purchases an insurance policy to cover accidental injuries, including skiing injuries, is handling the risk by purchasing insurance, thereby transferring the risk to an insurer.

Insurance professionals focus on loss exposures when discussing risk. A loss exposure is any condition or situation that presents the possibility of a loss. This chapter introduces risk management as a formal process for handling loss exposures and covers some of the more widely used risk management techniques. Informal risk management occurs each day in everyone's life and in every business.

Everything people or organizations do exposes them to possible accidental losses. Whenever accidental losses occur, they can create serious financial consequences for the individuals, households, or organizations that suffer the loss. Such losses can also prevent persons or organizations from achieving their goals. Identifying and finding ways to deal with these potential losses is what risk management is all about. Insurance, which cannot prevent accidental losses, works best when it is part of a well-designed risk management program tailored to the unique loss exposures of each insured.

THE RISK MANAGEMENT PROCESS

Risk management is essentially the process of managing exposures to accidental losses. Whether those practicing risk management are company executives,

Risk management
The process of managing exposures to accidental losses.

individuals planning for themselves or their families, or professionals working with clients, the primary goal of risk management is the same—to minimize the adverse effects of loss exposures by reducing the frequency and severity of losses. Risk management is not just a process used by large corporations. Risk management concepts are also used, consciously or not, by small and medium-sized companies, communities, families, and individuals.

The risk management process needs specific attention in every household or organization, regardless of its nature or its size. The person who performs the risk management function differs, depending on the household or organization. The responsible person in an organization may be an employee known as the risk manager, as the director of risk management, or by some other title. In other organizations, risk management may be performed by someone outside the firm—for example, a risk management consultant. An insurance agent or broker (producer) can assist organizations with their risk management process by helping them identify what loss exposures they have and by suggesting the types and amounts of insurance they need; however, decisions should be made by the client, not by the agent or broker (producer).

In a household, the person who performs risk management may be the primary wage earner or the person who handles the household finances. In this chapter, the term risk manager refers to anyone who is primarily responsible for risk management, regardless of title or status within the organization or household. The term household refers to any household unit, whether an individual, a traditional family, or individuals living together in a single household. The term organization refers to a business or entity operating for-profit or not-for-profit. Risk management concepts are valid for all types of households and organizations.

Risk managers in households or organizations are responsible for all six steps in the risk management process. Those steps are as follows:

1. Identifying loss exposures
2. Analyzing loss exposures
3. Examining the feasibility of risk management techniques
4. Selecting the appropriate risk management techniques
5. Implementing the selected risk management techniques
6. Monitoring results and revising the risk management program

Step 1: Identifying Loss Exposures

Identifying loss exposures involves developing a thorough list of possible accidental losses that can affect a particular household or organization. The key to identifying these loss exposures is understanding how the household or organization operates. The risk manager can start with a physical inspection of the premises and then use other techniques, such as loss exposure surveys, financial statement analysis, loss history analysis, flowcharts, and interviews. Three of the more common techniques are examined next.

Physical Inspection

A family or an organization's risk manager generally cannot gain a clear picture of possible loss exposures by sitting at a desk away from the source of risk. The most straightforward method of identifying loss exposures is to physically inspect all locations, operations, maintenance routines, safety practices, work processes, and other activities. For example, a risk manager in an industrial operation may observe that the guards have been removed from machines or that boxes of parts are stacked high on a storage shelf, creating an exposure for injury should the parts fall. Physical inspection alone may not be enough, however, because the risk manager may not have sufficient knowledge of the household or operations to identify all exposures or to ask others the right questions to uncover all loss exposures.

Loss Exposure Surveys

Loss exposure surveys, or checklists, are documents listing potential loss exposures that a household or an organization may face. Independent risk management consultants, as well as insurers, agents, and brokers, often design such surveys to be comprehensive enough to apply to almost any household or organization. However, a given household or organization is unlikely to face all of the loss exposures detailed in such surveys.

The risk manager usually discusses the items on the survey with managers, supervisors, and other employees familiar with the organization's exposures. If worded appropriately, the survey can also help familiarize the risk manager with the organization's operations. The survey's major weakness is that it may omit an important exposure, especially if the organization has unique operations not included on a standard survey form. Therefore, risk managers cannot depend solely on surveys. Rather, risk managers should use the survey as a guide to develop a comprehensive picture of the organization's operations and loss exposures.

Exhibit 10-1 presents a sample of questions frequently asked on loss exposure surveys for organizations. Such surveys usually group similar exposures together, such as exposures from manufacturing operations, from the sale of products, from the use of vehicles, and so forth. Similar but less extensive surveys are available from insurers to help households identify the loss exposures they face.

EXHIBIT 10-1

Sample of Questions Frequently Asked on Loss Exposure Surveys

Yes   No

☐   ☐   1. Do you have a brochure or other written material that describes your business operations or products?

☐   ☐   2. Is your business confined to one industry?

☐   ☐   3. Is your business confined to one product?

☐   ☐   4. Do you own buildings?

☐   ☐   5. Do you lease buildings *from* others?

☐   ☐   6. Do you lease buildings *to* others?

☐   ☐   7. Do you plan any new construction?

☐   ☐   8. Are your fixed asset values established by certified property appraisers?

☐   ☐   9. Do you own any vacant land?

☐   ☐   10. Are any properties located in potential riot or civil disturbance areas?

☐   ☐   11. Are any properties located in potential flood or earthquake areas?

☐   ☐   12. Do your properties have security alarm systems? (Fire-sprinkler discharge, burglary, smoke detection, and so forth)

☐   ☐   13. Are there any unusual fire or explosion hazards in your business operation? (Welding, painting, woodworking, steam boilers or pressurized machinery, and so forth)

☐   ☐   14. Do you take a physical count of inventory at least once a year?

☐   ☐   15. Do you lease machinery or equipment other than automotive?

☐   ☐   16. Do you stockpile inventory, either raw or finished?

☐   ☐   17. Could you conveniently report inventory values on a monthly basis?

☐   ☐   18. Do you buy, sell, or have custody of goods or equipment of extremely high value? (Radium, gold, and so forth)

☐   ☐   19. Do you use any raw stock, inventory, or equipment that requires substantial lead time to reproduce?

☐   ☐   20. Do you export or import?

Loss Histories

Loss histories provide another method for identifying an organization's loss exposures. Loss histories deal with an organization's past losses which can assist a risk management professional in identifying that organization's exposures to future accidental losses.

The quality of loss histories depends on whether they are complete, organized, consistent, and relevant. For example, data quality is reduced whenever a loss is omitted; whenever any item of information normally collected about losses (such as where or when they occur) is omitted; whenever the conditions under which an organization operates or those operations themselves change in some fundamental way; or whenever a new cause of loss emerges. Past events or conditions that were not recorded, inaccurately recorded, or made irrelevant by changing environments have little, if any, value for forecasting future events.

Step 2: Analyzing Loss Exposures

Analyzing loss exposures requires estimating how large the losses may be and how often they may occur. Such an analysis helps to determine how losses may interfere with the activities and objectives of the household or organization and what their financial effect may be. To determine the financial effect of losses, a risk manager needs to measure both the likely frequency and likely severity of those losses. This analysis enables the risk manager to give priority to the most significant loss exposures.

Loss Frequency

Loss frequency indicates how often a loss occurs in a particular period. Frequent losses include abrasions and minor lacerations of employees at a manufacturing plant, minor auto accidents with a large fleet of autos, and spoilage of produce at a supermarket. Other losses, such as those caused by earthquakes, tornadoes, and hurricanes, occur much less frequently.

Loss frequency
How often a loss occurs in a given period.

Accurate measurement of loss frequency is important because the proper treatment of the loss exposure often depends on how frequently the loss is expected to occur. If a particular type of loss occurs frequently, or if its frequency has been increasing in recent years, the risk manager may decide that procedures for controlling the loss are necessary.

Loss Severity

Loss severity is the monetary amount of damage that results from a loss. It is much easier to gauge the potential severity of property losses than of liability losses. Most property losses have a finite value. Whether the property is partially or completely destroyed, the severity of the loss is usually calculable. Conversely, the severity of liability exposures is much harder to calculate. For example, a paint manufacturer sells paint that produces toxic fumes when used, the severity of the potential liability loss is almost unlimited.

Loss severity
Monetary amount of damage that results from a loss.

Likewise, the severity of the property loss from an airplane crash may equal several million dollars, a calculable amount. However, if an aircraft loaded with passengers crashes in a densely populated metropolitan area, the potential severity of the liability loss is difficult, if not impossible, to estimate accurately.

Properly estimating loss severity is also essential in treating the loss exposure. The potential severity of losses is a major consideration in determining whether the household or organization should insure a particular exposure or retain all or part of the financial consequences of the loss.

Step 3: Examining the Feasibility of Risk Management Techniques

Once loss exposures have been identified and analyzed, the risk manager should examine all possible techniques for handling the exposures. These techniques are grouped into two broad categories—risk control and risk financing. Following is a discussion of some of the more common risk management techniques under each of these categories.

Risk Control

Risk control is a risk management technique that attempts to decrease the frequency or severity of losses. Risk control techniques include the following:

- Avoidance
- Loss prevention
- Loss reduction
- Separation
- Duplication

Avoidance eliminates a loss exposure and reduces the chance of loss to zero. For example, a manufacturer of sports equipment may decide not to sell football helmets to avoid the possibility of large lawsuits from head injuries. Likewise, a family may decide not to purchase a motor boat to avoid the potential property and liability exposures that accompany boat ownership.

The advantage of avoidance as a risk control technique is that the probability of loss equals zero—there is no doubt or uncertainty about the loss exposure because a loss is not possible. Avoidance has the disadvantage of sometimes being impractical and is often difficult, if not impossible, to accomplish. For example, suppose Priya is contemplating the purchase of her first automobile, but she is worried about the exposures inherent in automobile ownership. She may believe the chance of damage to the car is too great. Further, Priya may be unwilling to assume the chance of liability imposed by law, or perhaps she cannot afford automobile insurance. However, avoidance of these exposures may pose additional problems for Priya. Does she need a car for commuting to work or for other activities? If so, she will have to exchange the exposures of automobile ownership for the exposures inherent in some other type of transportation. Renting or leasing a car may be more expensive than auto ownership, and Priya would still be liable for any accidents she may cause. Foregoing a car would mean traveling by public transportation, by bicycle, by motorcycle, or on foot; any of these alternatives could prove more hazardous to Priya than riding in her own car. Priya may decide that avoidance is not a feasible technique and would thus choose to purchase a car and buy automobile insurance to cover her automobile loss exposures.

Risk control
A risk management technique that attempts to decrease the frequency or severity of losses.

Avoidance
A risk control technique that eliminates a loss exposure and reduces the chance of loss to zero.

Loss prevention seeks to lower the frequency of losses from a particular loss exposure. Examples of loss prevention are commonplace and include the following:

- Keeping doors and windows locked to prevent burglaries
- Maintaining a regular program of vehicle maintenance to prevent accidents due to faulty equipment

Loss reduction seeks to lower the severity of losses from a particular loss exposure. Common loss reduction measures include the following:

- Installing a sprinkler system, which does not usually prevent fires, but can limit damage should a fire occur
- Installing a restrictive money safe that a store clerk cannot open

Many insurers have a loss control department that includes risk management professionals who attempt to reduce an insured's frequency and severity of losses. Insureds often use loss control measures because the insurer has recommended them. Insurers direct much loss control effort to commercial insurance accounts. The loss control programs recommended by insurers are generally based on inspection reports prepared by the insurers' loss control representatives. An inspection report is one of the best sources of underwriting information and it supplements the application.

When an underwriter receives an application for a commercial account, one of the underwriter's first tasks is often to request an inspection report from the insurer's loss control department. A loss control engineer or representative visits the applicant's location or locations to inspect the premises and operations and submits an inspection report.

An inspection report usually has the following two main objectives:

- To provide a thorough description of the applicant's operation so that the underwriter can make an accurate assessment when deciding whether to accept the application for insurance.
- To provide an evaluation of the applicant's current loss control measures and recommend improvements in loss control efforts. The underwriter may require that the applicant implement the loss control recommendations in order for the application to be accepted.

Separation isolates loss exposures from one another to minimize the adverse effect of a single loss. For example, an organization may store inventory in several warehouses for valid business reasons, as well as for risk control. Another example of separation is using several suppliers for raw material purchases. Using multiple suppliers may also enable the organization to obtain competitive pricing.

Duplication uses backups, spares, or copies of critical property, information, or capabilities. For example, an organization may make copies of key documents or information, which can be stored at another location. Another example of duplication is maintaining an inventory of spare parts for critical equipment.

Loss prevention
A risk control technique that seeks to lower the frequency of loss from a particular loss exposure.

Loss reduction
A risk control technique that seeks to lower the severity (decrease the dollar amount) of losses.

Separation
A risk control technique that isolates loss exposures from one another to minimize the adverse effect of a single loss.

Duplication
A risk control technique that uses backups, spares, or copies of critical property, information, or capabilities.

Risk control techniques are rarely used alone, and are most often effective when used in conjunction with risk financing techniques discussed next.

Risk Financing

Risk financing is an effective risk management technique that includes steps to pay for or transfer the cost of losses. Risk financing techniques include the following:

- Retention
- Transfer (noninsurance transfer and insurance)

As a risk management technique, **retention** simply means that the household or organization retains all or part of the financial consequences of a loss exposure. The financial consequences of any loss exposure that has not been avoided or transferred are invariably retained.

Retention can be intentional or unintentional. After thoroughly analyzing the alternatives, a risk manager may decide that retention is the best way to handle a given exposure, perhaps because insurance is not available or is too expensive. For example, a risk manager may decide that purchasing collision coverage on a fleet of older vehicles is not worth the premium and may thus decide to retain the organization's exposure by paying for any collision losses from the company's operating funds. Unintentional retention may result from inadequate exposure identification and analysis or from incomplete evaluation of risk management techniques. For example, a restaurant may not identify its liability exposure for serving too much alcohol to a customer and therefore may fail to purchase liquor liability insurance to cover this exposure.

Retention can be partial or total. Examples of partial retention are a $500 deductible on a personal auto policy or a $10,000 per building deductible on a commercial property insurance policy. An example of total retention would be a husband and wife choosing not to purchase flood insurance on their lake-side home because they think it is too expensive. They are therefore retaining their entire exposure to flood losses.

In the long run, retention is less expensive than insurance. While retention involves absorbing the cost of losses, insurance premiums are used to cover losses and the insurer's overhead, taxes, expenses, and other costs of policy and claim handling.

Retention is usually used in combination with other risk management techniques, particularly loss control and insurance. A deductible in a business auto policy is an example of the combination of retention and insurance. If the risk manager also implements a driver safety program to lower the frequency of corporate auto accidents, the combination of loss control, retention, and insurance can handle the exposure economically.

Businesses often treat loss exposures by transferring the potential financial consequences of loss to another party. When the other party is not an insurer, this method is called **noninsurance transfer**. For example, the landlord of

Risk financing
A risk management technique that includes steps to pay for or transfer the cost of losses.

Retention
A risk financing technique that involves retaining all or part of a particular loss exposure.

Noninsurance transfer
A risk financing technique in which one party transfers the potential financial consequences of a particular loss exposure to another party that is not an insurer.

a commercial building may wish to transfer the financial consequences of a liability exposure arising out of activities of a tenant. The landlord accomplishes this transfer by having the tenant sign a hold-harmless agreement. The agreement can be a separate contract but is usually a provision included in the lease. A hold-harmless agreement states that one party (in this case, the tenant) agrees to hold the other party (the landlord) harmless, or not legally responsible, for any liability arising from the tenant's use of the premises. Because a person can possibly sustain an injury on the rented property, the landlord has transferred this liability exposure to the tenant, who will be responsible for any such loss.

In addition to other techniques for handling loss exposures, households and small businesses depend heavily on insurance, which is another transfer technique. Most medium-sized and large businesses also rely on insurance as a major component of their risk management programs, but they may be less dependent on insurance and employ other risk management techniques more systematically than households and small businesses.

Even large businesses face loss exposures that they can handle most economically by purchasing insurance. No viable alternative exists for highly unpredictable loss exposures that could result in catastrophic financial consequences. Such businesses may use large retention amounts (deductibles or self-insurance) and purchase insurance policies to provide coverage above these amounts to protect them against large losses.

By working closely with the organization's insurance producer, a risk manager can develop an insurance program tailored to the company's needs and coordinate the insurance program with risk control and risk financing to form a complete risk management program.

Exhibit 10-2 summarizes the various risk management techniques, explains what each technique does, and gives an example of each.

Step 4: Selecting the Appropriate Risk Management Techniques

If it were possible to predict accidental losses accurately, selecting risk management techniques would be easy: prevent or avoid the losses that are most likely to happen and buy insurance against the losses that cannot be prevented or avoided. However, because no one can predict accidental losses with such accuracy, selecting risk management techniques must be based on predictions of expected losses—where they are most likely to happen, how often they are likely to occur, and how large they will probably be.

Businesses that are accustomed to reaching decisions based on expected profits or other financial criteria will probably use these same financial standards to select the most promising risk management techniques. Organizations that are less financially oriented are more likely to apply informal guidelines in choosing risk management techniques. These two types of decision making are discussed next.

EXHIBIT 10-2

Risk Management Techniques

Risk Control Techniques

Technique	What the Technique Does	Example
Avoidance	Eliminates the chance of a particular type of loss by either disposing of an existing loss exposure or by not assuming a new exposure.	A family decides not to purchase a boat and therefore avoids the loss exposures associated with boat ownership.
Loss prevention	Lowers loss frequency (number of losses).	A business installs bars on windows and door deadbolts to prevent burglaries.
Loss reduction	Lowers loss severity (dollar amount of losses).	A business installs a sprinkler system to reduce the amount of fire damage from potential fires.
Separation	Lowers loss severity.	A business buys multiple small warehouses to contain the effects of a single loss.
Duplication	Lowers loss frequency.	A taxi firm maintains a few spare vehicles to keep all drivers on the road even if one vehicle needs repair.

Risk Financing Techniques

Technique	What the Technique Does	Example
Retention	Retains all or part of a loss exposure (intentionally or unintentionally), which means that losses must be paid for with available funds or other assets.	A business decides not to purchase collision coverage for its fleet of vehicles and sets aside its own funds to pay for possible collision losses.
Noninsurance transfer	Transfers potential financial consequences of a loss exposure from one party to another party that is not an insurer.	In a lease, a landlord transfers the liability exposures of a rented building to the tenant.
Insurance	Transfers financial consequences of specified losses from one party (the insured) to another party (the insurer) in exchange for a specified fee (premium).	A family purchases homeowners and personal auto policies from an insurer.

Decisions Based on Financial Criteria

Financial management decisions are typically made with the objective of increasing profits and/or operating efficiency. Risk management decisions can be based on the same objectives. When an organization undertakes an activity to achieve profit goals or other objectives, it also assumes the exposures to accidental loss that are inherent in that activity. How the organization deals with those loss exposures affects the profits or output from the activity. By forecasting how a particular risk management decision will affect profits or output, an organization can choose the risk management technique that is likely to be the most financially beneficial. For example, a corporation may analyze its financial position and decide that it does not want any retained loss exposures to affect annual corporate earnings by more than five cents per share of stock. If the corporation has one hundred million shares outstanding, the risk management department can retain up to $5 million for all exposures in a fiscal year. The risk management department makes its retention decisions for the coming year based on this strategy of protecting corporate earnings.

Decisions Based on Informal Guidelines

Most households and small organizations follow less formal guidelines in selecting risk management techniques. Four such guidelines are the following:

1. *Do not retain more than you can afford to lose.* Setting an upper limit on the proper retention level is an important guideline. The amount that a household or organization can afford to lose depends on its financial situation. For example, if a family has only $500 in its savings account and has little remaining from each paycheck, it probably cannot afford to carry a $1,000 deductible on either its homeowners or personal automobile policies. Unless the family wishes to borrow money to pay a deductible, the family will probably choose to carry whatever minimum deductibles the insurer offers, despite the fact that the family could save premium dollars by choosing a higher deductible. The family simply cannot afford to sustain any loss greater than a few hundred dollars.

2. *Do not retain large exposures to save a little premium.* A risk manager should not retain a loss exposure with high potential severity, such as auto liability, in order to save a small amount of insurance premium. Depending on market conditions, certain types of liability insurance coverage, such as some umbrella policies (designed to cover large liability losses), can cost relatively little because the potential frequency of large liability losses is low. However, such coverage can be priced much higher given different market conditions.

   Exposures with the potential of low frequency but high severity should generally be insured because they are highly unpredictable. For example, the probability of a building suffering a total fire loss is low because total fire losses happen infrequently; however, if a family's residence does burn to the ground, the severity of the loss would be great. One such loss would cost the family many times a year's insurance premium, so the family should fully insure the residence.

3. *Do not spend a lot of money for a little protection.* Risk managers should spend insurance dollars where they will do the most good. If the exposure is almost certain to lead to a loss during the policy period, the insurer must charge a premium close to the expected cost of the loss plus a portion of the insurer's overhead, premium taxes, and profit. It is better to retain exposures of this type because the household or organization could absorb the cost of a loss almost as easily as the cost of the insurance. For loss exposures with high frequency and low severity, retention and loss control are usually the best alternatives. For example, a family may choose a higher deductible on auto physical damage coverage and use that savings to buy umbrella insurance to provide coverage for the infrequent but severe liability losses exceeding their homeowners or auto policy liability limits.

4. *Do not consider insurance a substitute for loss control.* A risk manager may evaluate a particular exposure, such as automobile collisions, and discover that the frequency of accidents has been increasing in recent years. If the company has a $1,000 collision deductible for each accident, the risk manager may decide to take action to reduce the organization's total annual retention for auto accidents. One approach may be to lower the deductible to $500 so that the company retains less of the loss exposure on each accident. This step would not solve the real problem, however, which is the increase in loss frequency. The insurance cost increases with the lower deductible, and the loss frequency is likely to remain high. In this case, the risk manager would be using the purchase of insurance in lieu of loss control.

A better option would be for the company to implement a loss control program to prevent accidents from occurring. This program could include more careful screening of company drivers, periodically reviewing drivers' motor vehicle records, training employees in safe driving practices, ensuring vehicle safety through regular vehicle maintenance, and implementing other loss control activities to reduce the frequency of collisions. If the program works and fewer accidents occur, the organization's overall retention from absorbing deductibles decreases, although the cost of the loss control program must also be considered. Future insurance premiums may be lower as well, because the insurer may offer a lower premium for the improved accident record.

When insurance takes the place of loss control, the insured simply passes the cost of absorbing additional losses to the insurer. It may be more economical to spend dollars on a loss control program that will prevent and reduce losses and lower the long-term cost of insurance and the risk management program.

Step 5: Implementing the Selected Risk Management Techniques

Implementing the risk management techniques that an organization has chosen requires that the risk manager make decisions concerning the following:

- What should be done
- Who should be responsible
- How to communicate the risk management information
- How to allocate the costs of the risk management program

Deciding What Should Be Done

Once the risk manager has decided what risk management techniques to use, he or she must implement them. For example, Helen, the risk manager of a supermarket, has decided that the store needs a sprinkler system. She must now decide how much the supermarket can afford to spend on the system, what kind of system should be installed, and which contractor should install it. She might also need to check on the local water supply and building permits and decide what is necessary to comply with local ordinances. Because the executives of the store will certainly want to minimize customer disruption, Helen must decide how to accomplish this objective. She must also consult with the store's insurance agent to make sure that appropriate property and liability coverages are in place during and after the installation and that the insurer gives an insurance credit for the sprinkler system. Helen must take into account these considerations and many others before deciding exactly how to implement the loss control technique she has chosen.

Deciding Who Should Be Responsible

The risk manager usually does not have complete authority to implement risk management techniques and must depend on others to implement the program based on the risk manager's advice. Larger organizations may have a written risk management statement and a risk management manual outlining guidelines, procedures, and authority for implementing risk management techniques. In smaller organizations and in households, the person making risk management decisions is often the person implementing the program because that person is the organization's owner or the household's primary wage earner.

Communicating Risk Management Information

A risk management program must include a communications plan. Risk management departments of large organizations generally rely on a manual to inform others of how to identify new exposures, what risk management techniques are currently in place, how to report insurance claims, and other important information. Management and other employees must communicate information to the risk manager so that the program can be modified for new exposures and evaluated for effectiveness.

Allocating Costs of the Risk Management Program

Determining how to allocate the costs of the risk management program is also important. In large organizations the costs of loss control, retention, noninsurance transfers, and insurance, as well as the expenses of the risk management department, must be spread appropriately across all departments and locations.

In smaller organizations or within households, allocating costs is also feasible. For example, an employee of a small business may be required to pay the deductible arising from damage she caused to a company car, or a teenager may have to pay to fix a neighbor's window that he accidentally broke.

Step 6: Monitoring Results and Revising the Risk Management Program

Monitoring the risk management program is an ongoing activity that a risk manager must carefully perform. Because the needs of all households and organizations change over time, a risk management program should not be allowed to become outdated. Monitoring the program ranges from handling routine matters, such as updating fleets of vehicles by replacing those less roadworthy, to making complex decisions concerning new activities to initiate or avoid.

The household or organization should review its insurance program with its agent or broker each year. Because decisions regarding insurance are usually associated with other risk management techniques, any change in insurance will affect the other areas.

The last step in the risk management process is actually a return to the first. In order to monitor and modify the risk management program, the risk manager must periodically identify and analyze new and existing loss exposures and then reexamine, select, and implement appropriate risk management techniques. Thus, the process of monitoring and modifying the risk management program begins the risk management process once again.

BENEFITS OF RISK MANAGEMENT

Few businesses, individuals, or families are financially able to retain all their loss exposures and must transfer much of the financial burden. Therefore, insurance is an essential part of almost all sound risk management programs. However, insurance must be considered in its proper role in a well-balanced program of risk management that also includes other risk management techniques. Risk management has many advantages over merely buying insurance. These advantages benefit businesses, individuals, families, society, and insurers, as discussed next.

Benefits of Risk Management to Businesses

Making insurance part of an overall risk management program instead of relying solely on insurance provides many benefits to an organization, including the following:

- Improved access to affordable insurance because insurers often prefer to insure an organization that practices good risk management rather than one that relies solely on insurance for protection against the financial consequences of accidental losses. An insured who combines insurance with the risk management techniques of avoidance, loss control, retention, and noninsurance transfer usually has fewer and smaller losses than do other insureds. Therefore, insurers are likely to generate better loss ratios and underwriting results by insuring policyholders having sound risk management programs. Consequently, such insureds are often able to obtain broader coverage at lower premiums than insureds who do not practice risk management.

- Increased opportunities because uncertainty about future losses from new business activities is diminished. The fear of uncertain future losses tends to make many business owners and executives reluctant to undertake activities they consider too risky. This reluctance deprives a business of the benefits that undertaking certain activities could bring. A business having an effective risk management program is better prepared to seek other opportunities that may increase its profits. For example, if a business is confident in the way it has managed its present property and liability loss exposures, it may be in a better position to consider a proposal to manufacture a new product or to expand its present sales territory.

- Achievement of business goals through better management of large loss exposures. Risk management makes it possible for a business to achieve its business and financial goals in a cost-effective manner and can thus help improve profitability. The potential costs of a loss exposure can be disruptive to a business, and risk management techniques can be used to minimize the chance that the business must absorb such a large loss. Profits can be increased directly by reducing expenses. For example, a firm may reduce its insurance costs because the risk manager chooses to retain a loss exposure instead of insuring it.

Benefits of Risk Management to Individuals and Families

Like businesses, individuals and families benefit in the following ways from effective risk management:

- Coping more effectively with financial disasters that may otherwise cause a greatly reduced standard of living, personal bankruptcy, or family discord.

- Enjoying greater peace of mind from knowing that their loss exposures are under control.

- Reducing expenses by handling loss exposures in the most economical fashion.

- Taking more chances and making more aggressive decisions on ventures with the potential for profit, such as investing in the stock market, changing careers, or starting a part-time business. Though this may seem inconsistent with the purpose of risk management, many such decisions can have long-term value when made with a full knowledge of costs and potential benefits.

- Continuing activities following an accident or other loss, and thus reducing inconvenience.

Benefits of Risk Management to Society

By helping themselves through effective risk management, businesses, individuals, and families also benefit society in various ways as follows:

- Stimulating economic growth because fewer and less costly losses mean that more funds are available for other uses, such as investment, which can spur economic growth.

- Reducing the number of persons dependent on society for support because businesses and families plan for financial crises through risk management. For example, families who buy flood insurance need less help from charitable agencies or the government for federal flood relief after a flood event.

- Causing fewer disruptions in the economic and social environment because companies and families are not subject to the big and sudden expense of bearing the cost of a loss.

Benefits of Risk Management to Insurers

From an insurer's point of view, risk management is beneficial in many ways as follows:

- Creating a positive effect on an insurer's underwriting results, loss ratio, and overall profitability because insureds who practice sound risk management tend to experience fewer or less severe insured losses than those who do not.

- Providing more thoughtful consumers of insurance because those who practice risk management are likely to combine insurance with other techniques for handling loss exposures, and therefore may incur and submit fewer claims.

- Creating innovative products and competitive prices and services because professional risk managers seek to get the most for their insurance dollars and are often willing to pay higher premiums in exchange for greater insurance value. As a result, these risk managers may encourage insurers to be more innovative and competitive in the products and services they provide.

- Obtaining the respect and business of risk managers and business partners that have a risk management program.

AN EXAMPLE OF A RISK MANAGEMENT PROGRAM

To show that a risk management program need not be complicated, this example applies the risk management process to a family situation. Keep in mind, however, that risk management programs for organizations can be more sophisticated. These programs become more complex as organizations increase in size and their loss exposures become more extensive and complicated.

A typical household faces many loss exposures, such as various property and liability exposures from home and automobile ownership. For example, Tony and Maria Garcia both work outside their home, and they have three school-aged children. The Garcias own two automobiles and a home with a pool, have a modest savings account, and have invested in the stock market. After attending a seminar at his company on risk management, Tony has decided that the family should initiate a risk management program of its own. Remembering the steps in the risk management process, Tony knows that the family must:

1. Identify its loss exposures
2. Analyze its loss exposures
3. Examine the feasibility of risk management techniques
4. Select risk management techniques appropriate for the family
5. Implement the selected techniques
6. Monitor and revise the family's risk management program

Tony and Maria identified loss exposures by listing the exposures they could think of and then inspecting their home, looking for other exposures they had not yet considered. For example, when Tony spotted his son's hockey stick, he realized that they have a liability exposure arising from the children's various athletic activities. His daughter's saxophone in her bedroom reminded Tony that the saxophone was not specifically insured and that they did not have the funds readily available to replace it if it were stolen or damaged. As Tony viewed their swimming pool full of neighborhood children, he realized that they needed higher liability limits than their current homeowners policy provided. After physically inspecting their home and property, Maria called their insurance agent and obtained a household inventory form that they used to inventory their household contents and other possessions to determine their property loss exposures. The agent also sent them a survey form to complete, which they used to list potential liability exposures for the family. Maria and Tony then analyzed all the loss exposures they had identified and attempted to determine which ones could cause the most frequent or most severe losses.

After identifying and analyzing their property and liability exposures, the Garcias' third step was to examine risk management techniques. Tony knew from the seminar that the possible techniques included avoidance, loss control, noninsurance transfer, and retention, as well as insurance. The Garcias had been thinking of buying a new home near the local river, but Tony and Maria were concerned that the exposure to flooding was too great; therefore, they decided not to buy the house, thus using avoidance to eliminate this exposure. In an attempt to practice sound loss control, they installed deadbolt locks on all their doors and locks on all their windows. They also installed smoke detectors in several places in their home, and they are contemplating installing a burglar alarm system if they can find one that is both effective and affordable.

Tony and Maria explored noninsurance transfer by considering leasing a car, but they found that they would still be responsible for all liability connected with the use of the vehicle and would therefore still have to purchase insurance, so they decided this was not a good risk management technique.

Because the Garcias do not have much disposable income after they pay their mortgage, car payments, and other household bills each month, they know that they must rely heavily on insurance to cover their loss exposures. Although they cannot afford to retain much of their exposure, they did raise the deductibles on both their homeowners and personal auto policies from $250 to $500, thereby reducing the costs of their premiums.

They decided not to specifically insure their daughter's saxophone because their homeowners policy already covered it for fire, theft, lightning, and other causes of loss. They also decided to apply the retention technique if their daughter simply lost or damaged the saxophone; in other words, they would replace the saxophone from their personal funds, make their daughter earn money to replace it, or not buy a new one.

Further, they decided to purchase an umbrella policy to cover large liability losses such as those that might arise from use of autos, the children's sporting activities, or the pool exposure. The increased deductibles and retention of the property loss exposures for the saxophone were about all the retention Tony and Maria thought they could handle. Thus, as in most households, insurance will play a dominant role in treating loss exposures for the Garcia family.

By deciding not to purchase the house near the river, installing locks and smoke detectors, purchasing umbrella insurance, and deciding to retain some exposures, the Garcias effectively completed the third and fourth steps in the risk management process: selecting and implementing their risk management techniques.

The last step in the Garcias' risk management program was to periodically monitor and modify their program. For a family, an annual review of the program is probably sufficient unless the family's circumstances change significantly. An ideal time for the Garcias to do another physical inspection and inventory would be at the renewal of their homeowners policy, or if either Tony or Maria changes jobs, receives a large bonus, has a salary increase, or purchases any type of high-valued property. When Tony first began to monitor their risk management program, he realized that they had neglected to consider their personal loss exposures, such as death, illness, injury, or unemployment.

Tony and Maria immediately took steps to modify their risk management program to include their human loss exposures and thus began the process of exposure identification and analysis all over again.

SUMMARY

Risk management is the process of making and implementing decisions to deal with loss exposures. It involves identifying loss exposures and then applying various techniques to eliminate, control, or finance those exposures.

Insurance is one of the fundamental techniques of risk management, but it is not the only one. Risk management can enable a person, family, or business to handle loss exposures. Risk management is the process of making and carrying out decisions to minimize the adverse effects of accidental losses and involves the following steps:

1. Identifying loss exposures
2. Analyzing loss exposures
3. Examining the feasibility of risk management techniques
4. Selecting the appropriate risk management techniques
5. Implementing the selected risk management techniques
6. Monitoring results and revising the risk management program

A risk manager can conduct a physical inspection to identify loss exposures and can also use tools such as loss exposure surveys and loss history analysis. Analyzing loss exposures includes measuring loss frequency (how often losses occur) and loss severity (the monetary amount of losses).

After identifying and analyzing loss exposures, the risk manager must examine possible risk management techniques to handle the loss exposures. These techniques include the following:

Risk control techniques:

- Avoidance
- Loss prevention
- Loss reduction
- Separation
- Duplication

Risk financing techniques:

- Retention
- Transfer (noninsurance transfer and insurance)

Selecting the most appropriate techniques involves making decisions based on financial criteria as well as informal guidelines. Implementing the chosen techniques requires making decisions on what should be done, who should be responsible, how to communicate risk management information, and how to allocate costs of the risk management program.

The final step in the risk management process is actually a return to the first. To properly monitor and revise the program, the risk manager must return to step one and once again begin to identify new and existing loss exposures.

Risk management has many advantages over merely buying insurance. Although formal risk management programs are used primarily by businesses, individuals and families can also benefit from applying risk management to their loss exposures. While a risk management program for a large business can be complex, a risk management program for a family can be simple and is well worth the time and effort to implement.

Index

Page numbers in boldface refer to definitions of Key Words and Phrases.

V

W